Sitcom Factfinder,
1948–1984

Sitcom Factfinder, 1948–1984

Over 9,700 Details from 168 Television Shows

by VINCENT TERRACE

McFarland & Company, Inc., Publishers
Jefferson, North Carolina, and London

Library of Congress Cataloguing-in-Publication Data

Terrace, Vincent, 1948–
    Sitcom factfinder, 1948–1984 : over 9,700 details from 168 television
shows / by Vincent Terrace.
        p.   cm.
    Includes index.
    ISBN 0-7864-1243-7 (softcover : 50# alkaline paper) ♾
    1. Comedy programs—United States—Miscellanea.   I. Title.
PN1992.8.C66   T46   2002
791.45'6—dc21   2002004808

British Library cataloguing data are available

Manufactured in the United States of America

McFarland & Company, Inc., Publishers
    Box 611, Jefferson, North Carolina 28640
    www.mcfarlandpub.com

Contents

Contents

Contents

Preface

Before becoming head writer for Alan Brady, Rob Petrie (*The Dick Van Dyke Show*) worked as a disc jockey at radio station WOFF. Lurch of *The Addams Family* was not the first person to use the catchphrase "You Rang": Maynard G. Krebs (*Dobie Gillis*) did so five years earlier. Gloria's birth in 1944 on *All in the Family* cost Archie and Edith $131.50. Before working for *Cheers*, Carla was a barmaid at the Broken Spoke Bar.

These are just a few of the more than 9,700 facts that can be found in *Sitcom Factfinder*, a book that covers a neglected area of television—the facts that make characters interesting and add special interest to a program. Whether it's called trivia, nostalgia or useless information, you will find such facts in this volume from 168 series broadcast from 1948 to 1984.

All of the information that appears in this book has been compiled from the actual programs themselves. It was impossible to include every sitcom that was broadcast during this time frame. Copies of some no longer exist; others have only several existing episodes available. The resulting 168 programs are a combination of well-known series and rare series for which only a few episodes are known to exist. Appropriate entries also contain origin, spinoff, update and extension series information (for example, on *Father Knows Best* you will find its radio origins, TV beginnings and TV movie updates).

This book covers programs broadcast on ABC, CBS, DuMont, NBC and in syndication (cited as "Syn.") from January 1, 1948, to December 31, 1984. Specific programs broadcast after this date are included only to supplement original program information and are listed in the entry for the original program (for example, details on *The New Gidget* will be found under *Gidget*). A performer index, keyed to the program numbers, is also included.

If you are looking for details such as television characters' addresses, telephone numbers, or license plates, the names of their pets or their favorite foods (to name a few), then this work (along with its sister volume, *Television Sitcom Factbook, 1985–2000*) is the source you are seeking.

The author would like to thank James Robert Parish, Steve Eberly and Jennifer Mormile for their help in making this book possible.

THE SHOWS

1.   The Abbott and Costello Show Syn., 1952–1954

The Fields Rooming House at 214 Brookline Avenue in Hollywood, California, is owned by Sidney Fields (Himself), a patient and understanding man who tries to run "a nice, quiet and decent" establishment. He tries but the tenants complain about "those two hoodlums you have living here." Those "hoodlums" are Bud Abbott and Lou Costello (Themselves), out of work actors who are struggling to survive on what jobs they can find (or more aptly put, what jobs Bud can find for Lou).

Bud and Lou pay $7 a week in rent and their telephone number is Alexander 4444 (also given as Alexander 2222). Lou was born in Paterson, New Jersey, and mentioned that he helps support his sister and three nieces. Bud, who gets the hiccups when he's nervous, mentioned that he was a professional loafer (one who makes bread; not, as Lou believes, one who gets paid for doing nothing). Lou was also a Junior G–Man (a graduate of a through-the-mails detective school) and carried a toy cap pistol around with him for protection.

"We've got to raise some money" is often said by Bud, as he and Lou are always behind in their rent and finding work becomes a priority. (When they can't find work they sell what little valuables they have to Harry at Hock Shop Harry's.) Bud and Lou did have a number of jobs throughout the series run. These mostly one-day employment opportunities included being waiters at Brodie's Sea Food Restaurant; wallpaper hangers; pest exterminators; pet store owners; delivery boys for the Susquehanna Hat Company on Flugel Street; soda jerks; pot and pan demonstrators; door-to-door vacuum cleaner and "No Peddlers Allowed" sign salesmen; and roller-skate salesmen ("Abbott and Costello Cheap Skates"). Bud and Lou also appeared on the TV game show "Hold That Cuckoo" (where Lou performed a stunt before the cuckoo sounded and won the grand prize—a box of bubble gum). When there is a situation that involves a friend (or stranger) who is in trouble, Bud always remarks "Costello will get you out of this." Bud and Lou also tried their hand at becoming cops by attending police rookie school.

While the rules of the rooming house are quite strict ("no cooking cabbage in the apartment; no door slamming; no loud radio playing after 9:30; no pets; no babies") Lou most often breaks the no-pet rule with Bingo the Chimp, a chimpanzee he adopted while working in the pet shop. Bingo dresses like Lou (trademark checkered jacket and gray hat), eats watermelon for breakfast, 50 pounds of bananas a week and a side order of popcorn. The six-year-old Bingo and Lou argue each night over who is going to take their bath first. Lou mentioned that Bingo's mother was working with a circus and his father was in the Belgian Congo.

When Bud and Lou are out of town, Lou's girlfriend, Hillary Brooke (Herself), babysits for Bingo. Hillary, a gorgeous blonde, held jobs in accordance with what the episode called for (for example, nurse, dental assistant, waitress, lawyer's office receptionist, owner of the B-Bar-B Ranch in Texas, and owner of a haunted castle at Goblins Knob, which she inherited from her Uncle Montague). When Hillary calls on Lou she brings him cream puffs.

While Sidney Fields was primarily the landlord, he also played a number of relatives who were supposed tops in their fields (for example, Professor Melonhead, the judo expert; Lawyer Claude Melonhead; Judge Melonhead). Other regulars were Mike Kelly (Gordon Jones), the neighborhood police officer who was called "Mike the Cop"; Stinky Davis (Joe Besser), Lou's friend, a 30-year-old "kid" who loved to play games like football, hopscotch and cops and robbers with Lou; and Mr. Botchagalupe (Joe Kirk), the neighborhood's enterprising street vendor (seen selling fruit, vegetables, ice cream — whatever the episode called for).

The song "The Jazz Babies Ball" is used as the show's second season theme (over which a montage of Bud and Lou's movie clips is seen).

2.   The Addams Family ABC, 1964–1966

The haunted-looking Victorian residence at 000 Cemetery Lane in the town of Cemetery Ridge is home to Gomez Addams (John Astin), his wife, Morticia (Carolyn Jones), their children, Wednesday and Pugsley (Lisa Loring, Ken Weatherwax), Morticia's Uncle Fester (Jackie Coogan), Gomez's mother, Grandmama (Blossom Rock), and their butler, Lurch (Ted Cassidy).

Gomez is a wealthy defense attorney who has put more people in jail than any lawyer in U.S. history. He dabbles in the stock market and has made a fortune on a stock called Consolidated Fuzz. He owns an elephant herd in Africa, a nut plantation in Brazil, and a salt mine and animal preserve in Nairobi (which he keeps for its subterranean bat caves). For relaxation, Gomez enjoys crashing and blowing up Lionel electric O-gauge trains. He is a member of the Zen Yogi Society and Ivan the Terrible is his favorite person in history. His ancestry dates back to ancient Egypt when Maumud Kali Pashu Addams set fire to the library at Alexandria. "The second d in our name," says Gomez, "distinguishes us from the embarrassingly famous and historic John Adams and family."

Morticia, like Gomez, enjoys gloomy weather, thunderstorms, moon bathing and exploring caves. Gomez and the former Morticia Frump were 22 years old when they met and married. Blue-eyed Morticia's favorite color is black ("It's so soothing and mysterious") and she always wears a tight, floor length black dress (on their wedding day Gomez was driven wild by it and she promised "I'll never wear another"). Morticia's ancestry dates back to the early witch-burning days of Salem, Massachusetts. She loves to paint and smoke (literally), and is famous for her dwarf's hair pie and animal imitations, especially the bullfrog, which drives Gomez wild. Gomez also becomes romantic when Morticia speaks French. When she first spoke it, it cleared up his lifelong sinus condition. As a child Morticia had a doll (Anne Boleyn) and now has a pampered, carnivorous plant (an African Strangler) she calls Cleopatra (who likes zebra burgers). Morticia and Gomez enjoy fried eyes of newt, fried yak and barbecued turtle tips. Morticia struggles to keep their home "nice and gloomy" (she places rose stems in vases for that lived-in look) and is called "Tish," "Cara Mia" and "Caita" by Gomez (she calls Gomez "Bubala").

Wednesday and Pugsley attend the Sherwood Elementary School. Wednesday has a headless doll (Marie Antoinette) and a spider (Homer). Pugsley has an octopus (Aristotle), a jaguar (Fang) and loves to play with dynamite caps. He shocked his family when he joined the Boy Scouts.

Morticia's Uncle Fester thrives on electricity and needs to be recharged when he runs low. Fester considers himself to be an explosives expert and has a Revolutionary War rifle named Geneviere (his philosophy is "Shoot 'em in the back") and cures his headaches by forcing out the pain with a vise. Morticia mentioned that Fester once worked as an advice-to-the-lovelorn columnist but quit when everybody started suing him.

Grandmama attended Swamp Town High School and first voted in 1906—even before Women's Suffrage ("It didn't stop me"). She uses love potions to spark romances. Lurch, the six foot, nine inch tall butler, loves to play the harpsichord and responds with a somber "You Rang" when he is summoned.

Thing, Gomez's childhood companion, is a human right hand that has become a family servant. He lives in boxes placed around the house, and "Beware of Thing" is posted on the front of the iron gate that surrounds the house. Ophelia Frump (Carolyn Jones in a dual role) is Morticia's attractive but flaky sister. She loves flowers, cooking and washing dishes. She also loves water ("She is always jumping in fountains, brooks, even tubs and sinks") and dressing in flowing white dresses.

Cousin Itt (Felix Silla, Roger Arrovo) is the family intellectual. He is covered with blonde hair from head to toe and speaks a language all his own. He considers himself a ladies' man and when Gomez asked Itt what was under all that hair he responded "Roots." Itt held a job as a zoo keeper (although he was mistaken for one of the exhibits), and his favorite nooks are the chimney and the broom closet.

Kit Kat, also called Kitty, is the family's cowardly pet lion. Pierre is the lopsided moose head on the living room wall; the leg sticking out of the shark's mouth belongs to Cousin Ferouke. Thing's lady love is Lady Fingers, a human left hand who is the handmaiden of Gomez's Aunt Millicent (Elvia Allman). Vic Mizzy composed *The Addams Family* theme.

Update

The New Addams Family, Fox Family, 1998–2002. The spooky house with the "Beware of Everything" sign on the front gate is home to the Addams family: Gomez (Glenn Taranto), his wife, Morticia (Ellie Harvie), and their children, Wednesday and Pugsley (Nicole Fugere, Brody Smith). Also living with them are Fester Addams (Michael Roberds), Gomez's brother in this version; Eudora Addams (Betty Phillips), Gomez's Grandmama; Lurch (John DeSantis), the tall, zombielike butler; and Thing (Steven Fox), the servant (a human right hand).

Gomez is a wealthy eccentric who can't figure out how the Brothers Grimm can get work when they write such happy fairy tales. To solve this dilemma, Morticia wrote her own fable—"Hansel and Gretel, a Play by Morticia Addams" (wherein the witch is kind and the children are wicked). Gomez, who is of Spanish ancestry, is an excellent swordsman ("I can slice, dice and julienne" he says. But when it comes to fencing, Morticia feels he "has the skill of a demented artist"). Gomez, who dabbles in the stock market (which appears to account for his wealth), reads *Torture Times* and *Gentleman's Drawn and Quartered* magazines. He and Morticia celebrate Halloween and Bastille Day as major holidays and once a year Gomez and Fester celebrate "Gotcha Week" (where they play practical jokes on each other). After witnessing the crazy things Gomez does (like blowing up his electric trains), most people remark "You must be insane" (to which Gomez responds "Not yet but someday").

Morticia makes a curse on a shooting star, carves statues out of stone, and uses swamp water in her tea "for that special taste." She has a carnivorous plant she calls Cleopatra and cuts the rose flowers off the stems "because bare stems cheer up a room." In high school, Morticia (then Morticia Frump) received rave reviews for her role as Hamlet, and she dreads the time when the children go to bed early "because they get up bright and cheery."

Wednesday, 11, and Pugsley, 8, attend the Sherman School (they also attended the Warbridge School for a short time). Wednesday has a pet lion (Kitty), a doll (Marie Antoinette), and likes to see people betrayed and tortured (something she inherited from her father—who hopes that when the doorbell rings it is a disgruntled neighbor). Wednesday, who dresses in black and is growing up to be a beautiful young lady, claims she has a primary goal in life—"to devise a means by which to kill Pugsley" (many episodes show Wednesday seeking to do away with Pugsley). She considers Pugsley to be "an expendable guinea pig" and says "The post office relies on my family to make sure their carriers quit before retirement" (delivering mail to the Addams house is a letter carrier's worst fear). Pugsley's favorite comic book is "Galactic Enforcer" and when he gets upset he hides in the dumb waiter.

Fester is an explosives expert (or so he thinks) and buys his dynamite at Weapons 'R' Us. He is a member of the Global Mercenaries and the Iron Maiden Society (where he is in charge of sharpening spikes). He has a hangman's noose collection and he last vacationed at the lava pools at Mount St. Helens. Fester generates his own electricity, sleeps on a bed of nails and likes to lie down after dinner to keep his cholesterol up. In his grade school production of "George Washington," Fester played the cherry tree.

Grandmama is a gourmet cook (her specialty is slug stew and leech pudding) and she likes the TV soap opera "The Old and the Pulseless" for its "anguish and despair." Eudora gives useless presents, especially on the Ides of March Day—so she can get bad luck. "If it's something you don't want, she'll buy it for you" says Gomez.

Platypus perogies is Lurch's favorite food. He plays the piano (the Borgendoffer Piano) and responds with "You Rang" when the family summons him. When Gomez thought Lurch's gravel voice had "a beautiful tone" to it, he made a recording of him singing "You Rang" and launched him on a singing career (but when Lurch discovered he was going to be replaced as the family's butler, he gave up show business). Gomez and Fester also made Lurch a helper, Simon the Robot, when they thought he was working too hard.

John Astin appeared as Grandpapa Addams (Gomez's father) and horror director Steven DeVille used the Addams home (and family) in a movie called *Mansion of the Undead*.

Other Versions

1. *The Addams Family*, NBC, 1973–1975. An animated version that follows the Addams family as they leave Cemetery Ridge and embark on a motor tour of America. *Voices:* Lennie Weinrib (Gomez Addams), Janet Waldo (Morticia Addams and Grandmama), Cindy Henderson (Wednesday Addams), Jodie Foster (Pugsley Addams), Jackie Coogan (Uncle Fester), Ted Cassidy (Lurch).

2. *The Addams Family Fun House*, Syn., 8/73. An unsold pilot that presents the Charles Addams characters in various music and comedy situations with guest stars dropping by each week to share the fun (Jim Nabors guests in the pilot). *Cast:* Jack Riley (Gomez), Liz Torres (Morticia), Stubby Kaye (Uncle Fester), Noelle Von Sonn (Wednesday), Butch Patrick (Pugsley), Pat McCormick (Lurch), Felix Silla (Cousin Itt).

3. *Halloween with the Addams Family*, NBC, 10/30/77. A special wherein the Addams family celebrate their favorite holiday. *Cast:* John Astin (Gomez), Carolyn Jones (Morticia), Jackie Coogan (Uncle Fester), Lisa Loring (Wednesday), Ken Weatherwax (Pugsley), Ted Cassidy (Lurch), Jane Rose (Grandmama).

4. *The Addams Family*, ABC, 1992–1995. A second animated series that focuses on the activities of the Addams family, now residents of the town of Happydale Heights. *Voices:* John Astin (Gomez), Nancy Linair (Morticia), Rip Taylor (Uncle Fester), Debi Derryberry (Wednesday), Jeannie Elias (Pugsley), Carol Channing (Grandmama), Jim Cummings (Lurch), Pat Fraley (Cousin Itt).

3. Alice CBS, 1976–1985

Alice Spevak Hyatt (Linda Lavin), Vera Louise Gorman (Beth Howland) and Florence Jean "Flo" Castleberry (Polly Holliday) are waitresses who work for Melvin "Mel" Emory Sharples (Vic Tayback), the always yelling, stingy owner of Mel's Diner, a roadside eatery at 1030 Bush Highway in Phoenix, Arizona.

Alice, born in New Jersey, attended Passaic High School. She had her own singing group, Alice and the Acorns, and was voted "Girl with the Best Knees." She was also a bit overweight and called "Pudge Spevak" ("But I'm thinner now"). While working as a waitress at Vito's Bar and Grill in Newark, Alice met, fell in love with and married Donald Hyatt, a big rig trucker. Following Donald's death in a job-related accident, Alice decides to pursue her dream of becoming a singer. She and her son Tommy (Philip McKeon) leave New Jersey and head west. Car trouble strands them in Phoenix where Alice takes the job at Mel's as a temporary measure until she can get back on her feet.

Alice and Tommy first live at the Desert Sun Apartments (103) then the Phoenix Arms (Apartment 108). Alice performs at the local clubs (Herman's Hitching Bar, The Saddle Sore, Vinnie's House of Veal) and appeared in an unnamed musical revue at the local Palace Theater. She is still hoping for that big break but often feels depressed because she feels it will never happen. When working conditions forced Alice to quit, Mel replaced her with Blanche, the robot waitress (Lucille Benson; voice of June Whitley Taylor).

Alice had her job back when Mel's orders overworked the robot. Alice related a strange incident that occurred when she was eight. She was a brownie and became lost in the woods while gathering twigs for a campfire. A squirrel appeared before her and motioned for her to follow him. She did and was led back to the camp. When she looked back he was gone.

Mel, the diner's cook, is famous for his chili. Even on days when the diner is officially closed, Mel opens it so he can cook his dinner—"The neighbors complain about the smell if I cook at home" (634 Plainview Drive, Apartment 107. A poster of Farrah Fawcett is first on his living room wall; it is later replaced by a poster of Loni Anderson). Mel served a hitch with the Navy during the Korean War (he spent six months in Hawaii) and is landlord of the neighboring Mother Goose Preschool.

Mel keeps the diner's month-old bills in a Thom McAn shoe box; older bills are placed in a Buster Brown shoe box. His license plate reads NU 087 and Mel worries about his nose. In school, the kids called him "Hose Nose"; in the Navy his mates called him "Banana Nose"; when he was shipped overseas to Japan, the Japanese dubbed him "Hanasan" ("Mr. Nose"); and now he has the distinction of being called "Super Schnoz" by the men on his bowling team. (In another episode, Mel complained that in school he was called "Smelly Melly" and "Jelly Belly.")

Mel has an account at the Desert Bank and rented two guard dogs—Bobbie Joe and Billy Ray—to protect the diner at night. Mel's waitresses wear pink uniforms and earn $2.90 an hour. The only way Mel knows how to be nice to his waitresses "is to scream at them." Mel also stands up for what he believes "and it doesn't matter which waitress gets into trouble for it." In spite of the fact that Alice feels Mel's brownies "taste like asphalt," Mel is proud of his cooking and produced his own Mel's Diner T-Shirts (his picture on the front; the diner on the back). Mel attended pastry school (where he learned how to make roses for the tops of cupcakes), was "Be Boppin' Mel Sharples" for a 25th anniversary celebration at Vinnie's House of Veal, and took a temporary job with the R.J. Catering Company when he thought he should try something else (he quit when he couldn't be his own boss). Mel never married "because I'm married to this diner." In the back of the diner there is a large heart painted on a wooden fence with "Lynn Loves Bob" in it. Marty's Munch-A-Rama and Benny's Beanery are Mel's main competition. Mel buys his polyester suits at Syd's Stylist Shop and his third place bowling trophy sits on his desk in the diner's storeroom.

Vera, called "Dingie" by Mel, lives at the Sun Rise Apartments. She has a pet cat (Mel), two hamsters (Mitzi and Harold), a piggy bank (Irving) and a guppy (Sidney). She cares about animals, felt sorry for the shark in

Jaws, and rescued Sparky, a miniature horse, from the circus when its owner mistreated it.

Vera is shy, young and pretty but feels she has no sex appeal. She has the ability to count money by hearing it, plays the cello and tap dances (she took lessons at Miss Dana's Academy of Tippy Tappy Toe Dancing and dancer Donald O'Connor is her hero). In an attempt to make money by capitalizing on Vera's dancing ability, Mel initiated "Mel's Diner Presents The Vera Gorman Tap Dancing Marathon" (wherein Vera broke the world tap dancing record of 26 hours, 54 minutes by dancing non stop for 27 straight hours).

Vera's favorite cartoon is Daffy Duck. She has a poster from the movie *Watch on the Rhine* on her living room wall and has seen the film *The African Queen* 14 times. "One Day After Another" is Vera's favorite TV soap opera. She believes everything she sees on TV is real (for example, when "Kojak" caught a cold, she sent him a toupee; when Mary Richards of *The Mary Tyler Moore Show* quit her job, Vera cried for her). Due to a fear of missing her soaps, Vera quit her day job at Mel's to work the night shift at Big Herb's 24-Hour Gas Station. She soon quit that job, though, when she realized she was losing her friends at the diner.

When Vera finds herself in a situation that requires her to be in a high place, she tells her brain that she is on the ground floor "So I don't get scared." Yum Nutties are Vera's favorite candy. She refuses to serve Mel's Boston Clam Chowder "because the clams came from Seattle" and gets upset when she has to open a bottle of baby gherkins (she believes farmers sneak into the fields at night to snatch the baby pickles from their mothers). Vera believes trees are Mother Nature's condominiums and she doesn't go to drive-in movies "because I don't have a car. I'd look foolish standing there with the soundbox around my neck."

In the 1960s, Vera was a student at Berkeley. She was content and would paint peace signs on rocks. One day, while walking on campus, she ran into a crowd of protestors. She was pushed and shoved, and her handbag, filled with peace rocks, hit a policeman in the head. The incident so upset her (she was arrested) that she quit school and moved to Boston to live with her Aunt Agatha. Vera later married Phoenix police officer Elliott Novak (Charles Levin).

"Kiss My Grits" is the comeback line used by Flo, the wisecracking, sassy waitress who wears sexy, tight pants while not working and "peek-a-boo" nighties at bedtime. Flo lives in a mobile home at the Desert Trailer Park and frequents a bar called Shake Chug-a-Lug. Flo's prized possessions include an imitation leopard bedspread, a black velvet painting of Johnny Cash and a plush rabbit she won at the Corpus Christi State Fair.

Lookout Mountain is Flo's favorite makeout spot, and Flo says of Vera, who keeps a memento of every date she has, "If I did that, I'd have to open a museum." Mel objects to Flo's personal calls at the diner; and Flo taught Alice, who knows how to drive an eighteen-wheeler, how to insult Mel. Flo was the first waitress to leave Mel's. She is offered a job as hostess at the Thundering Herd Restaurant in Houston, but after a return visit to her hometown of Cowtown, Texas, she decides to stay and open her own bar, Flo's Golden Rose. The spinoff series, "Flo," followed (CBS, 1980–81) with Geoffrey Lewis as Earl Tucker, the bartender; Joyce Bulifant as Mirian Willoughby, the waitress; Lucy Lee Flippen as Fran Castleberry, Flo's sister; and Sudie Bond as Velma, Flo's mother.

Marie (Victoria Carroll) was the first waitress Mel hired to replace Flo. Marie and Mel date, fight, breakup and get back together again. Marie calls Mel "Barrel Bottom," "Cookie Nose" and "Puppy Toes"; he calls her "Cuddle Cups" and "Snookie Tookie." When Marie receives a job offer at the Shake Chug-a-Lug bar for a salary that Mel can't match ($400 a week), she quits. Shortly after, Belle DuPree (Diane Ladd), a former waitress of Mel's ("The best waitress I ever had"), returns to Phoenix to further her dream of becoming a country and western singer by offering a song she wrote to Tammy Wynette and Waylon Jennings (who are performing in town). When she fails to impress their manager, she returns to Mel's and is offered the waitress job.

Belle, originally from Mississippi, now lives at 1112 Aston Drive in Phoenix. She likes honey in her coffee and claims she has a little voice in her head that calls her Isabelle (Vera says she also has a voice in her head "that calls me 'hey'"). Belle, who wears bells in her earrings ("because my name is Belle") believes there is a soft spot in Mel "somewhere." Mel says "Don't let it out. I have to protect my image."

Belle is on vacation in Nashville when Jolene Hunnicutt (Celia Weston) wanders into Mel's Diner after a fight with her truck-driving partner (who wanted to be more than just a friend). Shortly after, Mel receives a phone call from Belle telling him that her cousin Larry is starting a band and she is going to be a backup singer. Jolene happens to be in the right spot at the right time and gets the waitress job. Jolene, born in South Carolina, now lives at the Pine Valley Apartments and dreams of opening her own beauty shop. She worked previously in a "Stuffing Factory" ("Stuff, staple, stuff, staple," she says) and as a big-rig trucker. Mel calls Jolene "Blondie" and when he yells at her he says "Bag it, Blondie." Jolene hates to wear a hair net ("It makes your hair look like sofa stuffing"), reads mystery novels and the magazines *True Romance* and *Modern Crime*. Jolene believes a coffee break "is a teensy weensy vacation with pay" and at the laundromat, she uses washers six and nine ("Because number eight wobbles") and dryers 16 and 35. She sleeps on Snoopy sheets.

As a kid Jolene pretended that her treehouse was a plane and she was a stewardess. (Vera pretended her treehouse was a dressing room and she was an actress.) To make that childhood dream become a reality, Jolene attended flight school and became a stewardess for Desert Airlines. After her first assignment (on flight 12) she quit when she found she was afraid to fly. Jolene, along with Alice and Vera, appeared on a name-that-tune TV show called "Go for It."

Tommy had his first crush on Brooke Shields (although Vera believes she was his first crush). He attended an unnamed high school where he was on the school's basketball team, the Coyotes, coached by Earl Cox (Dave Madden). He later attends Arizona State College, where he is a member of the Sun Devils basketball team. Tommy also worked as a short order cook at Mel's and played guitar and sang at the Dry Gulch Saloon (which serves soda and fruit punch). He is a sophomore when the series ends.

Henry Beismeyer (Marvin Kaplan) is Mel's most loyal customer (although he constantly complains about how bad Mel's cooking is). He is married to the domineering Chloe (Ruth Buzzi) and works for the phone company (he dreams of becoming the first intergalactic telephone repairman so Chloe can say "H.B. phone home"). Henry has two lunches each day: one at Mel's for loyalty and one at Benny's Beanery for pleasure. Henry wears Porky Pig pajamas and Chloe has to sing him a lullaby ("Rockabye Henry on the tree top ...") before he goes to sleep. In the last-season episodes, Henry and Chloe become the parents of twins.

In the series' last episode, Mel sells the diner, which he has owned for 27 years, to the Ferguson Brothers (who plan to tear it down). Alice finally gets her big break and moves to Nashville to sing with Travis Marsh. Vera discovered she was pregnant at the same time Elliott was promoted; and Jolene opened her own beauty parlor with money she inherited from her grandmother.

Linda Lavin sings the theme, "There's a New Girl in Town."

4.   **All in the Family** CBS, 1971–1979

In a quiet neighborhood at 704 Houser Street in Queens, New York, live Archie and Edith Bunker (Carroll O'Connor, Jean Stapleton), their married daughter, Gloria (Sally Struthers), and Gloria's husband, Mike Stivic (Rob Reiner).

Archie paid $14,000 for his home in 1951 and says "It's the only house on the block with a paid-up mortgage." He works as a dock foreman for the Prendergast Tool and Dye Company and drives a cab to make extra money. Archie drinks Schlitz beer, reads the New York *Daily News* and believes that credit is the American Way ("You can buy anything you can't afford"). He bowls on Tuesday nights and is a member of the Royal Brotherhood of the Kings of Queens Lodge (phone number 555-4378). His blood pressure varies between 168/95 and 178/90 and cigars are his only vice.

During World War II (the "Big One" as he calls it), Archie was first stationed at Fort Riley in Kansas. He later served 22 months in Italy with the Air Corps (where he was second in command of the motor pool). His hitch in the service earned him the Purple Heart, a good conduct medal and "a butt full of shrapnel—which is why I ain't danced with my wife for 30 years." "Whoop-dee-doo" is his catchphrase.

Archie grew up during the Great Depression. As a child he was called "Shoebootie" by the other kids (he wore one shoe and one bootie when his destitute family couldn't afford to buy him a pair of shoes). He is, today, a bigoted, uncouth, loud-mouthed conservative. Many of these traits come from his early upbringing where he was erroneously taught to believe in the superiority of his own race and to distrust foreign-born people of all kinds. Archie is not terribly intelligent. He is of normal intelligence and this, coupled with his environment, prevents him from learning much of anything new (he feels very threatened by all things he was never taught to fear). Archie is a strict conservative and pro law and order at any price. Archie considers the day that Sammy Davis, Jr. came to his house to be the greatest thing that ever happened to him (Sammy was permitted to sit in Archie's favorite easy chair by the TV—a privilege few can claim).

Archie first fell in love with Edith Baines in 1941 when he met her at the Puritan Maid Ice Cream Parlor. They dated and married shortly after. With the advent of television in 1948, Archie and Edith could not afford a set; they would watch "The Milton Berle Show" standing in front of the window of Tupperman's Department Store. Two years later they purchased their first set—a console with a six-inch screen.

Archie loves Edith very much and strayed only once, nearly having an affair with a woman named Denise (Janis Paige). Archie lovingly calls Edith "Dingbat" and often tells her to "stifle it" for talking too much. Edith is a simple housewife who takes life as it comes and sees only the good in people. She is totally honest and intuitive. Her best defense for survival with Archie has been her ability to know when to turn off, when to make a comment or when to say nothing.

Edith attended Millard Fillmore High School. In 1946 she held a job with the Hercules Plumbing Company. Her most "despicable act" occurred when she was six years old. She stole a five-cent O'Henry bar from the candy counter at F. W. Woolworth (she went back to make restitution but had to pay a dime as the price had gone up). "As the World Turns" is her favorite TV soap opera. Edith buys her meat at Klemer's Butcher Shop and earns $2.65 an hour as a Sunshine Lady at the Sunshine Home for the Elderly (she received the Citizen of the Week award for saving the life of an elderly man). Archie and Edith have joint accounts at the First Friendly Bank of Queens. Edith has three additional accounts that total $78: the Magic Potato Cutter Account; a Christmas Club account; and an account for her grandson, Joey. Edith was the first sitcom character to openly face menopause— a situation that caused the doctor to prescribe pills for Archie (who can't deal with "female problems").

Gloria was born at Bayside Hospital in Queens in 1944 (the hospital bill was $131.50). She earns $80 a week as a salesgirl at Kresler's Department Store and is called "Little Girl" by Archie. Gloria quit high school when she was 16 to take a secretarial course. She has been babied all her life, ever since Edith learned that she was anemic. Edith has protected Gloria and consequently, Gloria has rarely washed a dish or ironed a blouse. She is accustomed to being pampered and likes it. (Why she doesn't move out? If she does, she'll have to grow up and she is not ready for that.)

Gloria is married to Mike Stivic, a liberal who is Archie's exact opposite. Gloria met Mike in Manhattan and Archie first met him when Gloria invited him over for dinner (a later flashback finds Gloria meeting Mike, a hippie, when her girlfriend sets her up on a blind date). Mike is a dedicated humanitarian who hopes to become a social worker and change the world (as the series progressed, this was altered as Mike became a teacher). Gloria believes Mike is the most intelligent person she knows and is constantly torn between him and her father (she often sides with Mike because he is her husband and that is where her loyalties lie).

Gloria, 21 years old when the series begins, has led a sheltered life but is beginning to learn about the world from Mike. She is also realizing that her parents are wrong about a lot of things. Mike lives in a vacuum. He has no job, doesn't have to support a wife and has no responsibilities; he lives off Archie (who calls him "Meathead" and "You dumb Polack"). Mike believes Archie is harmful to what he is trying to do for the world. He believes Edith is ignorant, but sweet and harmless and he hopes to make Gloria more liberal (which he succeeded in doing when he gave her permission to pose nude for an artist—then became as uptight as Archie when she did it).

When the house next door becomes vacant, Mike and Gloria purchase it (at which time Gloria gives birth to a son they name Joey [Corey and Jason Drager]). Mike and Gloria had planned to name him Stanislaus, but changed their minds when Archie objected ("Kids are mean; they're gonna call him louse"). When Mike becomes a college teacher and a better paying job comes his way, he, Gloria and Joey move to Santa Barbara, California. Shortly after, Danielle Brisebois joins the cast as Stephanie Mills, the daughter of Edith's "no good" cousin, Floyd. Stephanie has been living with Floyd since the death of her mother in a car accident. When Edith learns that Floyd's drinking problem has been affecting Stephanie's welfare, she convinces a defiant Archie to let her live with them. Stephanie is Jewish and a member of the Temple Beth Shalom (Edith is Episcopalian; Archie mentioned that he is a Christian). Stephanie was born in May and attends Ditmars Junior High School.

Archie's neighbor and best friend is Barney Hefner (Allan Melvin), a bridge inspector for the city of New York. He is married to Blanche (Estelle Parsons) and has a dog named Rusty (who has a knack for messing up on Archie's front lawn). Teresa Betancourt (Liz Torres) is the nurse who comes to live with the Bunkers when Archie rents out Gloria's old room at $100 a month. She calls Archie "Mr. Bunkers" (although with her Spanish accent it comes out "Mr. Bonkers").

Carroll O'Connor and Jean Stapleton sing the theme, "Those Were the Days."

Note: Two unaired pilots were produced for ABC based on the British series "Till Death Us Do Part." The first, made in October 1968, was titled "And Justice for All." Carroll O'Connor was cast as a prejudiced elevator operator named Archie Justice. Jean Stapleton was his wife, Edith; Kelly Jean Peters was their daughter, Gloria; and Tim McIntire was Gloria's husband, Richard (not Mike). A second pilot, "Those Were the Days," was taped in February 1969. Carroll O'Connor and Jean Stapleton were Archie and Edith; Candace Azzara, Gloria; and Chip Oliver, Richard. When CBS expressed interest, producer Norman Lear shot a third pilot called "All in the Family" (wherein he changed Archie's last name to Bunker and Richard to Mike). Rob Reiner and Sally Struthers became Mike and Gloria and CBS bought the series.

Spinoffs

1. *Archie Bunker's Place*, CBS, 1979–1983. Archie buys his favorite watering hole, Kelsey's Bar (in Astoria, Queens), and reopens it as Archie Bunker's Place. In September 1979, Archie becomes a widower when Edith suffers a fatal stroke in her sleep. Barbara Lee "Billie" Bunker (Denise Miller)

joins Archie's household as his second ward. Billie is Archie's niece (his brother Fred's daughter). When Fred is unable to care for Billie he persuades Archie to help him (Archie figures she can help him with Stephanie and avoid those "womanly situations" he fears facing).

The bar is open from 9 A.M. to 4 A.M. daily. The printing on the front window says "Ladies Invited" and "Wine-Beer-Cocktails."

Billie works as a waitress at the bar. She does the cooking at home and shares a bedroom with Stephanie. Stephanie has her lunch at the bar (peach halves on cottage cheese "because it's healthy for me") and uses sliced peaches on her morning cereal; she and Billie drink Nestlé's Quik chocolate drink mix. Stephanie's favorite rock group is the Goo Goos and algebra is her most difficult course in school.

Billie was 12 years old when she first fell in love "with my orthodontist. I wanted to see him so badly I would go to see him every Saturday just to have my braces tightened." Stephanie would talk about cartoons, stuffed animals and roller-skates around Archie. "Now it's boys, boys, boys" he says. "She's growing up" explains Billie. "Not while I'm around she ain't," says Archie. Archie will let Stephanie have a boy who's a friend "but not a boy-friend." He feels she is only 13 and going to ruin the best years of her life— "Your obsolescence" as Archie puts it. Archie would prefer that Stephanie wear loose fitting clothes instead of clothes that show off her developing figure. It is at times like these, when Archie becomes involved with the girls and gets upset, that he heads for the kitchen for his relaxer—a beer. Archie is also a fan of John Wayne movies and believes that "if it appears in the *Enquirer*, it's true."

2. Gloria, CBS, 1982–1983. Before becoming a series (9/26/82) the pilot, "Gloria Comes Home," aired on "Archie Bunker's Place" (2/28/82). When Mike is unable to deal with society he leaves Gloria and Joey (Christopher Johnston) and moves to a commune in Humboldt, California. Gloria returns to Archie's home in Queens. Shortly after, Joey's pet turtle, Murphy, becomes ill. For unexplained reasons, Gloria travels 300 miles to Dutchess, New York, where she finds Dr. Willard Adams (Burgess Meredith), an elderly vet with a small practice in a community called Fox County. She becomes his assistant and the new series begins when she and Joey relocate. Joey has a dog named Archie.

3. Maude, CBS, 1972–1978. Maude Findlay (Bea Arthur) first appeared on the "Cousin Maude's Visit" episode of "All in the Family" (12/11/71). A second episode, "Maude" (3/11/72), became the actual pilot for the series (wherein Archie and Edith attend the wedding of Maude's daughter, Carol, played by Marcia Rodd). The series, set in Tuckahoe, New York, began on

September 12. Maude, a liberated, outspoken woman, lives at 30 Crenshaw Street (later 271 Elm Street) with her husband, Walter (Bill Macy), and her sexy, divorced daughter, Carol (Adrienne Barbeau). Carol is the mother of Philip (Brian Morris, Kraig Metzinger). Walter, Maude's fourth husband, owns the Findlay Friendly Appliance Store. Maude held various jobs and became a U.S. Congresswoman in the episode of 4/3/78. Walter retired to become Maude's aide in Washington, D.C. and the series ended. See "Good Times" for information on this series spinoff.

4. *The Jeffersons*, CBS, 1975–1985. See entry for information.

5.   The Amos 'n' Andy Show CBS, 1951–1953

Hoping to better their lives, Amos Jones (Alvin Childress) and Andrew "Andy" Halt Brown (Spencer Williams, Jr.) leave their home in Marietta, Georgia, and head for New York City. Amos is intelligent and level-headed; Andy is naive and easily manipulated. One day, while watching the construction of a new skyscraper in Manhattan, Andy meets George "Kingfish" Stevens (Tim Moore), a con artist, when Andy catches him trying to pick his pocket (or as George explains "One of my solid gold cufflinks must of gotten caught on your jacket sleeve"). Andy accepts the explanation and tells George that he and Amos have $340 to invest in a business. Before Andy realizes that he has been taken, George sells him a cab that is missing a door and its roof. Although disappointed in Andy's investment, Amos makes the best of it and starts the Fresh Air Taxi Cab Company of America, Inc. (Amos drives the cab; Andy oversees its operations. They eventually replace the cab's missing parts.)

Amos met his future wife, Ruby Taylor (Jane Adams), after a Sunday church social. They married and set up housekeeping at 134th Street and Lenox Avenue. Andy is single and lives in a small apartment on 134th Street. George has been married to the always nagging Sapphire (Ernestine Wade) since 1931 and lives with her and her mother, Mama (Amanda Randolph), at 134 East 145th Street. George is henpecked and can't get out from under the iron rule of Sapphire. She asks little of him, but that little, to find a steady job, is just too much for George to accept. George is a schemer and lives on cons. He tries to find work "but there ain't no jobs around for a man like me." George explained that his interest in money came at an early age. He attended a Christening and noticed that his uncle, Clarence, gave $500 to the parents when a baby was born into the family. Watching other people acquire Uncle Clarence's money gave George the notion that he too could make money by being clever. George's favorite activity is sleeping (which he does whenever he can) and he is the owner of a lot in New Jersey that he bought for $1,000 in 1932 ("figurin' New York would spread to New Jersey" and make him rich). Sapphire works for the Superfine Brush Company and is treasurer of the neighborhood Women's Club of Lenox Avenue.

Amos, the most stable member of the group, Andy and George are members of the Mystic Knights of the Sea Lodge (located at 127th Street and Lenox Avenue). George is the "Kingfish" and Andy, the entertainment chairman. Andy considers himself a ladies' man and supposedly had many girlfriends. He is most famous for his romantic involvement with Madame Queen (Lillian Randolph), the overbearing woman who stole his heart then sued him for breach of promise after they had planned to marry and she caught him with another woman.

George and Andy eat lunch at the Beanery, the diner next to the lodge hall. They both have accounts at the Lenox Savings Bank and the New Amsterdam Savings Bank. Andy's net worth, figuring in his life insurance policy, investments, Christmas Club, savings and checking accounts, amounts to nine dollars.

Algonquin J. Calhoun (Johnny Lee) is the totally inept lawyer Andy always hires to get him out of legal entanglements; Lightnin' (Nick O'Demus) is the slow-moving cab company janitor who doubles as the lodge hall janitor. He calls George "Mr. Kingfish" and Andy "Mr. Andy."

The series was adapted from the radio program of the same title wherein two white men, Freeman Gosden and Charles Correll, played Amos and Andy. Clarence Lucas and Joseph Breil composed the theme, "The Perfect Song."

6.   The Andy Griffith Show CBS, 1960–1968

Mayberry is a small, mythical town in North Carolina. Its people are friendly and most businesses are run by people everyone knows. There's Wally's Filling Station, Weaver's Department Store, Floyd's Barber Shop, The Junction Cafe and the courthouse where justice of the peace and sheriff Andrew Jackson "Andy" Taylor (Andy Griffith) and his deputy, Bernard "Barney" Fife (Don Knotts), have their base of operations. (Barney's middle name was given as Milton, Milton P. and Oliver.)

Andy's office is a bit old-fashioned. There are no submachine guns or tear gas grenades, though the office does have a wall rack with five to seven rifles (depending on the episode) and some emergency equipment—a rake and shovel that Andy carries in the trunk of his squad car (license plate JL 322; later JL 327). Crime is virtually nonexistent and upholding the law includes patrolling the streets after dark (to make sure each businessman has locked his door), helping children across the street, handing out parking tickets and replacing lids on garbage cans. Barney has the added duties of fly swatting and changing the pillow cases at the office jail.

Andy does not carry a gun (he is called the "Sheriff Without a Gun" by the national sheriffs' magazine). Barney wears a gun—but he is not allowed to keep it loaded (he carries the one bullet Andy permits him to have in his shirt pocket; sometimes in the right, sometimes in the left). Barney weighs 132 pounds, is easily excited and not taken seriously by lawbreakers (he waves his arms, makes speeches and rants). When Barney is permitted to use his gun, he does so to start the potato race at the Mason's Picnic.

Andy and Barney are actually cousins and graduates of Mayfield Union High School (class of 1945; orange and blue are the school colors). Barney has been a deputy for five of the 12 years Andy has been sheriff. Andy's address was given as both 322 Maple Street and 14 Maple Street. Barney lives at 411 Elm Street. Andy sings and plays the guitar; Barney plays the harmonica. Barney's birthstone is the ruby and he and Andy eat at the Junction Cafe (also called the Diner. Juanita is the unseen waitress; catfish casserole is the Friday special). Barney calls Andy "Anj" (Andy calls him "Barn") and he fears that one day "Mayberry is going to turn into a sin town." When a better opportunity comes his way, Barney leaves Mayberry (1965) to take a job in traffic with the Raleigh Police Department (he is later promoted to the position of staff detective). Andy replaced Barney with Deputy Warren Ferguson (Jack Burns), a character that just didn't work and was dropped—without a replacement—after four months (10/11/65–1/31/66). Raleigh and Mt. Pilot are Mayberry's neighboring towns; Capital City is the area's major metropolis.

When Andy wants to know what is going on in town, he asks his Aunt Bee, who seems to know all the town gossip. Beatrice Taylor (Frances Bavier) cares for Andy (a widower) and his young son, Opie (Ronny Howard). Aunt Bee is noted for her cooking and her ability to maintain a vegetable garden. She is famous for her homemade pickles and pies (apple and butterscotch pecan being Andy and Opie's favorites). Aunt Bee won assorted prizes for her cooking knowledge on the TV game show "Win or Lose" and she was awarded a trip to Mexico for winning the Tampico Tamale Contest. She is a member of the church choir, the Greater Mayberry Historical Society and the garden club. She claims that "Andy is meaner than a bear that backed into a beehive when he doesn't get his supper" and wrote the town's sentimental song, "Mayberry, My Home Town" with her friend Clara Edwards (Hope Summers). Aunt Bee's catchphrase is "Oh, fiddle-faddle."

Before dinner Opie washes his hands and face, empties the dirt from his pants cuffs and puts his lizard, Oscar, outside in his lizard house. Opie also has a dog (Gulliver) and a parakeet (Dinkie). He attends the Mayberry School and enjoys fishing with his father at Meyer's Lake (where they are seen in the opening theme and where Andy has a small rowboat named "Gertrude"). When guests stay over, they use Opie's room; Opie enjoys sleeping on the ironing board between two chairs ("It's adventurous sleeping" he says).

Eleanor "Ellie" Walker (Elinor Donahue) was Andy's original girlfriend. Andy called her "Miss Ellie" and she worked as a pharmacist at the Walker Drug Store. Andy later falls for and marries Helen Crump (Aneta Corsaut), Opie's grade school teacher. Thelma Lou (Betty Lynn) is Barney's longtime girlfriend (her phone number is Mayberry 596).

Floyd Lawson (Howard McNear) owns the barbershop (next to the TV repair shop). He charges $1.75 for a haircut, 50 cents for a shave, and 25 cents for a shampoo. Floyd has been deputized to carry the flag in the yearly Veterans Day Parade. Leon (Clint Howard) is the little boy who offers his peanut butter sandwich to Andy and Barney.

Gomer and Goober Pyle (Jim Nabors, George Lindsey) are cousins who work at a gas station called both Wally's Filling Station and Wally's Service Station. Goober is deputized yearly to guard the cannon in the park on Halloween "to prevent kids from putting orange peels, taters and rotten tomatoes in it." The station sells Acme Gasoline, and Mayberry 371J is Goober's phone number. Gomer left the series to become a Marine in 1964 (see *Gomer Pyle, U.S.M.C.* for information).

Emmett Clark (Paul Hartman) owns Emmett's Fix-It Shop; Otis Campbell (Hal Smith) is the town drunk and has his own jail privileges (he locks himself up when he gets drunk and lets himself out when he is sober). Howard Sprague (Jack Dodson) is the county clerk and Ernest T. Bass (Howard Morris) is the troublemaking hillbilly.

On Sunday afternoons, the unseen 80-year-old Mendlebright sisters—Maude and Cora—visit by phone. Maude lives in Mayberry and Cora in Mt. Pilot ("It's kinda hard for them to get about" says Andy). Earle Hagen composed *The Andy Griffith Show* theme (also known as "The Fishin' Hole").

Origins: The pilot episode aired on *The Danny Thomas Show* on 2/15/60. Here Andy was the sheriff, justice of the peace and newspaper editor (there was no Barney). He and Opie were cared for by their unseen Aunt Lucy. Their housekeeper, Rose, was played by Mary Treen; Frances Bavier was a citizen named Henrietta Perkins. The town drunk was Will Hoople,

played by Frank Cady. The story found Andy arresting entertainer Danny
Williams (Danny Thomas) for speeding when he refused to pay the fine.

Spinoffs

1. When Andy, Helen and Opie move (1968), *Mayberry, R.F.D.* (1968–
1971) evolves to focus on Sam Jones (Ken Berry), a widowed farmer who
becomes a city councilman. Millie Swanson (Arlene Golonka) is his girlfriend (later wife) and Mike (Buddy Foster) is his son. Aunt Bee moved in
to become Sam's housekeeper but left after two years. She was replaced by
Alice Ghostley as Sam's cousin, Alice, who had just retired from the army
after a 20 year hitch.

2. NBC broadcast *Return to Mayberry*, a TV movie reunion, on 4/13/86.
Andy and Helen return to Mayberry where Andy runs for the office of sheriff
without knowing that his opponent is acting sheriff Barney Fife (who, after
25 years, is still engaged to Thelma Lou). Opie is now married to Eunice
(Karlene Crockett) and is the editor of the Mayberry *Courier-Express* (orig-
inally the *Gazette*). Gomer and Goober now own their own gas station, the
G&G Garage. Otis, the former town drunk, is now an ice cream truck driver;
Howard Sprague is now Opie's assistant.

3. *Goober and the Trucker's Paradise*, CBS, 5/17/78. An unsold pilot
in which Goober Pyle (George Lindsey) moves to a small town outside Atlanta
where he and his sister, Pearl Pyle (Leigh French), open a truck stop cafe
(The Trucker's Paradise). Charlene (Sandi Newton) is the waitress; Becky
Pyle (Audrey Landers) is Goober's niece; and Toni Pyle (Lindsay Bloom) is
Goober's younger sister.

7.   The Ann Sothern Show CBS, 1958–1961

The theme tells us that "all the fellas fall for Katie, 'cause Katie is the
gal they adore." The very feminine and attractive Katie, short for Kathleen
O'Connor (Ann Sothern), is the assistant manager of the Bartley House, a
fashionable hotel at 36 East 56th Street in Manhattan. Katie lives at 21 East
10th Street in Greenwich Village and shares Apartment 3B with her secretary and best friend, Olive Smith (Ann Tyrrell); their address is also given
as 15 Greenwich Place. James Devery (Don Porter), a 1938 graduate of Harvard, began his career as a bellboy before becoming manager of the hotel.
He was born on August 23, 1916, and his middle name was given as both
Aloysius and Arlington. Jason Macauly and his domineering wife, Flora
(Ernest Truex, Reta Shaw), were the original hotel managers (transferred to

India to manage the Calcutta Bartley Hotel in 1959). Ann Sothern and Bonny Lake composed the theme, "Katie."

Archie Bunker's Place *see* All in the Family

8. Arnie CBS, 1970–1972

The house at 4650 Liberty Lane in Los Angeles is owned by Arnie Nuvo and his wife, Lillian (Herschel Bernardi, Sue Ane Langdon). Arnie, a former dock worker for Continental Flange, Inc., now earns $20,000 a year as the head of New Product Development. Lillian, a former Perfect Figure lingerie model, cares for the house and is the mother of their children, Andrea and Richard (Stephanie Steele, Del Russell), students at Westside High School. Their neighbor, Randy Robinson (Charles Nelson Reilly), hosts the TV cooking show "The Giddyup Gourmet." Arnie's boss, Hamilton Majors, Jr. (Roger Bowen), is a tightwad ("Save!" is his favorite expression) and is a member of the Bayshore Polo Club. Harry Geller composed the *Arnie* theme.

9. Bachelor Father CBS, 1957–1958; NBC, 1958–1961; ABC, 1961–1962

Bentley Gregg (John Forsythe) is a sophisticated private-practice attorney with an office (106) in the Crescent Building on Crescent Drive in Los Angeles. He lives at 1163 Rexford Drive in Beverly Hills with his niece, Kelly (Noreen Corcoran), a pretty 13-year-old who became his responsibility after her parents were killed in a car accident. Also living with them is Peter Tong (Sammee Tong), Bentley's Chinese houseboy, and their dog, Jaspar. Bentley's license plate reads RXR 553.

Bentley, a graduate of Harvard Law School, sometimes wonders why he didn't take up medicine when clients give him a hard time ("one of my professors said 'Why Bentley, with hands like that you'd make a brilliant surgeon'"). Bentley is not only sophisticated, but is a smooth and brilliant conversationalist. Girls swoon as he always manages to say the right thing. Peter calls him "the greatest general in the romancing department" and when Kelly sees her uncle dressed in a tuxedo she says "Gosh Uncle Bentley, you look beautiful." Bentley plays golf and tennis and treats his dates to dinner at the Coconut Grove and dancing at the Ambassador Room. While Bentley dates the most gorgeous women on TV, he says "The toughest thing about being a bachelor is remaining one" (his married friends are trying to find him a wife).

Kelly and her friends Howard Meechim (Jimmy Boyd) and Ginger (Bernadette Withers) attend Beverly Hills High School. Kelly's favorite subject is math, and Bill's Malt Shop is the after-school hangout. Kelly has an 11 P.M. curfew (at age 15) and every so often Bentley gives her "a cost of living increase in her allowance." He also says that he can't figure her out: "She's too young for mink and too old to ride bicycles." Bentley realized that Kelly, at age 15½, was growing up and becoming a responsible adult. He welcomed her into the adult world by giving her her own key to the house (something she had wanted for a long time). Kelly kisses Uncle Bentley on the forehead before she goes out; he kisses her on top of the head in the morning before he sits down to breakfast. Kelly doesn't like it when a boy calls on her by honking his car horn ("I like it when my boyfriends ring the doorbell"). She believes that the girls her uncle dates get all the breaks: "Imagine being able to spend an evening with a charming, sophisticated man of the world like you. I'm stuck with Howard." While Uncle Bentley says "What's wrong with Howard?" Kelly believes everything is wrong with him— from being immature to lacking Uncle Bentley's polish and finesse. Howard is more often than not Kelly's boyfriend. Kelly takes him for granted and he's always there for her when she needs him. Howard's idea of dressing up is wearing a suit with white sneakers ("My feet gotta breathe when I dance"). Kelly is determined to whip Howard into an Uncle Bentley—"The raw material is all there, he just has to be molded." Howard listens and tries, but can't and says "There's gotta be a better way." Howard is eventually dropped from the picture when Kelly falls in love with Warren Dawson (Aaron Kincaid), a young lawyer who joins Bentley's practice in 1962.

Ginger lives next door to Kelly and has three last names: Farrell (1957–58) with Catherine McLeod as her widowed mother, Louise; Loomis (1958–61) with Whit Bissell and Florence MacMichael as her parents, Bert and Amy Loomis (Bert owns a toy company); and Mitchell (1961–62) with Del Moore and Evelyn Scott as Cal and Adelaide Mitchell.

Peter has dinner ready every night at 7 P.M. He calls Bentley "Mr. Gregg" and Kelly "Niece Kelly." He attends night school to improve his knowledge of America and mutters in Chinese when he gets upset. He has many relatives and two of them, Grandpa Ling (Beal Wong) and Cousin Charlie (Victor Sen Yung), appear often. Peter calls Grandpa Ling "a 70-year-old juvenile delinquent." He doesn't understand the concept of American money and uses the barter system (whether the people he comes in contact with want to or not). He knows only three words of English: "Hello, Joe" and "Nice." Peter calls Cousin Charlie the "Beatnik of the family." He is always borrowing money from Peter and never pays him back ("He act like I U.S. Government and he foreign country," says Peter). Con artist Charlie was first introduced with the last name of Ling, then Fong.

The original pilot, *New Girl in His Life*, aired on "G.E. Theater" on 5/26/57. John Forsythe, Noreen Corcoran and Sammee Tong played the same roles; the proposed series title was *Uncle Bentley*. Johnny Williams composed the *Bachelor Father* theme.

10.   The Bad News Bears CBS, 1979–1980

Morris Buttermaker (Jack Warden) is a former minor-league ballplayer turned pool cleaner who coaches the Bears, the undisciplined little-league ball team of the W. Wendell Weaver School at 1647 Lorraine Court in Santa Barbara, California. Eleven-year-old Amanda Wurlitzer (Tricia Cast) is the star pitcher (jersey 11). She takes ballet lessons, wants to be a model and feels baseball is just a phase "because I'll be getting a bra soon and won't care anymore." She is famous for her 2½ foot curveball (which she learned from Morris). Mike Engelberg (J. Brennan Smith) is the overweight catcher who "eats for energy"; Timothy Lupus (Shane Butterworth) is the shy right fielder; and Ahmad Abdul Rahim (Christoff St. John) is the switch hitter and fastest runner (Hank Aaron is his idol). The Lions, coached by Roy Turner (Phillip R. Allen), are the Bears' rival for the championship. Based on the feature film.

11.   The Betty Hutton Show CBS, 1959–1960

Goldie Appleby (Betty Hutton), a former showgirl turned manicurist, lives at 346 West 41st Street (Apartment 18A) with her friends Lorna Patterson (Joan Shawlee) and Rosemary Zandt (Jean Carson). Lorna works with Goldie at the Mid Manhattan Beauty Salon; Rosemary is a waitress at the Pelican Club. Lorna is stingy; Goldie, frugal; and Rosemary somewhat flaky. "Cu-cu" is Goldie's catchphrase (which she says when something strikes her fancy). The pilot episode finds Goldie quitting her job to become the guardian of Patricia, Nicky and Roy Strickland (Gigi Perreau, Richard Miles, Dennis Joel), the spoiled children of a client whose sudden, unexpected death made her the head of the $60 million Strickland estate on Park Avenue. Patricia, a teenager, feels she is awkward, and she is struggling to become part of the social circle; Roy is the intellectual and, as Goldie puts it, "The Adolphe Menjou of the grade school set" (she feels he is more like a distinguished gentleman of 50 rather than a boy of 12). On Lorna's birthday, Goldie treats the girls to a night on the town; on Goldie's birthday, Rosemary treats them;

on Rosemary's birthday, it's Lorna's treat (and she seeks the cheapest way possible). Jerry Fielding composed the theme; the series is also known as *Goldie*.

12.   The Beulah Show CBS, 1950–1953

Beulah (Ethel Waters, Hattie McDaniel, Louise Beavers) is a black maid who considers her white employers, the Hendersons, "my family." Harry, the father (William Post, Jr., David Bruce), is a lawyer with the firm of Henderson and Associates, and lives at 213 Lake Street with his wife, Alice (Ginger Jones, Jane Frazee), and son, Donnie (Clifford Sales, Stuffy Singer). Beulah is looking for a husband and is a member of the Ladies Auxiliary Sewing Circle. She calls Harry "Mr. Harry" and Alice "Miss Alice." Harry enjoys playing golf on Saturday and has a prize rosebush in the front garden. Alice is a member of the local bridge club and Donnie, who enjoys hiking and catching frogs, races his soapbox racer, the "Fire Streak," down the 36th Street hill. Beulah's boyfriend, Bill Jackson (Percy "Bud" Harris, Dooley Wilson, Ernest Whitman), owns Jackson's Fix-It-Shop and eats at Slippery Joe's Diner. Beulah's scatterbrained girlfriend, Oriole (Butterfly McQueen, Ruby Dandridge), "knows everything about nothing." Based on the 1945–46 CBS radio series *The Marlin Hurt and Beulah Show*, wherein a white man (Marlin Hurt) played Beulah, the black maid to white businessman Marlin Hurt (Himself). The series was revised by ABC in 1947 as *Beulah* with a white man (Bob Corley) playing Beulah. When CBS picked up the series (1947–52), Hattie McDaniel, Louise Beavers and Lillian Randolph played the title role.

13.   The Beverly Hillbillies CBS, 1962–1971

Jedidiah "Jed" Clampett (Buddy Ebsen) is a poor, widowed mountaineer who lives in a small, run-down cabin near Blueberry Ridge in the Ozark community of Sibley. His cabin sits on a half acre of land "that is mostly stumps and rocks." His daughter, Elly Mae (Donna Douglas), and his mother-in-law, Daisy "Granny" Moses (Irene Ryan), also live with him. The Clampetts are eight miles from their nearest neighbor and are overrun with bobcats, possums, coyotes and skunks. They drink homemade moonshine, use kerosene lamps for light, cook on a wood-burning stove and wash with Granny's homemade lye soap. The outhouse is 50 feet from the cabin.

One day, while hunting for food, Jed shoots at a rabbit. The bullet misses its target and strikes the ground near his swamp. Oil emerges from the ground but Jed sees this as only another problem to deal with. A short time later, a wildcatter for the O.K. Oil Company in Tulsa, Oklahoma, spots the oil. John Brewster (Frank Wilcox), head of O.K. Oil, purchases "the headache" from Jed for $25 million. Jed's cousin, Pearl Bodine (Bea Benedaret), convinces Jed that he should live a better life and move to Beverly Hills (Jed likes the thought of "hills"). Jed's money is deposited in the Commerce Bank of Beverly Hills and the bank president, Milburn Drysdale (Raymond Bailey), purchases the mansion next to his for the Clampetts. With the help of Pearl's son Jethro (Max Baer, Jr.) and a loan of her 1920 Oldsmobile truck, Jed, Elly Mae, Granny and Jethro head for a new life out west.

The Clampetts' 32- (sometimes 35-) room, 14-bathroom mansion sits on nine to ten acres of land at 518 Crestview Drive (it was said to be owned by actor John Barrymore, who built it in 1933). The Clampetts call the $50,000 swimming pool in the backyard "The Cement Pond" and they believe that the steps leading to the water are for the wildlife when they come down from the hills for a drink. There is a stone figure of a woman pouring water into the pool they call the "Rock Lady." They call the pool table the "Big Fancy Eating Table" and the room in which it sits the "Fancy Eating Room." Jed uses the pool cues as "pot passers."

Despite the modern conveniences, Jed longs for the life he had in the Ozarks. He continues to dress in his shabby clothes and has also brought his hunting dog, Duke, with him. Mustard greens and possum innards are Jed's favorite foods ("There's one thing about possum innards—they're just as good the second day"). When something pleases Jed he says "Well Doggies"; when the front doorbell rings Jed remarks "There's them bells again" (the family is not aware of what doorbells are). Jed's late wife was named Rose Ellen. He attended Oxford Grammar School in Arkansas, and in 1963 his assets totaled $34,783,127.34 (by the time the series ended, the total grew to $80 million). Through Drysdale's investments, Jed became the owner of the Mammoth Film Studios in Hollywood. Jed also purchased a dress shop (The House of Renee) for Granny and reopened it as The House of Granny. He was swindled into buying "farmland" at the Happy Valley Cemetery and planned to take a job as a garbage man (for the "nifty uniform") until Drysdale talked him out of it and persuaded Brewster to make Jed an executive at O.K. Oil.

Elly Mae has a special place in her heart for animals (which she calls "critters"). She has a rooster, Earl (who can play dead), two chimpanzees, Skipper and Bessie (also called Beth), a jaguar (Jasper), raccoon (Elmer), squirrel (Nicky), cat (Rusty) and a duck (Charley).

Elly Mae is a beautiful young woman who dresses like a boy (when she got her first bra she thought it was "a store-bought lace-trimmed double-barreled sling shot"). Jed raised Elly Mae as best he knew how—like a boy (rough housing, fighting and fishing). Elly Mae was fearful of dressing like a girl because the boys called her "sissy." Jed wants her to become refined like her mother, but ever since she could walk, she has been climbing trees and "cuddlin' creatures." When someone mistakes Elly Mae for a boy she says "Why thank you." Granny claims that "the boys came a courtin' Elly Mae when she was 12 and she fought them off" (Elly Mae has to prove she is better than any man by "wrestlin'" them to the ground). Jed tried to teach Elly Mae about the birds and the bees but hasn't had much success as Elly Mae sees them in a literal light and says "Gee Paw, I'm fond of those little creatures."

"The big tree out front" is Elly Mae's favorite hiding place on the Clampett property. She attended the all-girl Willows Academy for Select Young Ladies and when she stretches, Granny remarks "Watch them buttons girl" (as they pop off her blouse).

Jethro, born on December 4, spent two years in the first grade, three years in the fourth grade and brags that he "was educated and graduated from the sixth grade" (at the Millicent Schyler Potts School, a private institution that teaches kindergarten to sixth grade; in the hills, Jethro attended the Oxford Grammar School). Jethro is considered "the educated one in the family" and is the only one who delights in the excitement of the big city. His main goal is to attract the opposite sex "and find me a sweetheart." Jethro had ambitions to be an astronaut ("to find Moon Maidens"), a streetcar conductor, a pig farmer, "do brain surgerin'," become a folk singer and a movie star (he did hold a job as a stunt double for film star Dash Riprock). Jethro, as a Marlon Brando type of lead, Elly Mae as the sexy Venus Adore, and Granny as the Dancehall Queen starred in an untitled film that was a ruse by a con artist to get money from Jed. When Jed feels Jethro has done something wrong, he remarks "I gotta have a long talk with that boy."

Jethro loves Granny's cooking (which he calls vittles) but is not permitted to indulge in Granny's moonshine until he gets married. At Oxford, Jethro was the champion crawdad eater. When something pleases Jethro he yells "Yee Haw."

Granny believes Jefferson Davis is the president of the U.S. She won "The Miss Good Sport Award" at the Bug Tussle Bathing Beauty Contest at Expo 1897 and has an all-around cure for ailments called Granny's Spring Tonic. Granny, born in Tennessee, has a double-barreled 12-gauge shotgun she uses "to get rid of revenuers." She plays a 200-year-old lap organ and refuses to give up the customs of the hills. She has a still in the backyard (to brew her "Rheumatiz Medicine") and claims she is the only one in the family who can hold a grudge. Granny can predict when it is going to rain by "twinges" ("aches in my bones") and her life savings of $5,000 is in Confederate money. When Granny makes her lye soap, noxious vapors are emitted that peel the bark off trees, kill her neighbor's prize hibiscus plants and, as Jed says, "Can bring a full grown mule to its knees." Granny's perfume is "pure vanilly extract." She is not sure of her exact age and mentioned that her mother fell into a swamp and drowned. When Granny became homesick, Jed built her a replica of their hills cabin in the backyard so "Granny could live the good life again."

When Milburn Drysdale acquired Jed's money, making the Clampetts his largest depositor, he gave his secretary, Jane Hathaway (Nancy Kulp), a second job: to cater to Jed's every whim. When Jane first met the Clampetts she mistook them for the mansion's servants; when she got to know Jethro, she summed him up as "a magnificent skyscraper with an uncomplicated penthouse" (in a later episode she says he "is a lighthouse. Strong, tall and sturdy. Too bad his beacon isn't as bright"). Jane, a bird watcher, is a graduate of Vassar and calls Milburn "Chief" (the Clampetts call her "Miss Jane").

Milburn will do anything to please the Clampetts so they will not take their money out of his bank. He is a man of vision and is seeking to exploit the potential of the Clampett income. To Milburn, "Jed is my kind of people—loaded" (Jed's deposit made the Commerce Bank third in capital assets). It was said that Milburn's mother's family had feuded with Granny's family, the Moses, back in Tennessee. When Milburn is happy, his wife, Margaret (Harriet MacGibbon), isn't. She has a pampered French poodle (Claude) and seeks ways to get the Clampetts out of her life (she feels they are a disgrace to the neighborhood). "Mother's baby" is Milburn's stepson (Margaret's son), Sonny (Louis Nye). Sonny is pampered and has been in college for 17 years ("I'm trying to find myself"). He likes Elly Mae "even though she's not a blueblood" and "digs that crazy package she comes in." When Sonny dates a girl, he gives her a picture of himself instead of candy or flowers.

Jethro's mother, Pearl, was a recurring regular in early episodes (Bea Benaderet left in 1963 to star in "Petticoat Junction"). Pearl taught music and her specialty was yodeling (which Granny considered a punishment to hear). The original, unaired pilot for the series, *The Hillbillies of Beverly Hills*, has the same cast but the music (uncredited) is different (no singing and a different tune). The story line differs in that Jed knew about the oil in the swamp (the hunting aspect was not used) and he sold it just to rid himself of a nuisance. The only other change is the name of the bank (called the Beverly Hills Bank). Jerry Scoggins sings the theme, "The Ballad of Jed Clampett," with music provided by Flatt and Scruggs.

TV Movie Update

The Return of the Beverly Hillbillies, CBS, 10/6/81. After Granny's passing, Jed (Buddy Ebsen) divided his vast estate between his daughter, Elly Mae (Donna Douglas), and his nephew, Jethro (Ray Young). Jed moved back to the hills; Elly Mae opened her own zoo (Elly's Zoo) and Jethro became the owner of the Mammoth Film Studios in Hollywood. Jane Hathaway (Nancy Kulp), now an employee of the Energy Department in Washington, D.C., experiments with some of Granny's moonshine and discovers that it has the potential to double our country's output of gasoline and oil. The story follows Jane as she seeks the formula for the moonshine from the only person who knows its secret: Granny's Maw (Imogene Coca), a 104-year-old woman who is not about to give away any family secrets.

14. Bewitched ABC, 1964–1972

Darrin Stevens (Dick York, Dick Sargent) and his wife, Samantha (Elizabeth Montgomery), are newlyweds who live at 1164 Morning Glory Circle in Westport, Connecticut. Darrin, an account executive for the Manhattan advertising firm of McMann and Tate, and Samantha met by accident—by bumping into each other. It was on their honeymoon at Connecticut's Moon Thatcher Inn that Samantha revealed to Darrin that she is a witch, "a cauldron-stirring, broom-riding witch." To please Darrin, Samantha agrees not to use her magic. The decision upsets Samantha's powerful parents, Endora and Maurice (Agnes Moorehead, Maurice Evans), as well as the Witches' Council, who object to witch-mortal marriages. Their home, also said to be at 164 Morning Glory Circle, was purchased from the Hopkins Realty Company. Trash pickups are on Tuesday and Friday; 555-2134 is their phone number and 4R6 558 is Darrin's license plate (555-6059 is his office phone number).

Samantha, called "Sam" by Darrin, and Darrin enjoy meals at Cerino's Restaurant (beef stew and scrambled eggs with chicken livers are his favorite meals; ringtail pheasant is the only food that will satisfy Samantha when she has a craving). Joe's Bar and Grill (also called Mulvanney's Bar) is Darrin's favorite hangout (to drown his sorrows when Samantha uses her magic against his wishes). Samantha evokes her magic by wrinkling her nose. The musical effect that is heard, called "Samantha's Twitch," is performed by theme composer Warren Barker on the xylophone. When something troubles Samantha she says "Oh my stars."

When the Witches' Council becomes upset with Samantha, it short-circuits her by taking away her powers (so she can experience "a power failure"). Being an earthbound witch also exposes Samantha to a number of unusual conditions (like red horizontal stripes on her face, rhyming words, voracious appetite, uncontrollable laughing or crying, and a buildup of weight caused by unused magic called Gravititis Inflammitis).

Ordinary doctors are unable to help Samantha. When medical assistance is needed, she uses the atmospheric continuum to contact her family physician, Dr. Bombay (Bernard Fox): "Calling Dr. Bombay, calling Dr. Bombay. Emergency." Samantha has a knack of summoning the doctor in the middle of something (like chasing his nurse, dolphin riding) and has a difficult time contacting him on a Saturday (his day for buffalo polo). Although called a "witch doctor" by Darrin, Dr. Bombay's cures often work.

Samantha and Darrin became the parents of Tabitha, a witch (Erin and Diane Murphy), and Adam, a warlock (David and Greg Lawrence). Tabitha's birth on 1/13/66 also introduced Serena, Samantha's beautiful "goddess of love" cousin (played by Elizabeth Montgomery under the name Pandora Spocks). The mischievous Serena is a member of the Cosmos Club and entertainment chairwoman of the Cosmos Cotillion. Serena has a birthmark on her face that changes with each episode. Usually on the left side of her face near her lower eye lid, it takes the form of, among other things, an anchor, a question mark, a heart, a peace sign, and the letter S for Serena. Serena enjoys demonstrating her unperfected karate skills and doesn't trust anyone over 3,000 years old. Her favorite wine is Château Lafite Rothschild 1923 and she wrote a song called "Kisses in the Wind." A later episode changes Tabitha's birthday to Mother's Day (at which time Darrin gave Samantha the Weeping Willow tree that is in front of their house).

Endora's favorite breakfast is fried raven's eggs and she can temporarily lose her powers if she mixes eye of newt with oysters or is exposed to black Bavarian roses. Endora is chairwoman of the Witches' Council (also called the Witches' Committee) and frequents the Avant Garde art gallery. Her favorite color is purple and she often calls Darren "Dumbo," "Durwood" or "Dum Dum." When Darrin first met the 118-pound, five foot six inch Endora he asked, "Mrs. ...?" Endora responded with "You'll never be able to pronounce it." When a client of Darrin's became fascinated with Endora, he asked her to star in a series of commercials for Autumn Flame, "a perfume for older chicks." She refused.

Although married to Endora, Maurice lives a life separate from her. He is a powerful, distinguished warlock and feels Darrin does not meet his standards for the ideal son-in-law. He is a member of the Warlock Club and quotes Shakespeare. He calls Darrin "Duspin," "Dustin," "Dobbin" and "Duncan" and turns him into objects when he becomes upset (for example, a statute, an old pair of galoshes, a donkey, a raven and a monkey. Endora has also had fun with Darrin, casting spells on him which force him to do things like talk in rhyme, tell the truth, be unable to speak English, grant wishes without his knowledge, and slowly shrink).

"When I think of you as a blood relative, I long for a transfusion" says Uncle Arthur (Paul Lynde) about Endora. Arthur, Samantha's fun-loving, practical-joke-playing uncle, is famous for his table cloth trick (pulling the cloth out from under the dishes without breaking them; Sam can do the trick backwards—placing the cloth under the dishes). Uncle Arthur calls the Witches' Council the "Old Cronies," Endora the "Wicked Witch of the West," and Sam "Sammie." Serena calls Arthur "Unkie Pooh."

Samantha's Aunt Clara (Marion Lorne), an aging and bumbling witch, is famous for her doorknob collection. She was once lady-in-waiting to Queen Victoria and when she casts a spell the wrong things happen. She has trouble remembering the spell she used to reverse it and Sam calms an upset Darrin by telling him "Aunt Clara will think of the spell and everything will be right again."

Esmerelda (Alice Ghostley) is the shy witch who usually appears as a piece of clothing (for example, a hat, a coat, a pair of shoes) before the rest of her materializes. When she gets nervous she sneezes and something unexpected pops in (for example, a palm tree, a goat). She feels Darrin doesn't like her and pops out whenever she hears his voice.

The Happy Time Bar is the favorite hangout of Darrin's boss, Larry Tate (David White). Larry, president of the ad agency, is married to Louise (Irene Vernon, Kasey Rogers). Larry takes credit for Darrin's ideas, has silver hair (red in his youth) and is called "Peter Cotton Top" by Serena.

Abner Kravitz (George Tobias) and his wife, Gladys (Alice Pearce, Sandra Gould), are Sam and Darrin's neighbors. Gladys is convinced there is something weird going on at the Stevens house; she sees things no one else does. Abner pays little attention to her (he reads the newspaper or plays chess by himself) and the police consider her a kook for her reports which they see as imagined incidents.

At the age of one, Tabitha first showed evidence of being a witch. She touched her nose and levitated a toy. When a client of Darrin's saw Tabitha, he signed her up as a model for his company, Robbins Truck Transmissions. On April 24, 1976, a pilot for a *Tabitha* series aired on ABC. In it, Liberty

Williams played Tabitha as a 24-year-old editorial assistant at a fashionable San Francisco magazine called *Trend*. Bruce Kimmel was her warlock brother, Adam, and Barbara Cason was Roberta, Tabitha's boss. A second *Tabitha* pilot (ABC, 5/7/77) led to a 12-episode ABC series (9/10/77–1/14/78) with Lisa Hartman as Tabitha, now a production assistant at KXLA-TV in Los Angeles. David Ankrum was her brother, Adam, and Karen Morrow her Aunt Minerva.

15.   The Bickersons Syn., 1951

Apartment 22 at 123 Engelwood Drive is home to John and Blanche Bickerson (Lew Parker, Virginia Grey), a married couple who argue about everything. John is a vacuum cleaner salesman for Household Appliances; Blanche, a housewife, says that "John doesn't act human until he gets his morning coffee" (which he enjoys with duck eggs and reindeer milk). John is a chronic snorer ("It's like trying to sleep next to Cape Canaveral" says Blanche) and Murphy's Bar and Grill is John's favorite hangout. Blanche and John have been married eight years and they have a cat named Nature Boy (originally Joy Boy). They keep their money in the sugar bowl; the ironing board doubles as the kitchen table and they have a humongous refrigerator (then called an icebox) with six doors. Adapted from the radio series of the same title (NBC, 1946–47; CBS, 1947–48; 1951) with Don Ameche and then Lew Parker as John, and Frances Langford and then Marsha Henderson as Blanche.

16.   The Bing Crosby Show ABC, 1964–1965

Bing Collins and his wife Ellie (Bing Crosby, Beverly Garland) live at 168 Valley Tree Lane in Los Angeles. They are the parents of 15-year-old Joyce (Carol Faylen) and ten-year-old Janice (Diane Sherry). Bing is a former singer-musician turned engineer who is now a member of the teaching staff of Colbert University (originally, Taylor University). Ellie is a former singer; Joyce attends Richmont High School; and Janice, called "Champ" by Bing, attends Gorman Elementary School. Bing Crosby sings the opening theme, "That's Life," and the closing signature, "It All Adds Up to Love."

17.   Blansky's Beauties ABC, 1977

"The Major Putnam Spectacular—La Plume de la Putnam" is a stage show produced by Nancy Blansky (Nancy Walker) for the Oasis Hotel in

Las Vegas. Nancy lives at 64 Crescent Drive with her dog, Blackjack, chore-ography assistant, Joey DeLuca (Eddie Mekka), and his brother, Anthony (Scott Baio). Joey is the cousin of Carmine Raguso (of *Laverne and Shirley*) while Nancy is the cousin of Howard Cunningham (of *Happy Days*). The main showgirls are Bambi Benton (Caren Kaye), who was named after the title character in her mother's favorite movie, *Bambi*; Ethel Akalino (Lynda Goodfriend) is from Witchita, Kansas, and nicknamed "Sunshine" ("because I smile a lot"); Arkansas Baits (Rhonda Bates), a farm girl, says "I don't sing too good and I don't dance too good but I can sure do a mean hog call—suuuu-weeee!"; Hilary Prentiss (Taaffe O'Connell) is a stunning blonde; Sylvia Silver (Antoinette Yuskis) is a streetwise but sweet girl from the Bronx; and Bridget Muldoon (Elaine Bolton) is the prime and proper British girl. Pat Morita plays Arnold Takahashi, the owner of Arnold's Coffee Shop. Joey's favorite sandwich is peanut butter and bologna. Cyndi Grecco sings the theme, "I Want It All."

18.　**The Bob Newhart Show** CBS, 1972–1978

Bob Hartley and his wife, Emily (Bob Newhart, Suzanne Pleshette), live in Apartment 523 in a building managed by the Skyline Management Corporation. Bob, a Virgo, works as a psychologist in the Rampo Medical Arts Building (352-22-7439 is his Social Security number; his office is seen as both 751 and 715). Emily, maiden name Harrison, was born in Seattle, Washington, and married Bob on 4/15/70. She first taught third grade at Gorman Elementary School; later she is vice principal of Tracy Grammar School. Bob served with the 193rd Combat Support Orchestra during the Korean War and yearned to become a professional drummer (until orchestra leader Buddy Rich told him "You stink, man"). Their neighbor, Howard Borden (Bill Daily), was originally a 747 navigator for the major airlines. When he was replaced by a computer, he found work at an airline called EDS (European Delivery Service). Jerry Robinson (Peter Bonerz) is the children's orthodontist with an office opposite Bob's; Carol Kester (Marcia Wallace) is Bob and Jerry's secretary. She was born in Collinsville, Iowa, lives in Apartment 7, and has a tape recording of a barking dog named Lobo that is activated when the doorbell rings. Henrietta and Lorenzo Music composed the theme, "Home for Emily."

19.　**Bosom Buddies** ABC, 1980–1982

In order to live at the Susan B. Anthony, a hotel for women at 3191 Broadway, and pay only $150 a month in rent, Henry Desmond and Kip

Wilson (Peter Scolari, Tom Hanks) pose as their sisters, Hildegard Desmond and Buffy Wilson. Kip and Henry reside in Apartment 312 and work for the Livingston, Gentry and Mishkin Ad Agency in Manhattan (Kip is a graphic artist; Henry a copywriter; they use clothes from a campaign for Blouse City and Dresses for Women). Also residing at the hotel are their friends Amy Cassidy (Wendie Jo Sperber), a copywriter at the agency; Sonny Lumet (Donna Dixon), a nurse at Memorial Hospital; and Isabella Hammond (Telma Hopkins), a model who hopes to become a singer (she performs at Budd Shore's Spotlight Club). Kip and Henry are 1975 graduates of Edgar Allan Poe High School in Shaker Heights, Cleveland. In second-season episodes, Kip, Henry and Amy open their own ad agency, 60 Seconds Street. The pilot finds Kip and Henry posing as sisters Buffy and Hilda (not related to Kip and Henry) who were working in a Canadian logging camp before moving to New York.

20.   **The Brady Bunch** ABC, 1969–1974

Carol Ann Tyler Martin (Florence Henderson) is a widow and the mother of Marcia (Maureen McCormick), Jan (Eve Plumb) and Cindy (Susan Olsen). Michael "Mike" Paul Brady (Robert Reed), a widower, is the father of Greg (Barry Williams), Peter (Christopher Knight) and Bobby (Michael Lookinland). The families become one when Mike and Carol wed. Mike, an architect (for an unnamed company), designed the four-bedroom, two-bathroom Los Angeles home they live in (at 4222 Clinton Avenue); 762-0799 (later 555-6161) is their phone number. They have a housekeeper named Alice Nelson (Ann B. Davis), a sedan (plate TEL 635), a station wagon (plate 746 AEH), a dog (Tiger) and, in the pilot only, a cat (Fluffy).

Very little information is given about the adults. Mike, who enjoys playing golf, received the 1969 "Father of the Year Award" by the local newspaper, the *Daily Chronicle*. He was the checkers champion of Chestnut Street as a kid. Carol attended West Side High School and was called "Twinkles" as a kid. She wrote an article about her family for *Tomorrow's World* magazine. Alice had been working for Mike for seven years when he and Carol married. Her boyfriend, Sam Franklin (Allan Melvin), owns Sam's Butcher Shop. Joyce Bulifant was originally cast as Carol and Monte Margetts was originally cast as Alice.

Marcia, the eldest girl, takes ballet lessons (with her sisters) at the Valley School of Dancing. She was a member of the Sun Flowers Girl Scout Troop, and at Fillmore Junior High School she was senior class president and editor of its paper, the *Fillmore Flier*. Marcia yearned to attend Tower

High School but was unable when her family moved into the Brady home (outside the school zone). She attended Westdale High where she became a cheerleader for the Bears football team and found history to be her worst subject ("I get confused with dates"). Marcia held an after-school job as a countergirl at Hanson's Ice Cream Parlor and hangs out at the Pizza Parlor. As Marcia progressed into young womanhood and found an attraction to boys, she also found herself being spied upon by Jan and Cindy, whom she called the "nosey Bradys."

Greg, the eldest boy, attends Westdale High School (where he is a member of the basketball team). He had a pet mouse (Myron) and was a Frontier Scout. Greg sings and plays guitar and attempted to break into showbusiness as a singer named Johnny Bravo. Greg first had a band called the Banana Convention, then with his siblings formed the Brady Six (later changed to the Brady Bunch Kids); "Time to Change" was the first song they sang. This singing and dancing TV act became a reality when the group produced two albums: *Meet the Brady Bunch* and *The Brady Bunch Christmas Album*). Greg also attempted to become a filmmaker (using his family as Pilgrims in a production of the first Thanksgiving) and was caught smoking a cigarette by his parents.

Jan, the middle girl, plays practical jokes and loves cinnamon spice cookies. She was voted "Most Popular Girl" in her class at Fillmore Junior High; she later attends Westdale High. Jan describes herself as "pretty, smart and kind" but because she wears glasses, she feels "I'm not as beautiful as Marcia." She invented a boyfriend ("George Glass") to show everyone that boys liked her, and wore a brunette wig to change her personality "so I'm not a blonde Brady." Jan worked at Hanson's Ice Cream Parlor and looks forward to the Fillmore Junior High Carnival.

Peter, the middle boy, shares some of Jan's insecurities. When it comes to girls, he feels he has no personality and is dull. He likes science fiction movies and his hero is George Washington. Peter attended Clinton Elementary School then Fillmore Junior High and was a member of the Treehouse Club.

Cindy is the youngest girl. She attends Clinton Elementary School and has two pet rabbits (Romeo and Juliet). She also has a doll (Kitty Carry-All), and Joan of Arc is her hero. She has a habit of eavesdropping and tattling and often gets into trouble for doing it.

Bobby, the youngest boy, claims his hero is outlaw Jesse James. He attends Clinton Elementary School and has a pet parakeet (Bird). He is school safety monitor and tried to make money by selling Neat and Tidy Natural Hair Tonic for $2 a bottle (the product turned hair orange).

The family appeared in a TV commercial for Safe laundry detergent. The opening theme shows the Bradys in a Tic Tac Toe board. Marcia, Carol and Greg form the top square, left to right; Jan, Alice and Peter (the middle); and Cindy, Mike and Bobby (the bottom). The Peppermint Trolley Company (first season) and then the Brady Kids sing the theme, "The Brady Bunch."

Spinoffs

1. *The Brady Kids*, ABC, 1972–1974. An animated version in which the Brady kids (voices of the series regulars) find adventures in a world without adult supervision.

2. *The Brady Bunch Hour*, ABC, 1977. A musical hour in which the Brady family sing, dance and act in skits. Geri Reischl replaced Eve Plumb as Jan Brady.

Updates

1. *The Brady Girls Get Married*, NBC, 1981. Marcia is a fashion designer for Casual Clothes; Jan is majoring in architecture in college. Greg is a doctor; Peter has joined the Air Force. Cindy and Bobby are college students. Mike is still an architect; Carol works for Willowbrook Realty. A double wedding occurs when Marcia and Wally Logan (Jerry Houser) and Jan (now Eve Plumb) and Philip Covington III (Ron Kuhlman) marry.

2. *The Brady Brides*, NBC, 1981. Continues the above storyline as Marcia and Wally (a designer for the Tyler Toy Company) and Jan and Philip (a college chemistry professor) pool their resources and share a house.

3. *A Very Brady Christmas*. A 1988 CBS TV movie that reunites the Bradys for a Christmas celebration. The original cast appears, except for Cindy, who is now played by Jennifer Runyon. Marcia and Wally have two children, Jessica and Mickey (Jaclyn Bernstein, J.W. Lee); Greg is married to Nora (Caryn Richman) and the father of Kevin (Zachary Bostrom). Peter is engaged to Valerie Thomas (Carol Huston); Carol now works for Advantage Properties Real Estate.

4. *The Bradys*, CBS, 1990. Mike (Robert Reed) has retired and is a Fourth District City Councilman; Carol (Florence Henderson) sells real estate. Marcia (Leah Ayres) and Wally (Jerry Houser) own the Party Girls Catering Company. Jan (Eve Plumb) has taken over her unnamed father's company; she and Philip (Ron Kuhlman) have an adopted daughter, Patty (Valerie Ick). Cindy (Susan Olsen) hosts "Cindy at Sunrise" at radio station KBLA. Greg (Barry Williams) is a doctor and his wife, Nora (Caryn Richman), is a nurse at the same unnamed hospital. Peter (Christopher Knight)

assists his father; Bobby (Michael Lookinland) is a racecar driver and married to Tracy (Martha Quinn). Other cast changes are Jonathan Weiss as Greg's son, Kevin, and Michael Melby as Marcia's son, Mickey.

21. The Brian Keith Show NBC, 1972–1974

Drs. Sean Jamison and his daughter Anne (Brian Keith, Shelley Fabares), both graduates of Harvard Medical School, operate the Jamison Clinic for Children in Kahala, Hawaii (their rent is $450 a month; 555-6606 is their phone number). Sean enjoys fishing and has a parrot named Sam. Anne doubles as the local vet and is manager of the Children's Theater Group. Millar Gruber (Nancy Kulp), the landlady, is a graduate of Audubon University and has been married six times. Dr. Austin Chaffey (Roger Bowen) is an allergist who rents office space from Sean for $250 a month. He dislikes children and has a collection of frog-jumping trophies that he won with his now stuffed frog, Big Hopper of Webfoot. Originally titled *The Little People*.

22. Bridget Loves Bernie CBS, 1972–1973

Bridget Theresa Mary Colleen Fitzgerald (Meredith Baxter), a Catholic school fourth grade teacher at the Immaculate Heart Academy, and Bernie Steinberg (David Birney), a Jewish cab driver who hopes to become an actor, are newlyweds struggling to overcome the problems of a mixed religious marriage. Bridget and Bernie live above his parents' deli, Steinberg's Delicatessen, on Manhattan's Lower East Side (next to Goldstein's Bakery). Sam and Sophia Steinberg (Harold J. Stone, Bibi Osterwald) are Bernie's hardworking parents; Walter and Amy Fitzgerald (David Doyle, Audra Lindley) are Bridget's wealthy parents, the owners of a company called Global Investments. Bernie drives Cab 12 (number IC-56); rates are 60 cents for the first fifth of a mile, ten cents for each additional fifth of a mile. Jerry Fielding and Diane Hilderbrand composed the theme, "Love Is Crazy."

23. Car 54, Where Are You? NBC, 1961–1963

Car 54, license plate 973 664, is a patrol vehicle attached to the 53rd Police Precinct on Tremont Avenue in the Bronx, New York. Captain Martin Block (Paul Reed) heads the precinct and officers Francis Muldoon (Fred Gwynne) and Gunther Toody (Joe E. Ross) are partners assigned to Car 54 (in early episodes, 54 is seen as the license plate).

Toody and Muldoon were teamed on August 16, 1952, and officials find that only they can ride with each other (Toody constantly talks and drives other partners crazy; Muldoon rarely speaks and makes other partners uneasy— "It's like riding with a spook," they say). Gunther and Francis are members of the precinct's Brotherhood Club and Singing Whippoorwills. They coach the Wildcats, a PAL (Police Athletic League) basketball team. Nailing Benny the Bookie was the first arrest they made together.

Francis comes from a long line of police officers; his father was a police captain and his grandfather was a deputy police commissioner. He is single and lives with his mother (Ruth Masters) and sisters Peggy and Cathy (Helen Parker, Nancy Donahue) at 807 East 157th Street (also given as 175th) in the Bronx. Francis, badge number 723 (787 in the pilot) attended Holy Cross High School and was a member of the basketball team (he was also said to have attended Bryant High School and Newtown High School). In grammar school he felt inferior (the kids called him "Horse Face") and he is afraid of girls ("I'm six feet, five inches tall and five feet, six inches is all face"). Francis weighs 183¾ pounds and was named after his mother's idol, film star Francis X. Bushman. Francis, famous for his homemade salad dressing, is called "My Big Baby Boy" by his mother. He has a mind like a computer (he can recall any police regulation) and wrote a play for the Policeman's Benefit called *Tempest in the Tropics*. Francis collects stamps and is a member of the Bronx Stamp Club.

Peggy, an aspiring actress, performed in a Broadway play called *Waiting for Wednesday* (later called *Copper's Capers*). Nancy is attending Columbia University.

Gunther and his wife, Lucille (Beatrice Pons), live in a five-room, rent-controlled apartment in the Bronx. They have been married for 15 years and pay $45 a month rent. Gunther is five feet, eight inches tall and wears badge number 432 (camera angles and lighting make it also look like 1432 and 453). When Gunther was in the army and attended dances at Fort Dix, he was called "Lover Lips." In high school Gunther played football and was called "Bull." When Toody attended rookie school, the lieutenant at the academy said that if Toody ever graduated he would shoot himself (Toody graduated and the lieutenant is fine).

Before becoming a police officer, Toody worked for the Department of Sanitation. He hopes to become a detective and "studies" by watching *Dragnet, Checkmate* and *Perry Mason* ("I've gotten so good that I can solve the crime by the third commercial"). Toody's favorite sport is bowling. If he misses a game, his teammates say "He must not only be sick, he must be on the critical list." Gunther was born on August 15 and his catchphrase is

"Oooh ooh, jumpin' Jehoshaphat" (which he says when something excites him). The gravel-voiced Gunther is from a famous family of singers (the Singing Toodys) but has not inherited a singing voice.

Lucille, maiden name Hasselwhite, attended Fairview High School (where she met Gunther) and Hunter College. She is forever yelling at Gunther for all the stupid things he does (she lets off steam by yelling out the window "My husband is a nut"). Francis calls Lucille, whom he treats like a sister, "Boo Boo." Gunther reads a daily paper called the *News Journal* and he and Francis have accounts at the Bronx Home Savings Bank.

Officer Leo Schnauser (Al Lewis), badge number 1062, is married to the former Sylvia Schwarzcock (Charlotte Rae). Leo was born on Friday the 13th and has been on the force for 20 years (he has been married to Sylvia for 15 years and believes that when he was born a black cat crossed his path for all the bad luck he has). Leo has six sisters, yet he is considered the pretty one in the family. Leo and Sylvia are also an argumentative couple. She believes that every time Leo goes out with the boys he is having a secret affair with Marilyn Monroe. Leo hates night duty "because I get home in time to see Sylvia getting out of bed."

Leo and Sylvia live in Apartment 6A. Leo was a mounted policeman (horse named Sally) for 12 years before becoming a patrolman at the 53rd. He coaches a basketball team called the Tigers. Sylvia was an actress and ballet dancer, and tried painting before marrying Leo. She is working on a book based on the 53rd called *Precinct Place*. She also believes in psychics and what the tea leaves tell her. Leo calls her "Pussycat." In the pilot episode, Al Lewis (Grandpa on *The Munsters*) played Al Spencer, a building contractor.

The stern Captain Block believes that when Toody and Muldoon come off patrol "it is like Tinkerbell and Peter Pan returning to Never Never Land." He believes Muldoon is intelligent, but he knows Toody is "gullible, stupid and simple-minded." He feels that his life has been plagued since the day Toody became a part of his precinct and longs for the day that Toody will be transferred. In high school, Martin (also called Paul) starred in a play called *Vagabond King*. Louise Kirtland and Patricia Bright played Martin's wife, Claire (also called Elsie).

Mr. Eisenberg (not seen) is the notorious Bronx jaywalker. Reforming Charlie the Drunk (Larry Storch) is the chief project of the Helping Hand Committee of the Precinct (of which Toody and Muldoon are members). In the opening theme, Toody and Muldoon are seen driving Car 54. Muldoon is at the wheel; Toody does the following: reads a newspaper; plays checkers; eats an ice cream cone; handcuffs himself to Francis; pretends to be a snake charmer; jiggles a fake spider in front of Francis; talks into an unplugged telephone; disguises himself as a woman to catch a mugger. John Strauss and Nat Hiken wrote the theme.

24. The Cara Williams Show CBS, 1964–1965

Cara Wilton (Cara Williams) is a file clerk for Fenwick Diversified Industries, Inc. who protects her job by devising her own complicated filing system. Frank Bridges (Frank Aletter) is the company's top efficiency expert and Damon Burkhardt (Paul Reed) is their stern boss. Stories originally focused on Cara and Frank's efforts to keep their marriage a secret when they marry against company policy ("Fenwick prohibits employees from marrying each other"). Cara then convinced the president, Mr. Fenwick (Edward Everett Horton), to change the rule ("Without marriage there would be no babies and no market for Fenwick baby products"). Fenwick is located at 9601 West Beverly Boulevard in Los Angeles; Cara and Frank live at 6758 Riverdale Lane; 736-8876 is their phone number; T1204 is Cara's license plate number. Damon lives at 790 Parker Way. Kenyon Hopkins composed "Cara's Theme."

25. Charles in Charge CBS, 1984–1985; Syn., 1987–1990

Charles (Scott Baio), a Copeland College student without a last name, is the live-in helper to Jill and Stan Pembroke (Julie Cobb, James Widdoes), a married couple with three children: Lila (April Lerman), Douglas (Jonathan Ward) and Jason (Michael Pearlman). When the Pembrokes move to Seattle in 1987, they sublet their home (at 10 Barrington Court, New Brunswick, New Jersey) to the Powell family and Charles finds himself caring for Jamie (Nicole Eggert), Sarah (Josie Davis) and Adam (Alexander Polinsky), the children of Ellen and Robert Powell (Sandra Kerns, James O'Sullivan).

Charles was born in Scranton, Pennsylvania. At the age of 11, he won a spelling bee with the word *quixotic*; in the fifth grade he had a ventriloquist act with a dummy named Muggsy. In high school he had a band called the Charles Tones, and his mother, Lillian (Ellen Travolta), calls him "Doodlebug." Lillian first owned Sid's Pizza Parlor then the Yesterday Cafe. Charles, majoring in education, left the Powells to get his teaching degree at Princeton (the final episode). When he bumps his head, Charles takes on the identity of motorcycle hood Chazz Lambergini.

Charles is best friends with Buddence "Buddy" Lembeck (Willie Aames), a political science major at Copeland (although aptitude tests rated Buddy as a Jack of no trades and best suited for jury duty). The Lamplight (CBS) is their favorite eatery; and "Charles Are Us" was their misguided efforts to make money by marketing clones of Charles as live-in housekeepers.

Buddy, born in California, had a dog named Kitty and a hand puppet called Handie as a kid. He now lives in the campus dorm (where he is banned from performing chemistry experiments and bringing livestock into the room). He has a pet lizard (Lloyd) and ant (Arlo). He once smashed 57 cans of beer against his forehead before passing out ("I could have done more if the cans were empty"). He had his own radio program, *The Buddy Lembeck Show*, on WFNZ. In high school Buddy was voted class flake. He has an autographed Mickey Mantle baseball that he signed on behalf of Mickey (who wasn't around at the time). Buddy is afraid of clowns (one scared him as a child) and is a member of Copeland's Scuba Club. Of all the troublesome situations in the world, Buddy worries most about why the park ranger won't let Yogi Bear have a picnic basket.

Jillian Ann "Jill" Pembroke is a theater critic for the New Jersey *Register*. Her favorite eatery is Willie Wong's Chinese Palace. In high school Jill was called "Pixie" (her father called her "Jillybean"). Stanley Albert "Stan" Pembroke is one of 49 vice presidents in an unnamed company. Lila Beth is "sweet and lovely and dots her *i*'s with hearts." She first attended Lincoln Elementary School then Northside High School. Lila reads *Co-ed* magazine and is a member of the Circle of Friends Club. She calls Buddy "Goon Machine" and loves to wear makeup and high heels. Douglas and Jason attend Lincoln Elementary. Douglas is smart and Jason, who loves to wear Halloween masks, is mischievous. They have a never-seen feline named Putty Cat and eat Kellogg's Bran Flakes for breakfast.

Ellen Powell works as a real estate broker and her husband, Robert, is a naval commander stationed in the South Seas. Jamie is the oldest of the Powell children. She attends Central High School and yearns to be a model. She and her sister, Sarah, did a commercial for Banana Cream Shampoo and Hair Lotion. Jamie, who wears a size five shoe, is a cheerleader and called "Little Scooter" by her father. She won the "Yesterday Cafe Beauty Pageant" and, under the sponsorship of Jeannie's Boutique, entered the "Miss New Brunswick Beauty Pageant." Jamie worked as a waitress at Sid's Pizza, took classes at the Better Image School of Modeling, and joined the Followers of Light, a phony religious sect she thought was legit.

Sarah, the middle child, attends Central High School and longs to be a writer. She is a reporter for the *Herald* and had her first story, "What It Is Like to Be a Teenager," published in *Teen* magazine. Sarah, the sensitive child, has a pet turtle (Ross) and a favorite doll (Rebecca). She is a member of the Shakespeare Club, and Elizabeth Barrett Browning is her favorite poet (she later says Emily Dickinson). Adam, the youngest and most mischievous, attends an unnamed grammar school. He is closest to his grandfather, Walter Powell (James Callahan), a retired naval officer who lives with them. He is a member of the John Paul Jones Society for Retired Naval Men and is hoping Adam will follow in his and Robert's footsteps. Michael Jacobs, Al Burton and David Kurtz composed the *Charles in Charge* theme.

26.   **Cheers** NBC, 1982–1993

The place "where everybody knows your name" is Cheers, a neighborhood bar at 112½ Beacon Street in Boston. It was established in 1889 as a bordello called Mom's and became a bar six years later. It has a legal capacity of 75 people; Tecumseh is the wooden Indian that stands to the right of the front door; and Melville's Fine Sea Food is the restaurant above Cheers. Gary's Old Towne Tavern is the bar's competition. A real Boston bar, the Bull and Finch, is the model for Cheers.

Sam Malone (Ted Danson) is the first owner of Cheers we see (he bought it from a Gus O'Malley in 1976). In 1987, when Sam becomes bored with Cheers, he sells it to an unnamed corporation that appoints Rebecca Howe (Kirstie Alley) the manager. When Rebecca is fired (falsely accused of letting her boyfriend, Roger Colcord [Roger Reese] use her secret computer code, "Sweet Baby," to access corporation information), the corporation sells Cheers back to Sam for 85 cents. Sam puts up a sign that reads "Under Old Management."

Sam, jersey 16, was a former relief pitcher for the Boston Red Sox. It was at this time that he found a bottle cap on the field that became his good luck charm. He appeared in a TV commercial for Field's Beer and has a dream of opening a waterfront bar called Sam's Place. When Sam sold the bar, he used the money to buy a ketch and sail around the world. Shortly after, his ketch sank in the Caribbean and he discovered an uncharted atoll he named "No Brains Atoll" (for selling the bar that he now missed). When Sam returned to Boston and told Rebecca his pathetic story, she took pity on him and hired him as a bartender (at $6 an hour). While Sam was somewhat of a ladies' man, most of his romantic escapades revolved around Diane Chambers (Shelley Long), the prim and proper barmaid. Diane, an art student and substitute teacher at Boston University, is a dreamer "and I have a habit of making those dreams come true."

Diane, who previously worked at the Third Eye Bookstore and Hurley's Market, used the pen name Jessica Simpson Bordias, to help Sam write his memoirs for a book that never materialized. Sam and Diane had planned to marry but when Diane received a book deal from Houghton Mifflin Publishers, Sam postponed the wedding to give Diane the opportunity to pursue her dream of becoming a writer. The book project fell through and Diane never returned for Sam. (When the publisher rejected her novel, her agent suggested she trim several thousand pages and turn it into a screenplay. Six years later, while watching Cable's Ace Awards, Sam sees Diane accepting an award for writing the TV movie *The Heart Held Hostage*.)

Diane won the 45th Annual Miss Boston Barmaid title. She gets a facial tic when she gets nervous. She is interested in rare, first-edition books and wanted to become a ballerina (but abandoned it to become a novelist). As a kid, Diane's father called her "Muffin" and she had a cat named Elizabeth Barrett Browning (after her favorite poet).

Rebecca also found romance at the bar when she met and fell in love with Don Standtree (Tom Berenger), the plumber Sam hired to fix the beer dispenser (they married in the final episode, 5/20/93). Rebecca was born in San Diego and is easily exasperated. She smokes and accidentally damaged Cheers when she tossed a lit cigarette into a trash can (the bar regulars found a temporary home at Mr. Pubbs). When Rebecca lost her job at Cheers, she first worked at the Auto Show as the Miracle Buff Girl (Miracle Buff is a wax that preserves a car's shine). When she quit, Sam took pity on her and hired her as his bar manager (at $6 an hour). Rebecca attended the University of Connecticut; her father, a naval captain, calls her "Pookie"; her mother is a concert cellist. *Spenser for Hire* is Rebecca's favorite TV show and its star, Robert Urich, her favorite actor.

Carla Maria Victoria Angelina Teresa Appollona Lozupona Tortelli Le Bec (Rhea Perlman) is the three-times married, nasty barmaid (she worked previously at the Broken Spoke Bar). Carla was named after her grandmother's stubborn mule and as a kid was called "Muffin" by her brothers (who stuffed her ears with yeast and tried to bake her face). Carla attended Saint Clete's School for Wayward Girls and danced on the TV show *The Boston Boppers* when she was 16. Carla calls Diane "Fish Face" and curtailed her nasty ways for one day in 1991 to win the Miss Congeniality award in the Miss Boston Barmaid contest. Her phone number is 555-7834.

Carla has eight children. Anthony (Timothy Williams), Sarafina (Leah Remini), Lucinda (Sabrina Wiener), Gino (Josh Lozoff) and Anne Marie (Risa Littman) are with her first husband, Nick Tortelli (Dan Hedaya). Ludlow (Jarrett Lennon) is by husband two, Dr. Bennett Ludlow (John Karlen), and twins Elvis and Jesse (Danny Kramer, Thomas Tulak) are by third husband Eddie Le Bec (Jay Thomas), a goalie for the Boston Bruins hockey team.

Carla's children are known to roll drunks, and Ludlow has an eight-foot boa constrictor named Mr. Tibbington. Nick is now married to the gorgeous but naive Loretta (Jean Kasem).

Carla used the "Le Mans" method of childbirth ("I screamed like a Ferrari") and refused to follow family tradition by giving her first-born son (Anthony) her father's name and her mother's maiden name (Benito Mussolini). Carla's humor is always at someone else's expense ("It makes me laugh").

Ernie Pantusso (Nicholas Colasanto), called "Coach," is Sam's bartender. He was the Boston Red Sox pitching coach and holds the record for being hit more than any coach in major-league history. Ernie was called "Red" in his youth ("Not because I had red hair, but because I once read a book") *Thunder Road* is his favorite movie and 1:37 A.M. is his favorite time of day ("I don't know why, I just like it"). Ernie coached the Titans, a little-league team, and bangs his head on the bar's serving area when he gets angry. After Coach's death, a picture of Geronimo that Nicholas kept in his dressing room was placed on the Cheers set to remind them of Ernie.

Hilary "Norm" Peterson (George Wendt) is the bar regular who enjoys eating and drinking beer. Norm was first an accountant for H.W. Sawyer and Associates, and then was "Corporate Killer" (fires people) for Talbot International Accounting, accountant with Masters, Holly and Dickson, and finally owner of his own home decorating business AAAA Painting (also called K&P Painting).

The Hungry Heifer Restaurant is Norm's favorite eatery and Ho-Ho's his favorite snack. In high school he was called "Moonglow" and is now married to the never-seen Vera (voice of Bernadette Birkett, Wendt's real-life wife). Norm is loyal to the bar first while Vera "is somewhere down the line." His license plate reads CR 4585.

Bar regular Clifford "Cliff" Claven (John Ratzenberger) has an opinion on everything and believes he is "the wingnut that holds western civilization together." He is a U.S. Post Office letter carrier (attached to the South Central Branch; works the Meadow View Acres route near the airport). He is later promoted to district supervisor, Subdivision A, Grid L. Cliff fears the Flanigan's dog (which is on his route) and the Sears Catalogue (which puts a strain on him). Cliff is a member of the Knights of the Semitar Lodge and watches the Weather Channel ("For the Weather Bunnies"). Twinkies are his favorite snack and he is prepared for the flooding that will occur if the Polar Ice Caps melt (his car trunk is stuffed with an inflatable raft and cans of tuna fish). He appeared on *Jeopardy* (lost $22,000 when he couldn't give the real names of Cary Grant, Tony Curtis and Joan Crawford). Cliff,

Norm and Sam lost money by investing in a coin-operated laundromat and tanning salon business called Tan 'n' Wash.

Huckleberry "Woody" Tiberias Boyd (Woody Harrelson) is the assistant bartender. He attended Hanover High School in Indiana and invented a game called Hide Bob's Pants. Woody, a hopeful actor, made a TV commercial for Veggie Boy (a vegetable drink mix of broccoli, cauliflower and kale juice). He had a dog named Truman and Small Pox was his first childhood disease. Blowing into an empty Good & Plenty candy box provides Woody with a duck caller when he goes hunting. He wrote "Kelly's Song" for the girl he eventually married, the rich and spoiled Kelly Susan Gaines (Jackie Swanson). In the last episode, Woody became third district councilman with the Boston City Council.

Dr. Frasier Crane (Kelsey Grammer) and his wife, Dr. Lilith Sternin (Bebe Neuwirth), are bar regulars. Frasier is a private-practice psychiatrist who considers himself "The solver of all problems personal." He collects first-edition books; Charles Dickens is his favorite author; and he has a dog named Pavlov. Frasier was first married to Nanette Goodsmith, a now famous children's singer called Nancy Gee. Frasier also conducts traveling self-help seminars called "The Crane Train to Mental Well-Being" (the cost is $350).

Lilith, a psychiatrist on call at Boston Memorial Hospital, "rides the roost in her bra and panties" says Frasier. Whitey and Whiskers are her favorite lab rats and she wrote the book *Good Girls, Bad Boys*. Frederick (Kevin and Christopher Graves), Lilith and Frasier's son, was born in the back of a cab ("The cab driver was nice enough to let me bite down on his foam dice," says Lilith of the incident). Frederick attended the Magic Hours Learning Center preschool. When Lilith enters the bar, Cliff yells "Frost Warning." In the episode of 11/5/92, Frasier discovers that Lilith has been having an affair with her research partner, Dr. Louis Pascal (Peter Vogt). "One minute we were feeding the lab rats and the next we were in a hotel room," says Lilith. Pascal, called "Googie" by Lilith, invented the Eco-Pod, a subterranean environmental bubble. Fraiser agrees to a yearlong separation to allow Lilith to work with Pascal in the bubble (the prototype for an eventual space station). On 2/18/93 Lilith returns to Frasier after "Pascal went crazy and the experiment was canceled." Frasier, too, dated someone else before marrying Lilith—Diane (Diane developed an allergic reaction to him, and Frasier's rude and snobbish mother, Dr. Hester Crane [Nancy Marchand] felt her son would ruin his life if he married "a pseudo intellectual barmaid").

Gary Portnoy sings the theme, "Where Everybody Knows Your Name."

27. The Cosby Show NBC, 1984–1992

Dr. Cliff Huxtable (Bill Cosby), his wife, Clair (Phylicia Rashad), and their children, Sondra (Sabrina LeBeauf), Denise (Lisa Bonet), Theo (Malcolm-Jamal Warner), Vanessa (Tempestt Bledsoe) and Rudy (Keshia Knight Pulliam), reside at 10 Stigwood Avenue in Brooklyn, New York.

Cliff, a graduate of Hillman College in Georgia, is a gynecologist-obstetrician with offices at home and the Children's Hospital and Corinthian Hospital. At Hillman Cliff was a member of the track team and called "Combustible Huxtable." Cliff, an expert on jazz music, calls himself "Mr. Jazz" and hangs out at Jake's Hardware Store (where Clair says he has no sales resistance). He likes western movies ("Especially *Six Guns for Glory* starring Colt Kirby") and first met Clair Hanks at Hillman (he called her "Lum Lum"; she called him "Baby Cakes"). They married on 2/14/64 and honeymooned at the Caralu Hotel in the Caribbean. As a kid Cliff had a bike he called Bob and a bird named Charlie (that he accidentally sat upon and killed). Cliff reads a daily paper called the *City Sun*.

Cliff has a tendency to gain weight and is often restricted by Clair to eating healthy foods, not junk foods. Clair wears a size eight dress and was a panelist on the Channel 37 TV show *Retrospective*. She is a lawyer with the firm of Greentree, Bradley and Dexter; she and Cliff celebrated her graduation from law school with dinner at Michael and Ennio's Restaurant.

Sondra attended Princeton University (at a cost of $79,648.72) and married Elvin Tibideaux (Geoffrey Owens); she later became the mother of twins Winnie and Nelson (Jessica Vaughn, Gary Gray). Sondra, a law student, met Elvin, a pre-med student, at Princeton. After marrying they put their careers on hold to open a business called The Wilderness Store. They first lived in a small apartment (5B) where the *K* from a Valley Fair Milk sign is against the window. They later move in with her parents and in 1990, to their own home in New Jersey. Elvin calls Sondra "Muffin." When their business failed, Elvin worked for Benrix Industries as Inspector 36 (checking pill bottles for their safety seals; he was fired when an efficiency expert said they didn't need 36 inspectors). Sondra was a stay-at-home mom. With Cliff's help, Elvin enrolled in medical school and became a doctor in 1990. Sondra also resumed her education and became a lawyer in 1991.

Denise, the most troublesome child, attended Central High School then Hillman College (see **Spinoffs** below). She worked at The Wilderness Store then at Blue Wave Records as the assistant to the executive assistant (for $25 a week). She later became a photographer's assistant and, while on a photo shoot in Africa, married Martin Kendall (Joseph C. Phillips), a divorced Navy lieutenant with a young daughter named Olivia (Raven-Samone). Denise next pursues her dream of teaching disabled children and begins taking education classes at the Medgar Evers College of the City University of New York. Martin is a graduate of Annapolis; Olivia's favorite song is "Pop Goes the Weasel." She has two invisible pets: Howard the parrot and Dwayne the dog. In the last episode, Denise announces she is pregnant.

Theodore "Theo" Aloysius, the only son, first attended Central High School (where he was "Monster Man Huxtable" on the wrestling team) then New York University (where he lives on campus in Apartment 10B in Greenwich Village). In 1991 he became a psychology major and acquired a job as a junior counselor at the Seton Hall Communications Center teaching the Rosa Parks Group. The following year Theo graduated from NYU with a bachelor's degree and enrolled in the school's department of psychology grad program. It cost Cliff and Clair $100,000 for Theo's education.

Vanessa first attended Central High School then Lincoln University in Philadelphia (where, at age 18, she met and fell in love with Dabnis Brickley [William Thomas, Jr.], a man 12 years her senior. Dabnis, a maintenance man, and Vanessa became engaged, but broke up in 1991).

Vanessa loves old movies and was a member of a band called the Lipsticks. Rudith "Rudy" Lillian, the youngest Huxtable, has a teddy bear named Bobo and a goldfish called Lamont. She loves vanilla ice cream and was called the "Gray Ghost" by Cliff when she became a sensation on the Pee Wee league football team (jersey 32). Schools for Rudy are not mentioned. Bill Cosby and Stu Gardner composed the theme.

Spinoff

A Different World, NBC, 1987–1993. Denise is a freshman at Hillman College in Georgia with an undecided major. She lives in the Gilbert Hall Dorm and shares room 204 with Jalessa Vinson (Dawnn Lewis) and Maggie Laughton (Marisa Tomei). Denise is a member of the track team and is called the "Little Engine." Maggie (bottom) and Denise (top) share a bunk bed while Jalessa has her own bed. Maggie is an army brat and majoring in journalism. She tends to rattle when she is nervous and was captain of her high school debate team. She works as a reporter for the college newspaper; Denise works with Jalessa in the cafeteria.

Jalessa, 26, was born in Camden, New Jersey. She was married to a man named Lamar for two years but the marriage broke up when he cheated on her. She later marries Colonel Bradford Taylor (Glynn Turman), the tough calculus teacher called "Dr. War." Jalessa went on to begin her own campus company, Jalessa Vinson May Temps.

Denise has a grade average of 1.7; she has, after three semesters, five D's, one C and seven incompletes. She decides to quit and returns to her home in Brooklyn. At this same time, Maggie leaves when her father is stationed overseas. The series continues with a focus on a number of students, most notably, Whitley Gilbert (Jasmine Guy) and Dwayne Wayne (Kadeem Hardison).

Whitley, born in Richmond, Virginia, is rich, beautiful and spoiled. She resides in room 20-S of Gilbert Hall (built by her grandparents) and was a child beauty queen (crowned "Miss Magnolia"). She considers herself "The Ebony Fashion Queen," uses a bar of soap only once and won't eat or let anyone eat cheese in her presence. She has taken jazz, ballet and tap lessons since she was a child and "my only flaw is my ability to sleep through anything." Whitley, an art major, is later an art buyer at E. H. Wright Investments. At this time she lives in the Dorothy Height Hall.

Dwayne, a math major, is from Michigan and lives in Matthews Hall. He works as the D.J. Darryl Walker at the school's radio station (WHZU) and later marries Whitley (who calls him "Pookie Bear"). She and Dwayne live off campus (Apartment 1) when Dwayne becomes a math teacher at Hillman.

Note: Bill Cosby and Phylicia Rashad continued their roles as man and wife (Hilton and Ruth Lucas) on *Cosby* (CBS, 1996–2000). Hilton, a baggage handler for National West Airlines, was downsized after 30 years on the job. Ruth and her friend Pauline Fox (Madeline Kahn) run the Flower Cafe. Hilton and Ruth are the parents of Erica (T'keyah Crystal Keymah), a law student then lawyer with the firm of Muldrew and Renwick who quit to become a chef, then a flight attendant, then a teacher. She married Darien (Darrian Sills-Evans), a flight attendant for National West.

Also living with Hilton at 1559 Blake Street in Queens, New York, is Griffin Vesey (Doug E. Doug), a sound engineer who later teaches at the Ralph Bunche Middle School (when Erica began practicing her cooking, she burned Griffin's house to the ground; Hilton allowed Griffin to move into the attic). Ruth and Pauline have run the cafe (later a coffee shop-bookstore) for 20 years. Pauline has a fear of leprechauns and even though she is an only child, she has a sister named Susie (whom her father made up for tax purposes). Hilton and Griffin have a beer at the Steinway Pub. Hilton banks at Trust Savings and Loan, and SBX 942 is his license plate. Erica, a vegetarian, has a cat named Sherman; Ruth, a lifeguard in her youth (at Lake Onawanamaga), saved five people from drowning when their boat overturned.

28.   The Courtship of Eddie's Father ABC, 1969–1972

The theme song talks about "my best friend." Eddie Corbett (Brandon Cruz), a six-year-old boy, and his father, Tom Corbett (Bill Bixby), are each others' best friends. Tom and Eddie live in Apartment C at 146 South Beverly Boulevard in Los Angeles. Tom, a widower, works as the editor of *Tomorrow Magazine*, a newspaper supplement; Eddie attends the Selmar Grammar School. Eddie lives by the last words his mother told him (to watch out for his father) and plays matchmaker by inviting "strays" home to meet "my kind, generous and handsome father." Tom calls Eddie "Sport," and Eddie "eats an awful lot of cookies before he goes to bed" (when they upset his stomach, he wears his "sick pajamas"—the ones with dive bombers on them). Their Japanese housekeeper, Mrs. Livingston (Miyoshi Umeki), calls Tom "Mr. Eddie's Father." Harry Nilsson sings the theme, "Best Friend."

29.   A Date with Judy ABC, 1951–1953

"I've got a date with Judy, a big date with Judy, oh jeepers and gee; I've got a date with Judy and Judy's got one with me" is the song Oogie Pringle (Jimmy Sommers) composed for his girlfriend, Judy Foster (Patricia Crowley, Mary Linn Beller), a 16-year-old who lives at 123 State Street in an unspecified town (the Bijou is the local movie theater; the *Gazette*, the town paper). Judy, the daughter of Melvyn (Frank Albertson, Judson Rees, John Gibson) and Dora Foster (Anna Lee, Flora Campbell) is a high school sophomore and receives an allowance of $2 a week; the after-school hangout is the Coke Parlor (later, Pop Scully's Soda Fountain). "Oh, caterpillars" or "Oh, butterflies" is what Judy says when something goes wrong. Judy's 12-year-old brother, Randolph (Gene O'Donnell, Peter Avramo), has an allowance of 75 cents a week and loves Humphrey Bogart and Boris Karloff movies. Melvyn owns the Foster Canning Company and met Dora when they were in college. Oogie has a band called the High School Hot Licks and first met Judy "when she ran me over with her tricycle." Based on the radio series (NBC, 1941–48; ABC, 1948–50) with Dellie Ellis, Louise Erickson and Ann Gillis as Judy, and Harry Harvey and Richard Crenna as Oogie.

30.   Dear Phoebe NBC, 1954–1955

Bill Hastings (Peter Lawford) is a journalist professor at UCLA who believes that psychology and science play a role in determining the outcome of a story. To test his theory he applies for a reporter's position on the Los

Angeles *Daily Star*. He becomes, however, Phoebe Goodheart, the "woman" who writes the "Dear Phoebe" advice-to-the-lovelorn column when a reporting position is not available. Bill lives at 165 La Paloma Drive and his girlfriend, Mickey Riley (Marcia Henderson), the paper's sports reporter, lives at 34 West Sunset. Clyde Fosdick (Charles Lane) is the managing editor and the paper, incorrectly called the *Blade* in *TV Guide*, is on Wilshire Boulevard. Raoul Kraushaar composed the theme.

31. December Bride CBS, 1954–1959

Lily Ruskin (Spring Byington) is a 60-year-old, young-at-heart widow who lives with her married daughter, Ruth (Frances Rafferty), and her husband, Matt Henshaw (Dean Miller), at 728 Elm Street in Westwood, California (the street, however, is lined with palm trees). Lily writes the "Tips for Housewives" and the "Let Yourself Go" columns for the Los Angeles *Gazette*. Ruth is a housewife and Matt an architect for the Coricon Company (later the Gordon Architectural Firm). Their next-door neighbor, Peter Porter (Harry Morgan), and his never-seen wife, Gladys, were spun off into *Pete and Gladys* (see for information). Eliot Daniel composed the theme.

32. Diana NBC, 1973–1974

Diana Smythe (Diana Rigg), newly arrived in New York from London following her divorce, lives at 4 Sutton Place, Apartment 11B. She works as a fashion illustrator for Buckley's Department Store (at 37 West 34th Street) and cares for Gulliver, her brother's Great Dane. Diana is 30 years old and her phone number is 555-7755. The original, unaired pilot finds Diana as the assistant to Mr. Vincent (Philip Proctor) the head designer at the store called Sue Ellen Frocks. Jerry Fielding composed the theme, "Diana."

33. The Dick Van Dyke Show CBS, 1961–1966

Rob and Laura Petrie (Dick Van Dyke, Mary Tyler Moore) are a young married couple who reside at 148 Bonnie Meadow Road in New Rochelle, New York (house number also given as 485). They are the parents of Ritchie (Larry Matthews). Rob works as the head writer of *The Alan Brady Show*, a mythical TV variety series that airs at 8:30 P.M. opposite a real CBS program called *Yancy Derringer*. The *Brady* series ranks 17 in the ratings in the U.S.; number one in Liberia.

Rob, born in Danville, Ohio, attended Danville High School (where he played the lead in a production of *Romeo and Juliet*). His middle name is Simpson and the freckles on his back form a picture of the Liberty Bell when connected. Franks and baked beans with sauerkraut are his favorite dinner; cold spaghetti and meatballs his favorite breakfast. Rob wears a size 10D shoe and is allergic to cats and chicken feathers. He ran for but did not win the position of ninth district councilman and carries a wallet with a picture of actress Paula Marshall in it (a calendar on the back of the photo came with the wallet but he never removed it).

Laura worked as a USO (United Service Organizations) entertainer before marrying Rob. She weighs 112 pounds and moo goo gai pan is her favorite meal. She hides the love sonnets written to her by her high school boyfriend behind some loose bricks near the furnace in the basement, and attempted to write a children's novel under the pen name Samantha Q. Wiggins. *Town of Passion* is her favorite TV soap opera and she sobs "Oh Rob" when something goes wrong. Rob embarrassed Laura by telling the host of *The Ray Murdock X-Ray Show* that her scatterbrained antics provide the inspiration for sketches on *The Alan Brady Show* (Laura, in turn, accidentally revealed on TV that Alan Brady was bald).

Rob and Laura paid $27,990 for their home, which has a large rock in the basement (protects against flooding when it rains). Their doorbell rings in the keys of E and G-flat minor and there are 382½ roses on their bedroom wallpaper. Rob and Laura met at the Camp Crowder Army base in Joplin, Missouri. He was a sergeant with Company A (Company E in some flashbacks); she was a dancer who won the camp title "Bivouac Baby." While dancing to the song "You Wonderful You," Rob stepped on Laura's foot and broke her toes. He visited her at the hospital, brought her flowers and recipes and they fell in love. Laura's maiden name was given as Meeker (later Meehan) and she was said to be 17 when she married Rob (not 19 as she told him; they remarried to make it legal).

The newlyweds first lived at the camp housing development, then in Ohio where Rob became a disc jockey for radio station WOFF. It was during an on-air promotion to stay awake 100 hours that Rob received the opportunity to audition for the position of head writer on *The Alan Brady Show* in New York City. Though dead tired and doing what he does best, "making a rotten first impression," Rob got the job. During his Army hitch Rob wrote the song "Bupkis" and was nicknamed "Bones." His mentor is Happy Spangler (Jay C. Flippen), a former comedy writer (now owner of a tie store), who called him "Stringbean."

Buddy Sorrell (Morey Amsterdam) and Sally Rogers (Rose Marie) are

Rob's coworkers; Melvin "Mel" Cooley (Richard Deacon) is the show's producer; and Alan Brady (Carl Reiner) is the show's star.

Buddy is married to a former showgirl named Pickles (Joan Shawlee). Her real name is Fiona "But all girls named Fiona in my hometown are nicknamed Pickles." She likes strawberry sundae on a stick ice cream and was previously married to a forger named Floyd B. Bariscale. Buddy plays the cello, has a German shepherd (Larry) and claims tomato juice is his favorite drink. He once overdosed on Dozy Doodles sleeping pills after an argument with Pickles. Buddy's real name is Maurice, and prior to joining Alan's staff he had his own series (*Buddy's Bag*) and wrote for *The Billy Barrows Show*.

Sally hides her loneliness with her sense of humor. She is single and looking for Mr. Right. She has a pet cat (Mr. Henderson) and a mother-dominated boyfriend named Herman Glimshire (Bill Idelson); in some episodes he is called Woodrow Glimshire. Sally attended Herbert Hoover High School and was a writer on *The Milton Berle Show* before joining Alan's staff. She wears a size 6½ shoe and discovered Randy Isenbauer, a teenager who invented a dance called the "Twizzle" (a cross between the Twist and the Sizzle). She and Buddy perform as a variety act called Gilbert and Solomon at Herbie's Hiawatha Lodge.

Alan lives at the Temple Towers on East 61st Street in Manhattan. Mel is his "yes man" and is tormented by Buddy with his constant barrage of "baldy jokes" (the only way Buddy knows how to be "nice" to Mel). Alan's business ventures pay the bills. The Ishomoto Motorcycle Company pays Rob's salary; Buddy and Sally were first paid by Tam-O-Shanter, Ltd. (makers of Dean Martin and Jerry Lewis coloring books), and later by Barracuda, Ltd. (Alan's mother-in-law's company). Brady Lady, Alan's wife's company, pays the band.

Rob pays his neighbors, Jerry and Millie Helper (Jerry Paris, Ann Morgan Guilbert), $37.50 a year so they can tar the back wall of their basement (that rock Rob has causes Jerry's basement to flood if the wall is not waterproofed). Jerry is a dentist and Millie a homemaker. They have an iron jockey on the front lawn and a pet mynah bird (Herschel). Millie keeps a porcelain bull on the mantel and carries a siren pen for protection. Together Rob and Jerry purchased a boat they agreed to call the "Betty Lynn" (Rob wanted "Shangri-La"; Jerry, the "Challenger").

When Laura was expecting Ritchie, everyone suggested a name. Laura wanted Robert or Roberta; Rob, Laura or Laurence; Mel, Allen, Alan, Allan; Sally, Valentino ("I was saving it for a parakeet, but you can have it"); and Buddy, Exit ("If the kid is an actor, it'll be in every theater in the country"). Rob and Laura give him the middle name "Rosebud" to please their relatives—

Robert-Oscar-Sam-Edward-Benjamin-Ulysses-David. *The Uncle Spunky Show* is Ritchie's favorite TV program and Stanley and Ollie are the names of his pet ducks. Rob's most unusual gift to Laura was the grotesque Empress Carlotta necklace; the Petrie family heirloom is a cumbersome brooch shaped like the U.S. (a jewel marks the birthplace for each family member). Rob and Laura's cemetery plots are at Rock Meadows Rest on the 15th hole of a golf course. Earle Hagen composed "The Theme from the Dick Van Dyke Show."

Origins

Head of the Family, CBS, 7/19/60. In the original pilot, Rob (Carl Reiner), Buddy (Morty Gunty) and Sally (Sylvia Miles) write *The Alan Sturdy Show* (Jack Wakefield plays Alan). Rob is married to Laura (Barbara Britton) and the father of Ritchie (Gary Morgan). Here *The Alan Sturdy Show* airs live on Sundays at 9 P.M. and Ritchie has a pet hamster named Buster.

A Different World *see* The Cosby Show

34.   Diff'rent Strokes NBC, 1978–1985; ABC, 1985–1986

The Manhattan Penthouse (A; sometimes B) at 679 Park Avenue is owned by Phillip Drummond (Conrad Bain) a widower with a daughter, Kimberly (Dana Plato), and two adopted, black sons, Arnold and Willis Jackson (Gary Coleman, Todd Bridges).

Phillip, the owner of Drummond Industries (also called Trans-Allied, Inc.), promised his former housekeeper, Lucy, that if anything should happen to her he would care for her sons. Following her death, Arnold and Willis became part of his family (they previously lived at 259 East 135th Street, Apartment 12, in Harlem).

Phillip's real last name is Van Drummond (changed when his Dutch ancestors first came to America). He is called "L&M" ("Lean and Mean") at the Riverside Athletic Club and attended the Digby Prep School as a child. He has given each of his children ten shares of Drummond company stock. In 1984 Phillip married Maggie McKinney (Dixie Carter, Mary Ann Mobley), a divorcee with a young son named Sam (Danny Cooksey).

Maggie hosts the daily TV show *Exercise with Maggie* and teaches aerobics at the Manhattan Health Club. Maggie mentioned that when she began working her first pay check amounted to $37; Phillip mentioned his first paycheck was for $1.8 million. Sam has a pet goldfish (Montgomery) and is a member of Scout Troop 14. He is on the Hawks baseball team and peanut butter with tuna fish is his favorite sandwich.

Kimberly, a prima ballerina, played the lead in her school's production of *Swan Lake* (the Peekskill, New York, academy for girls is first called Eastlake then Eastland). She later attends Garfield High School in Manhattan (where she is a member of the swim team). Kimberly receives an allowance of $10 a week and held a job at the Hula Hut (fast food). She developed bulimia when she became a fashion model at Baun's Department Store (she thought she was losing her slim figure) and received ice skating lessons from Dorothy Hamill (when she thought she wanted to be a world-class skater). Kimberly, called "Pumpkin" by Phillip, was a spokesgirl for a cleaner environment when the all-natural Mother Brady's Shampoo reacted with the acid-affected rainwater she used and turned her blonde hair green. Kimberly left the series to attend school in Paris.

Arnold, the younger brother, attended P.S. 89, P.S. 406, Roosevelt Junior High, Edison Junior High and Garfield High School. He loves model railroading (he had both "HO" and "O" scale layouts) and horror movies (he hates it when Kimberly watches love stories). "What you talkin' about?" is his catchphrase and as a baby he had a plush cow named Fuzzy Wuzzy Moo Moo. He also had a ratty doll (Homer) and now has a goldfish (Abraham) and cricket (Lucky). Hamburger Heaven, later called the Hamburger Hanger, is his after-school hangout and he is champ at the video game "Space Sucker" (scoring one million points). Arnold was a reporter for his P.S. 89 newspaper, *The Weekly Woodpecker*, and editor of Edison's paper, *The Beacon*.

Arnold, a member of the Super Dudes Gang, formed a band called Frozen Heads. He enjoys magic and fancies himself as the magician Arnoldo. His first job was handing out circulars for Guido's Pizza Palace on 63rd Street. The Gooch is the unseen bully who picks on Arnold.

Willis, the older brother, attended Roosevelt Junior High, Garfield High then an unnamed college. "Say What?" is his favorite expression and as a kid he had a doll named Wendy Wetems. He, Kimberly, and his girlfriend, Charlene DuPres (Janet Jackson), formed a band called the Afro Disiacs. Willis is a bit conceited and thinks he is a ladies' man. He likes looking in the mirror and tries to "act like Superfly with the girls but I come off like Big Bird." Willis was a member of the Tarantulas gang and worked at Kruger's Garage.

Phillip's housekeepers were Edna Garret (Charlotte Rae; see *The Facts of Life*), Adelaid Brubaker (Nedra Volz) and Pearl Gallagher (Mary Jo Catlett). Alan Thicke, Gloria Loring and Al Burton composed the theme.

35. **Dobie Gillis** CBS, 1959–1963

The setting is the mythical community of Central City. At 285 Norwood Street is the Gillis Grocery Store, a business that has been run by its owner, Herbert T. Gillis (Frank Faylen), since 1937. Herbert, his wife, Winnie (Florida Friebus), and their son, Dobie (Dwayne Hickman), live above the store (address also given as 285 Elm Street, 9th and Main and 3rd and Elm). Herbert is a member of the Benevolent Order of the Bison Lodge and always claims he is 46 years old. He is known as a cheapskate and was voted "The citizen most likely to hang onto his last dollar." Herbert first recalls meeting Winnie at a dance; later it is in high school when Winnie entered a beauty pageant (she finished 27th out of 29 contestants). They honeymooned in Tijuana, Mexico. Herbert frequents the Scarpitta Barber Shop and his competition is Fortunato's Grocery Store.

Dobie and his best friend, Maynard G. Krebs (Bob Denver), attend Central High School (later S. Peter Pryor Junior College). Dobie, a romantic, always falls for a girl who causes him heartbreak. He is most famous for his infatuation with Thalia Menninger (Tuesday Weld), a girl who knows Dobie is dirt poor and the son of a cheap father, but who has high hopes of his "making oodles and oodles of money" so he can support her family—"a 60-year-old father with a kidney condition, a mother who isn't getting any younger, a sister who married a loafer, and a brother who is becoming a public charge." Thalia is absolutely gorgeous. His rival for her affections is Milton Armitage (Warren Beatty), the rich, spoiled schoolmate who calls Thalia "Mouse" (for her inability to choose between him and Dobie). Thalia's favorite perfume is MMMM ($18 an ounce).

Dobie admits that "I'm not only penniless, but dimeless, quarterless and dollarless." Linda Sue Faversham (Yvonne Craig) is a beautiful girl with an excellent memory for numbers—"stocks, bonds and compound interest." "Linda Sue," Dobie says, "has the face of an angel, the body of a goddess and the soul of a cash register." She too became an obsession with Dobie. Like Thalia, Linda Sue needed to find a rich husband "to support my unemployable family." Linda Sue tempts men with her gifts, "This stunning body, these perfect teeth, this beautiful hair and this fabulous face." Linda Sue carries a bag of "Sneaky Tricks" around with her "that I collected over a lifetime of sneaky living."

Following in Linda Sue's footsteps is her equally gorgeous sister, Amanda Jean (Annette Gorman). She is being groomed by Linda Sue to marry money. At age five Linda Sue had Amanda Jean reading the *Wall Street Journal* ("I loved it," she says, "especially the parts where they foreclosed mortgages and threw everybody out on the street. It was thrilling"). Amanda Jean believes Dobie is a deadbeat and not worth her sister's time (although she fell for Dobie's poor cousin, Duncan Gillis [Bobby Diamond]). When Herbert gets mad at Dobie he turns to the camera and utters "I gotta kill that boy, I just gotta."

Zelda Gilroy (Sheila James) is a classmate who loves Dobie "with all my heart and soul." Pretty and intelligent, she taught Dobie how to play the guitar and is always there for him when a girl dumps him. She wants Dobie and feels he is not attracted to her because she is much smarter than he is. Dobie feels she is a pain and is constantly telling her to "get off my back."

Maynard calls Dobie "Good Buddy." When Dobie breaks up with a girl Maynard always says "You've got me good buddy" (to which Dobie replies "I'm afraid so Maynard, I'm afraid so"). Maynard is a beatnik and loves to play the bongo drums. He likes jazz and hangs out at Riff's Music Store. He has a stuffed armadillo (Herman) and says the *G* in his name stands for Walter. Maynard lives at 1343 South Elm Street and has a weekly allowance of 35 cents. His favorite activities are watching workmen paint a new white line down Elm Street and being there when they knock down the old Endicott Building (which must be done brick by brick as it is mentioned often). Maynard has been turned down 46 times in six years for his driver's license and claims that delicatessen is the longest word he can pronounce. His favorite movie is *The Monster That Devoured Cleveland* (apparently the only movie that the Bijou Theater ever shows) and he always responds with "You Rang?" when his name is mentioned. Maynard panics when he hears the word *work*, and when he sees a girl crying he says "I'd offer you my handkerchief if I had one." He claims to have the world's largest collection of tin foil.

Chatsworth Osborne, Jr. (Steven Franken), a schoolmate, is the spoiled son of the fabulously wealthy Clarissa Osborne (Doris Packer). Chatsworth claims to have type "R" (for royal) blood and is heir to the Osborne National Bank Fortune. He lives in a 47-room Louis XIV home ("the one with the broken glass embedded in the walls"), belongs to the Downshifters Club and is president of the Silver Spoons Club (for snobs) at Pryor College. He dreams of going to Yale, and "mice and rats" is his catchphrase. He calls Dobie "Dobie Doo" and his mother "Mumsey" (she calls him "You Nasty Boy").

Professor Leander Pomfritt (Herbert Anderson, William Schallert) teaches English. He refers to his students as "young barbarians." Pomfritt wrote nine unpublished novels (eight of which he destroyed). He wishes, at times, that he had gone into the aluminum siding business (in some episodes he mentions the air conditioning business).

Dr. Imogene Burkhart (Jean Byron) teaches biology and psychology. In early episodes Jean Byron played Ruth Adams, the math teacher. The Imogene Burkhart character was originally played by Jody Warner as a classmate on whom Dobie had a crush.

Dobie and Maynard's after-school hangout is Charlie Wong's Ice Cream Parlor (which serves 31 flavors of ice cream and strawberry won-ton sundaes, Thalia's favorite). In college Dobie was editor of the school's newspaper, the *Pryor Crier* (the radio station was KSPP). In 1961, Dobie and Maynard joined the Army (where Dobie gained 14 pounds; they were said to be with Company A, Company C and Company Q). Dobie comments to the audience while sitting or standing near a statue of the Thinker in the park. The series is also known as *The Many Loves of Dobie Gillis* (the 1959–60 title).

Updates

1. *Whatever Happened to Dobie Gillis?*, CBS, 5/10/77. An unsold pilot that finds Dobie (Dwayne Hickman) married to Zelda (Sheila James) and the father of Georgie (Stephen Paul). Maynard (Bob Denver) is an entrepreneur and Dobie and his father, Herbert (Frank Faylen), have an expanded Gillis Grocery Store.

2. *Bring Me the Head of Dobie Gillis*, CBS, 2/21/88. A TV movie that finds Dobie and Zelda (Dwayne Hickman, Sheila James) as owners of the Gillis Market and Pharmacy. Their son, Georgie, is now played by Scott Grimes. Maynard (Bob Denver) is a rich businessman, Chatsworth (Steve Franken) is the town banker, and Thalia (Connie Stevens) is a rich widow. The story finds Thalia seeking to win Dobie's love by offering to save his bankrupt town—if he will divorce Zelda and marry her.

36.   **The Donna Reed Show** ABC, 1958–1966

Dr. Alex Stone and his wife, Donna (Carl Betz, Donna Reed), live in the fifth district in the town of Hilldale. They are the parents of Mary and Jeff (Shelley Fabares, Paul Petersen) and Hilldale 4-3926 (later Hilldale 7281) is their phone number. Donna, the dedicated wife, loving mother and all-around problem solver, was a nurse (Donna Mullinger) when she met Alex, an intern. Alex, a pediatrician, works out of an office in his home (next to the kitchen). Alex was stationed at Fort Dix during World War II and reads a daily paper called the *Sentinel*. Mary, three years older than Jeff, first attended Hilldale High School and then an unnamed college 4 $\frac{2}{10}$ miles from her home. Mary wears a size eight dress, dances at the Round Robin, has meals at the Blue Lantern and soft drinks at Kelzey's Malt Shop. Jeff weighed

10½ pounds at birth, and has perfect pitch but no musical talent. He was a member of the Bobcats football team and had a hand puppet (Bongo) and mouse (Herman) as a kid. He attends Hilldale High (also called Central High) and *Gunbutt*, sponsored by Happy Gum, is his favorite TV show. In 1962, when Mary leaves for college, Donna and Alex adopt Trisha (Patty Petersen), a parentless girl who had been living unhappily with an uncle (she befriended the Stones during a game of touch football in the park). Her favorite TV show is *Jingo the Clown*. William Loose and John Seely composed the theme, "Happy Days."

37.   The Doris Day Show CBS, 1968–1973

Wanting to spend more time raising her sons, Billy and Toby (Philip Brown, Todd Starke), widow Doris Martin (Doris Day) relinquishes her career as a singer and takes on the role of mother when she moves in with her father, Buck Webb (Denver Pyle), the owner of a ranch at 32 Mill Valley Road in Mill Valley, California. In 1969, when she feels a need to help with expenses, Doris acquires a job in San Francisco as the executive secretary to Michael Nicholson (McLean Stevenson), the editor of *Today's World*, the "Now Magazine."

When commuting becomes difficult, Doris, the kids and her sheepdog, Lord Nelson, rent a $140 a month apartment above Palucci's Italian Restaurant at 965 North Parkway. In 1971, when Doris becomes a reporter, Cyril Bennett (John Dehner) becomes her editor. Doris's license plate reads 255 NOZ; Cyril's is 495 CCF. Doris Day sings the theme, "Que Sera, Sera" ("What Will Be, Will Be").

38.   Double Trouble NBC, 1984–1985

Identical twins Allison and Kate Foster (Jean and Liz Sagal) live at 1555 North Ridge Drive in Des Moines, Iowa, with their widowed father, Art (Donnelly Rhodes), the owner of Art's Gym (where the girls work as aerobic instructors).

Allison is quiet and serious; Kate is a bit wild and mischievous. After six episodes, the format found Allison and Kate moving to New York to pursue their dreams: Allison, as a fashion designer; Kate, as an actress. They now reside with their aunt, Margo Foster (Barbara Barrie), the author of the "Bongo the Bear" children's stories. Margo was first said to live at 49 West 74th Street; later at 51 West 74th Street; 555-7767 is her phone number. Ray Colcord composed the theme.

39.   **Duffy's Tavern** NBC, 1954

Duffy's Tavern is a rundown bar located on Third Avenue in New York City. It is "where the elite meet to eat" and where, with a beer, the free lunch costs 15 cents. Archie (Ed Gardner) runs the bar for the never-seen Mr. Duffy. Archie is a con artist and "the books are a little unbalanced." He is a graduate of P.S. 4 grammar school and is dating Peaches La Tour (Veda Ann Borg), a stripper at the Burlesque Palace (later the Bijou Burlesque). Keeping tabs on Archie is Miss Duffy (Patte Chapman), Duffy's daughter, whom Archie calls "Mother Nature's revenge on Peeping Toms." She works as the cashier and freely gives out her phone number (Murray Hill 3-8000) in an effort to find a husband. "Unfortunately," says Archie, "her phone ain't never rung." Clifton Finnegan (Alan Reed) is Archie's simple-minded friend ("When Clifton was born, the baby doctor was a little nearsighted and Finnegan got slapped on the head"). He enjoys collecting cigar bands. The Feinschmacker Brewery of Greater Staten Island services the bar (Duffy orders the Weehawken Lager Beer, Nectar). Based on the radio series (CBS, 1941–42; NBC, 1943–51).

40.   **The Dukes of Hazzard** CBS, 1979–1985

Hazzard County, Georgia, is home to the Duke family, the owners of a farm 18 miles outside of town on Mill Pond Road. Jesse Duke (Denver Pyle) owns the farm and lives there with his nephews, Bo and Luke Duke (John Schneider, Tom Wopat), and his niece, Daisy Duke (Catherine Bach).

Jesse, the Duke family patriarch, once ran moonshine in the Ridgerunner Association in a car he first called "Sweet Tillie," then "Black Tillie." He has a pet goat named Bonnie and believes that "the law is the law and us Dukes gotta obey it no matter what." The law, unfortunately, is Jefferson Davis Hogg (Sorrell Booke), a former moonshine runner (with Jesse) who is still corrupt (he owns most of the town and is called Boss Hogg and J.D. Hogg). Boss is the commissioner, president of the Hazzard County Bank and the justice of the peace. He also has a number of businesses: Road Hogg Towing, Hogg Used Cars, the Boar's Nest (a bar off Highway 30) and the radio station (WHOGG), and sells Hogg Alarm Systems, Hoggoco Motor Oil, J.D. Shocks, the Hoggo Car Charger Kit, Hoggamufflers and Hogg's Happy Burgers ("The only burger that makes you straighten up and fly right").

Boss has a plaque on his office wall that reads "Do Unto Others Before They Do Unto You" and the "J.D. Hogg War Memorial: Dedicated to J.D.

Hogg and Less Important War Heroes." He has a car called the "Gray Ghost" and the Hogg Celebrity Speed Trap (which catches famous country and western singers and forces them to perform at the Boar's Nest). Boss Hogg wants to further his ambitions by becoming the richest man in town but fears one man: his twin brother, Abraham Lincoln Hogg (Sorrell Booke), "the white sheep of the family." He is as honest as J.D. is dishonest and dresses in black (J.D. dresses in white). "How do you tell the difference? You hold up a dollar. The one who grabs it is Boss; the one who wants to give it away is Abe," says Jesse.

The Dukes have made it their goal to clean up Hazzard County by stopping Boss Hogg's endless array of corrupt moneymaking schemes (the most persistent of which is finding ways to make the Dukes late in paying the farm's mortgage so he can foreclose and sell the land to the Crystal Mountain Brewery).

Daisy works as a waitress at the Boar's Nest (Boss gives her 25 percent of the tips she makes). She also worked part time as a reporter for the Hazzard County *Gazette*. She entered "The Miss Tri Counties Beauty Pageant" and won the title "Best All Around Gal in Three Counties" (for her "beauty, mechanical abilities and driving skills"). Daisy shops at the Capitol City Department Store. She originally drove a yellow Dodge Charger (destroyed by Bo and Luke when they lost control, jumped out and the car went off a cliff) and then a white Jeep Golden Eagle she called "Dixie." Daisy is also den mother to the Junior Patrol, a girl scout troop. The bikini Daisy is seen wearing in the opening theme and the short shorts she wears during the show (the Daisy Dukes) were created by Catherine Bach.

Bo and Luke enjoy fishing at Sunset Lake and ride in the "General Lee," a souped-up 1969 orange Dodge Charger (with a Confederate flag on the roof, the racing number 01 on the door, and the license plate CNH 320). They found the car in a state of disrepair in a nearby Chickasaw County junk yard (the car had been used in a bank robbery). With the help of Cooter Davenport (Ben Jones), the owner of Cooter's Garage, they completely made it over with a powerful engine and welded-shut doors (like NASCAR racers). The car's horn plays a 12-note musical selection from the song "Dixie." Luke is famous for the "hood slide" (sliding across the roof from the driver's side to the passenger side). The car was originally black; Cooter had only orange paint in stock. Uncle Jesse suggested the name.

Bo and Luke do not use guns (they use dynamite-tipped arrows as weapons) and have C.B. codes when on the road: Jesse is "Shepherd"; Bo and Luke are "Lost Sheep" and Daisy is "Bo Peep" (they broadcast on frequency Channel 9). Luke is the older of the cousins and saw much of the world during his hitch with the Marines. Bo was a linebacker on the football team at Hazzard High School and can talk any girl into a date for Saturday night. Daisy was considered the wildest girl at Hazzard High. The "General Lee" is often in need of repairs and Cooter can "bang out the dents the same day it is damaged" ($987 was the most Bo and Luke have paid to have the car fixed; they also race it in the Cherokee County Dirt Road Classic and the Smokey Hollow Race). Cooter has a farm on Jessup Road and SU 0265 is the plate of his tow truck.

Sheriff Roscoe P. Coltraine (James Best) was an honest cop for over 20 years. When he was denied a pension, he joined Boss Hogg in abusing authority for fun and profit. His sister, Lulu (Peggy Rea), married Boss. Roscoe calls Boss his "Little Fat Buddy" and says to him "You've always got some devious little scheme in that fat head of yours." He rides in a patrol car with his lazy dog, Flash, and yells "Hot Pursuit" when he chases the Dukes.

"What Roscoe lacks in brains he makes up for in stupidity," says Boss of Roscoe. When Boss wanted to cut expenses, he instituted "Hoggonomics." He did away with patrol cars and put Roscoe and his deputy, Enos Strate (Sonny Shroyer), on horseback (the Hazzard Mounted Police); each horse had a siren and a flashing red light on its head. Lulu runs Hogg Enterprises and is the founder of H.E.R.S. (Hazzard Equal Rights Society). Roscoe's office is room 101 in the Hazzard County Police Department and his patrol car license plate reads 835 27.

The Hazzard County car wash is a hole in the road that fills up when it rains. The Hazzard Picture Palace is the local movie theater and the Boar's Nest sponsors the town's pee wee basketball team, the Boar's Nest Bears (it also has a one dollar cover charge "to keep out the riff raff"). April first is Sadie Hogg Day (when the women take over government jobs); the Lulu Hogg Stakes Horse Race is a highlight of the annual Hazzard County Fair and Bo and Luke also compete in the Annual Hazzard Drag-n-Fly Derby (auto race and car-jumping contest). In Hazzard County, hunting season is "three weeks for deer, two weeks for quail and open season on Dukes and moonshiners," says Boss.

The Dukes have a family history of running moonshine. When a contract dispute over merchandise tie-ins forced John Schneider and Tom Wopat to leave the show, their cousins Coy and Vance Duke (Byron Cherry, Christopher Mayer) were brought on in 1982 to help Uncle Jesse while they went on tour with the NASCAR circuit. Six months later (after the dispute was settled), Bo and Luke returned to Hazzard after they found the NASCAR circuit dull; Coy and Vance left to care for their Aunt Bessie and Uncle

Albert. Waylon Jennings provides the narration and sings the theme, "Good Ol' Boys."

Spinoffs

1. *Mason Dixon Girls*, CBS, 2/29/80. An unsold pilot about Mason Dixon (Dennis Rucker), a private investigator, and his two beautiful assistants, Tinker (Mary Margaret Humes) and Sam (Robin G. Eisenmann). Here, they seek a drug smuggler in Hazzard County.

2. *Enos*, CBS, 1980–1981. When Enos, the only law-abiding officer in Hazzard County, captures two of America's most wanted men, he is recruited by the L.A.P.D. and teamed with Turk Adams (Samuel E. Wright), a tough black cop. Both are with Division 8 of the Metro Squad.

3. *The Dukes*, CBS, 1983–1985. Denver Pyle narrates an animated series in which the Dukes (Coy, Vance and Daisy, first season; Bo, Luke and Daisy, second season) compete against Boss and Roscoe in an around-the-world car race for a cash prize that the Dukes need to save their farm. The series regulars provide their own voices.

TV Movie Update

The Dukes of Hazzard Reunion, CBS, 4/25/97. The original cast, with the exception of Sorrell Booke (who had passed away), return in a story that finds the corrupt Roscoe P. Coltraine planning to snatch the Duke farm to build a theme park.

41. The Egg and I CBS, 1951–1952

Betty Blake (Patricia Kirkland, Betty Lynn) and her husband, Jim (John Craven), are former city dwellers who purchase a chicken farm in Allagain County, a small farming community in upstate New York. Goods are purchased at Ed Peabody's General Store and Betty has a pet pig named Penny. Their neighbors are Ma and Pa Kettle (Doris Rich, Frank Tweddell), an elderly couple who own the nearby farm. Pa loves donuts and Ma's cooking, and is rather lazy (Ma says "The only reliable thing about Pa is his appetite"). Pa claims to have won the 1912 Allagain County Corn Husking Contest and was a hard worker before settling down. Alan Edwards is the announcer. Based on the book by Betty MacDonald.

42. Eight Is Enough ABC, 1977–1981

The white house with maroon shutters at 1436 Oak Street in Sacramento, California, is owned by Thomas "Tom" Bradford (Dick Van Patten), a columnist for the Sacramento *Register*, who is also the father of eight children (David, Mary, Joanie, Nancy, Susan, Tommy, Elizabeth and Nicholas).

Tom Bradford and Joan Wells (Diana Hyland) were married in 1950. It is with her that Tom had his children. To remember their names, Tom and Joan made up this saying (with each capital letter standing for a child's name): "Never Try Eating Nectarines Since Juice May Dispense." When they first married, Tom was the editor of a small magazine that went bankrupt; three months later he found a job with the *Register*. Joanie, as Tom called her, worked as a freelance photographer. She likes to read, enjoys poetry and buys Christmas gifts for the children months in advance. Joanie "died" shortly after the series began when Diana lost her life to cancer in 1977. Tom disliked the sound of Joanie filing her fingernails. He wears a size 39 regular suit.

Sandra Sue "Abby" Abbott (Betty Buckley) became the new woman in Tom's life (they married in 1979). Abby, a guidance counselor at Memorial High School, lived previously at 1412 Compton Place with her late husband, Frank (a P.O.W. who died in Vietnam). As a kid Abby had a horse named Blaze. She wrote her college thesis on "Modern Sex Roles."

David (Grant Goodeve), the oldest of the children, is a contractor. Before forming the Bradford Construction Company with his father, David worked for the Mann Construction Company and Joseph Jenkins and Associates. He graduated from Sacramento Central High in 1977. On the first Sunday in November, David and Tom observe a Bradford family tradition: duck hunting. David lives outside the family home (in Apartment 207) and married Janet McCarther (Joan Prather), a lawyer with the firm of Goodman, Saxon and Tweedy. Marital difficulties led to their separating and later divorcing (1981) but they remained friends. Janet lived at 2475 DeVanna Place and later worked for the firm of Ted O'Hara and Associates. Mark Hamill played David in the pilot.

Mary (Lani O'Grady), the most studious of the children, is in medical school struggling to become a doctor. She interns at Saint Mary's Hospital, where her mentor, Dr. Craig Maxwell (Michael Thoma), practices. Craig, a family friend called "Dr. Max," is also with Sacramento Memorial and Sacramento General Hospital. When the pressures of medical school made Mary unsure of her career choice, she ran for political office but lost (a seat on the 8th District School Board). When Mary was a student at Berkeley College, she was a radical and was arrested for protesting (she stands up for causes—even if they oppose Tom's beliefs). Mary enjoys cold pizza for breakfast.

Joanie (Lauri Walters), named after her mother, has her mother's eyes, smile and sensitivity. She also has something her mother didn't—frizzy hair (she uses Frizz Free shampoo). Joanie is first a researcher then reporter for KTNS-TV, Channel 8, in Sacramento. She also entertains (as a clown) at the Charles Street Children's Home. Before her job in television, Joanie had aspirations to be an actress. She shocked Tom ("I've never seen a look like that on Dad's face") when she appeared without clothes in a play called "Shakespeare in the Nude." Joanie, dressed as an ice cream cone, and Susan, a banana split, worked as walking advertisements for the Sweet Tooth Dessert Shoppe (at $3.25 an hour). All the Bradford children found it difficult to adjust to Abby at first; it was Joanie who felt the most out of place (Joanie believed that Abby resented her because she looked so much like her mother).

Nancy (Dianne Kay), the prettiest of the Bradford girls, attended Sacramento High School (where she was a cheerleader) and later State College (but dropped out when she couldn't handle the work load). Nancy first worked for Hot Wires (singing telegrams over the phone) then as a model (she appeared on the cover of *Epitome* magazine). She was also the "Sunshine Soda Girl" in TV commercials and gave up possible stardom when she refused to show her breasts in an ad campaign for Vernon Isley Jeans (Nancy felt she could break into modeling with "my outgoing personality and nice features"). Nancy plays tennis, rides horses, and uses extra body shampoo. She finds a steady job at the Bates, Callahan and Chester brokerage house (later called the Fenwick, Hargrove and Elliott brokerage house). Kimberly Beck played Nancy in the pilot.

Susan (Susan Richardson) is the most sensitive of the children. She attended Sacramento Central High School and traveled a different path to discover her goal. She attempted a number of jobs, but failing the physical endurance test to become a police officer was the most devastating for her. Susan has a fondness for children. When Nancy failed in an attempt to start a day-care center, Susan found her true calling when she took over the unnamed business. Susan married Merle "The Pearl" Stockwell (Brian Patrick Clarke), a pitcher for the Cyclones, a minor-league baseball team. In 1980, Merle became a pitcher for the New York Mets. His career ended a year later when he injured his arm while trick riding on a bike. He then became the athletic coach at Central High School and he and Susan became the parents of a daughter they named Sandra Sue.

Tommy (Willie Aames) is the most troublesome of the children (he constantly rebels against parental authority and longs to become a rock musician; he plays guitar). He attended Sacramento Central High and formed a band called Tommy and the Actions (they performed the song "Let's Be

Frank"). His hangouts are Bennie's Burger Bin and the Cluck 'n' Chuck (fast food chicken). Chris English played Tommy in the pilot.

Elizabeth (Connie Needham) is the youngest of the Bradford girls. She attends Sacramento Central High then Sacramento Junior College. She is studying dance and hopes to become a professional dancer. Although she is very pretty, she feels awkward around boys ("I'm like a cross between Marie Osmond and a kewpie doll"). Elizabeth uses shampoo with conditioner. If she misses her 11:30 P.M. curfew, she is grounded for two weeks "with no time off for good behavior." Elizabeth was not permitted to graduate with her class (she dropped a water balloon from a second floor and caused a teacher to fall and break her leg). In the fourth grade, Elizabeth wore braces and was called "Metal Mouth" by the boys (this caused her to fight with the name callers and become a hero with the girls; she was also elected blackboard monitor). In the pilot, Elizabeth is depicted as a troublesome Bradford (here, arrested for drug possession); not so in the series. When Joanie gets angry at Elizabeth and calls her "a baby," Elizabeth sulks and locks herself in the bathroom.

Nicholas (Adam Rich) is the youngest of the children. He attends the Goodwin Knight Elementary School and had a neighborhood courier service (N&M Delivery Service). When there is a water crisis in the state and people need to conserve, Tom appoints Nicholas the family's water monitor (there is a problem because, for example, Elizabeth takes two showers a day, and Joanie practices her lines in the shower). Nicholas loves basketball and was rejected for being too small for the youth-league basketball team (he wore jersey 32). Nicholas has two hamsters (Ron and Marsha) and won a racehorse named Royal in a contest. He also had a job selling a wrinkle remover called Guca Dew door to door. Nicholas was the ring bearer at Tom and Abby's wedding; best man at Susan and Merle's wedding.

The Bradfords' telephone number is first 555-0263, then 555-6023. Abby's car, Gwendolyn (a British MG), has the license plate YNH 872; Tom's license plate reads 460 EKA (station wagon) and 842 CUI (sedan). Tommy's license plate is 553 VFZ and David's van license plate is HIR 312. When Joanie produced the Unified Charities Telethon for Channel 8, the family pitched in: Abby performed a special song ("Travelers on a Star"); David sang "The Eyes of a Stranger"; Nancy and Nicholas sang "Me and My Shadow"; Mary and Susan were on the pledge phones; Tommy performed with his band; Tom observed from the audience.

Tom's cooking specialty is chili con Bradford. He is called "Tommy Bellybutton" by his wealthy sister, Vivian (Janis Paige); she is called "Auntie V" by the family. Joanie (the mother) mentioned to Mary that she and three other children (not named) were accidents ("Not that you're not loved, just not planned for").

Last-season episodes also feature Ralph Macchio as Jeremy Andretti, Abby's nephew, a student at Sacramento Central High, who came to live with the family (after his mother died and his father deserted him). He attempted to make money by selling health products he bought from an ad he saw in *Man's Man* magazine (the shampoo, for example, turned Nancy's blonde hair green). Grant Goodeve sings the theme, "Eight Is Enough."

TV Movie Updates

1. ***Eight Is Enough: A Family Reunion***, NBC, 10/18/87. The cast remains the same with the exception of Abby, now played by Mary Frann. The story finds the family reuniting to help celebrate Tom's 50th birthday. Tom is now the managing editor of the *Register*; Abby owns her own restaurant, the Delta Supper Club. Mary, now a doctor, is married to Chuck (Jonathan Perpich). Susan and Merle are the parents of a daughter they now call Sandy (Amy Gibson); Tommy is a struggling lounge singer; Elizabeth and her husband, Mark (Peter Nelson), own a car restoration business; David is an architect (still divorced from Janet). Joanie, who became an actress, married film director Jean Pierre (Paul Rosilli). Nancy is now married to a sheep rancher named Jeb (Christopher McDonald) and Nicholas is attending college.

2. ***An Eight Is Enough Wedding***, NBC, 10/15/89. The family reunites once again, this time to witness the wedding of David to Marilyn "Mike" Fulbright (Nancy Everhard). The cast remains the same with the exception of Abby, now played by Sandy Faison.

43.   The Facts of Life NBC, 1979–1988

The Eastland School is a private academy for girls in Peekskill, New York. Friendship and generosity represent the school spirit and uniforms are maroon and white with a yellow Eastland crest on the vest. Edna Garrett (Charlotte Rae) is the school's dietician; principal students are Blair Warner (Lisa Whelchel), Jo Ann "Jo" Polniaszek (Nancy McKeon), Dorothy "Tootie" Ramsey (Kim Fields) and Natalie Greene (Mindy Cohn).

Edna, a divorcee, worked previously for Phillip Drummond (*Diff'rent Strokes*) as his housekeeper. She was born in Appleton, Wisconsin, and drives a car with the plate 845 DUD. When her pension fund is lost through bad investments and she is unable to get a raise, Edna quits Eastland to begin her own business, Edna's Edibles, a gourmet food shop at 320 Main Street (in a store formally called Ara's Deli). When a fire destroys the shop, Edna uses the insurance money to open Over Our Heads, a novelty store. Blair, Jo, Tootie and Natalie work for Edna and live above the store. (Their building is next to a famous residence called the Blackbird Boarding House that, in the 1960s, served as a stopover for singers performing in Peekskill. The school was originally called the Eastlake School for Girls). George Burnett (George Clooney) is the handyman Edna employs. He lives at 918 Haight Street and worked previously in Kuwait "installing hot tubs in Kuwaiti homes."

In 1987, Edna married Dr. Robert Gaynes (Robert Mandan) and moves to Africa to help him in his work with the Peace Corps. Her sister, Beverly Ann Stickle (Cloris Leachman), becomes the girls' new guardian. Beverly Ann, a divorcee, is the adoptive mother of Andy (Mackenzie Astin) and guardian of Pippa McKenna (Sherrie Krenn), a foreign exchange student from Colunga, Eastland's sister school in Sydney, Australia. Andy attends South Junior High School. Beverly Ann tells stories from her past to help the girls overcome their problems.

Blair, the school's most beautiful girl ("I'm cashmere and caviar") was named after her grandfather, Judge Carlton Blair. She is heir to Warner Textile Industries and considered by others to be a snob. While she doesn't have to work ("I'm best at spending money"), Blair sold cosmetics (as a Junior Beauty Ambassador) for Countess Calvet (Zsa Zsa Gabor).

Blair, who won the Small Businesswoman's Association Award for inventing contour top sheets, reads *Vogue* magazine and is a member of the Fur of the Month Club. She was voted Eastland Harvest Queen and received a blue ribbon for being Most Naturally Blonde. Blair has a horse named Chestnut and hopes to become a lawyer. She later attends Langley College and becomes a member of the Gamma Gamma Sorority. The last episode, "The Beginning of the End," was a pilot for the unsold *Lisa Whelchel Show*. When Eastland files for bankruptcy, Blair uses the money she had been saving for her law office to buy the school. She becomes the headmistress and changes the enrollment to allow boys. Juliette Lewis and Mayim Bialik were set to play students Terry Rankin and Jennifer Cole.

Jo was born in the Bronx, New York, and is attending Eastland on a scholarship (her mother is a waitress; her father is in jail). She is pretty, but tough and burdened with an attitude problem (a constant source of friction between her and Blair). She rides a motorcycle and cares little about fashion and makeup (Blair calls her "Polyester and pretzels"). Jo is saddened by the fact that the school library "has no books on automotive engineering. You'd be surprised how many girls don't know how to drain a crank case."

When Jo isn't "mean and rotten" to Blair, Blair thinks Jo "must be coming down with something." Jo later attends Langley College (where she is a member of the Board of Regents; the school newspaper is the *Langlian*). Jo first works as a disc jockey for Langley's radio station, WLG, 90.8 FM; then as a counselor at the Hudson Valley Community Center. Jo, Natalie and Tootie made a failed attempt to start their own business—Mama Rosa's Original Bronx Pizza, Inc. The last episode finds Jo marrying her boyfriend, Rick Bonner (Scott Bryce).

Tootie, the youngest and most darling of the girls, lived on rollerskates during her first year at Eastland. She has a habit of meddling and hopes to become an actress (she was the first black girl at Eastland to play Juliet in *Romeo and Juliet*). She has a cat (Jeffrey) and two rabbits (Romeo and Juliet). Tootie is also the most ambitious of the girls (Blair calls her "My little helper") and oils her rollerskate wheels when she gets angry. She enjoys playing checkers with Natalie and believes Natalie is the most honest person she knows.

Natalie hopes to become a journalist and wears her thinking cap when she writes (a blue baseball cap with orange lightning bolts over each ear). She worked as a reporter for the *Peekskill Press* (where her first article, "An Eighth Grader Gets Angry," was published) and as a waitress at a taco stand called El Sombrero. Natalie washes her hair when she gets angry and is the peacemaker of the group (she resolves differences between Jo and Blair). The last episode finds Natalie moving to New York's Soho district to pursue her writing career and Tootie preparing to attend London's Royal Academy of Dramatic Arts.

Molly Parker (Molly Ringwald), Nancy Olson (Felice Schachter), Sue Ann Weaver (Julie Piekarski) and Cindy Webster (Julie Ann Haddock) are other first-season students at Eastland.

Molly is a photographer for the school's newspaper and has a ham radio with the call letters WGAIO. She chews on pencils when she gets angry. Nancy is a beautiful teenager who hopes to become a model. She is constantly talking about or to (over the phone) her boyfriend, Roger. Sue Ann, called "Thunder Thighs" by Blair, is the school's star runner (she won the silver-plated track trophy two years in a row and runs the mile in 4 minutes, 58 seconds). Cindy is the school's pretty tomboy. She loves baseball and tennis and when she gets mad, she jumps rope. She wears her blonde hair in pigtails and was called the "Eastland Streak" when she went out for track (her best mile time was 5 minutes, 3 seconds). Cindy wears jersey 14 and while she and Sue Ann sweat after a race, Edna claims "Eastland girls don't sweat, they humidify." A later reunion episode revealed that Cindy (not Nancy) had become a model; Nancy, a businesswoman; and Sue Ann, a gofer, not the company vice president she pretended to be. Charlotte Rae (first and second season) and Gloria Loring sing *The Facts of Life* theme.

44.   Family Ties NBC, 1982–1989

The Keatons are a family of six who live in the Leland Heights section of Columbus, Ohio. Steven and Elyse (Michael Gross, Meredith Baxter) are the parents; Alex, Mallory, Jennifer and Andrew (Michael J. Fox, Justine Bateman, Tina Yothers, Brian Bonsell) are their children.

Elyse Catherine O'Donnell was 15 years old when she first met Steven Richard Keaton. They dated, were engaged when she was 18 and married two years later. They were flower children and lived in a commune in Berkeley, California (another episode states that Elyse and Steven were students at Berkeley when they first met and they married after attending Woodstock in 1969). At college, Steven was president of the south campus aluminum can recycling program and wrote the play, *A Draft Card for Burning* (as a protest of the Vietnam War). Steven was a communication arts major; Elyse an architecture major. After the birth of their first son, Alex (whom they contemplated naming Moon Muffin), they moved to Columbus and lived in a small apartment on Rosewood Avenue.

Steven is now the manager of PBS TV station WKS, Channel 3, and Elyse works as a freelance architect (she previously worked for the firm of Norvacks, Jenkins and St. Clair). Elyse has a lifelong dream of becoming a folk singer. The Cavanaugh Building was the first structure she designed.

Alex P. Keaton is a staunch Republican and prides himself on being different (for example, he does extra homework on Saturdays—"It's what gives me my edge"). He always wears a shirt and tie and worships money. He was a student at Harding High School and prided himself on "being one of the smartest kids" in school; "I can't stand being average." Alex also had a strict policy against high school blind dates "unless I can see her yearbook picture first." After graduating with honors, Alex attended the prestigious Leland College and majored in economics. He was president of its Young Businessmen's Association, Young Entrepreneurs Club and the Young Republicans, and also won the Matthews, Wilson, Harris and Burke Scholarships. He carries his resume with him at all times.

Alex reads the *Wall Street Journal*, hosted *Syncopated Money* (blues music and business news) on Leland's radio station (WLEL) and held a temporary job at the Harding Trust Company and the American Mercantile Bank. The last episode saw Alex accepting a job with the Wall Street firm of O'Brien,

Mathers and Clark in New York City. The day school begins is Alex's favorite day of the year; he has a collection of report cards from nursery school through college.

Mallory is very pretty and bright in her own way (she is not as smart as Alex but finds solace in her dream of becoming a fashion designer). She has a hard time relaxing "because I'm nervous about everything" and believes that cooking means preparing everything with an oven setting of 375 degrees. Mallory wrote the advice column "Dear Mallory" for *Columbus Shopping Guide* and needs at least ten hours to prepare for a date ("Which is still cutting it a little close"). She first attended Harding High School then Grant College (which "is conveniently located near all the major highways"; Alex doesn't consider Grant "a real college because Mallory got in"). At Grant, Mallory majored in fashion design, was a member of the Gamma Delta Gamma Sorority and held a temporary job as an apprentice at David Campbell Fashions. Mallory has a "gift" to tell fabrics apart blindfolded and deplores polyester.

Alex thinks Mallory "is borderline interesting at best." Her hoodlike boyfriend, Nick Moore (Scott Valentine), finds Mallory's naivety intriguing. "Woman with a Half-eaten Hamburger" was the first painting Nick, a potential artist, sold. He has a dog (Scrapper) and greets people with "Heyyyy." His father owns a used car lot called Joe Moore's Motors and Nick later opened an art school for children.

When Mallory wears a short skirt she hears "You look cute wearing Jennifer's outfit" from Elyse and Alex. Jennifer, Mallory's younger sister, is as bright as Alex but wishes she could trade some of that intelligence for Mallory's fashion sense, beauty and popularity with boys. Jennifer was a member of the Sunshine Girls Club (troop 247, patch 27) and first attended Thomas Dewey Junior High School then Harding High and finally Leland College. She worked after school as an order taker at Chicken Heaven, a fast food store.

Andrew, the youngest Keaton, is a clone of Alex and attends the Harper Preschool. *Wall Street Week* is his and Alex's favorite TV show and Alex is grooming him to become a ruthless business tycoon. The theme, "Without Us," is first sung by Mindy Sterling and Dennis Tufano; later by Johnny Mathis and Denicse Williams.

45. **Father Knows Best** CBS, 1954–1955; 1958–1962; NBC, 1955–1958

The Andersons are a family of five who live at 607 South Maple Street in the town of Springfield (address also given as Main Street). Jim, the father

(Robert Young), is the manager of the General Insurance Company (also given as the Cavalier Casualty Insurance Company; 201 is his office number). He married the former Margaret Merrick (Jane Wyatt) on the 20th (no month given) at her parents home in nearby Lemon Falls. They are the parents of Betty (Elinor Donahue), Bud (Billy Gray) and Kathy (Lauren Chapin).

Jim, who is seen smoking a cigarette in the first episode, is known for his ability to solve virtually any problem his family may encounter (he says, however, "I'm just an ordinary guy who sells insurance"). At times, when Betty has a problem, he asks for Margaret's help because "You've had more experience being a high school girl than I have." Jim reads the *Springfield News*, and each year he and Margaret donate $25 to the Children's Home Society. Jim graduated from college in 1933. There are telephones in the hallway, kitchen and den.

Betty, the eldest of the children, is also the smartest (she was valedictorian of her senior class at Springfield High School). She later attends Springfield College and when she encounters a problem she is unable to solve, she retreats to her "secret thinking place," the stream by the shore of Sycamore Grove Park ("I don't know why they call it that," says Jim, "because the trees are live oaks and cottonwoods"). At that park, Betty asked Father (as she calls him) some tough questions, like, "Who Started God?" and "How do they keep the sun from burning up the sky?" Years later Jim confessed "that I haven't figured out those answers yet." In the episode "Betty's Double," Betty won *Photo Screen* magazine's "Donna Stewart Twin Contest" and was flown to Hollywood to meet the famous movie star (Elinor in a dual role). Jim calls Betty "Princess." The Malt Shop is Betty's after-school hangout.

James Anderson, Jr., nicknamed Bud, was born in 1941. He attended Springfield High School (later Springfield College) and hopes to become an engineer. He is fascinated by cars and was a member of a basketball team sponsored by the Crystal Paint and Glass Company. Bud held a number of jobs (from newspaper delivery boy to gas station attendant; gas was 25⁹⁄₁₀ cents a gallon) and earns two bits for each gopher he catches in the neighbors' vegetable gardens. Bud wears a size 8½ B/C shoe (his white bucks cost $11.98 plus tax) and when Betty isn't around, Margaret uses him to hem her dresses. For reasons which he can't explain, he just likes doing it. Bud calls Betty "Hey, ugly" when he yells for her.

Kathy, called "Kitten" by Jim and "Angel" by Margaret, is the youngest of the children. She attends Springfield Grammar School and is a member of the Maple Street Tigers baseball team. Bud calls her "Shrimp," "Squirt" and "Shrimpboat." The trellis by the house is Kathy's secret thinking place.

There, she and her teddy bear, Bear, try to think "but neither one of us has been able to think up anything to think about," she says. When Kathy thought she was adopted, she felt she was a stranger in the family and called her parents Mr. and Mrs. Anderson; Betty called her "Little Orphan Annie." In early episodes, Kathy receives an allowance of 35 cents a week.

Origins

Father Knows Best is based on the radio series of the same title (NBC, 1949–1954) that starred Robert Young (Jim Anderson), June Whitley, Jean VanderPyl (Margaret Anderson), Rhoda Williams (Betty), Ted Donaldson (Bud), Norma Jean Nilsson, Helen Strong (Kathy). It was first seen on television as the "Keep It in the Family" episode of NBC's *Ford Theater* on 5/27/54. Character names, however, were different. Robert Young was the father, Tom; Ellen Drew, his wife, Grace; and Sally Fraser, Gordon Gebert and Tina Russell their children Peggy, Jeff and Patty.

Updates

1. *The Father Knows Best Reunion*, NBC, 5/15/77. Betty, Bud and Kathy (Elinor Donahue, Billy Gray, Lauren Chapin) return to Springfield to celebrate the 35th wedding anniversary of their parents, Jim and Margaret Anderson (Robert Young, Jane Wyatt). Betty is now a widow with two children, Jenny and Ellen (Cari Anne Warder, Kyle Richards); Bud, married to Jean (Susan Adams), is the father of Robby (Christopher Gardner) and a professional motorcycle racer. Kathy, the youngest, is engaged to Dr. Jason Harper (Hal England), a man ten years her senior.

2. *Father Knows Best: Home for Christmas*, NBC, 12/18/77. The cast listed above is reunited to help Jim and Margaret celebrate Christmas—a celebration that is saddened by the prospect of Jim and Margaret selling their home, which is so rich in memories.

46. **Father of the Bride** CBS, 1961–1962

The modest house at 24 Maple Drive in Fairview Manor, Connecticut, is owned by Stanley and Ellie Banks (Leon Ames, Ruth Warrick). Stanley, a lawyer with the Manhattan firm of Bartham, Henderson and Peck, and Ellie, a member of the Garden Club, are the parents of Katherine "Kay" (Myrna Fahey) and Tommy (Rickie Sorensen). Kay, who calls her father "Pops" (and her mother "Moms"), is Stanley's favorite ("Even though I'm not supposed to have a favorite"). Kay, whom Stanley calls "Kitten," is "Daddy's Little Girl." He had 15 years of peace and solitude: she wasn't too interested in boys and boys, for some reason, just didn't notice her. But on her 15th birthday everything changed: she began dating. Soon boys were an important part of her life. Five years later, in a rather unexpected moment at dinner, Kay announces she is marrying Buckley Dunston (Burt Metcalfe), a man six years her senior. Buckley, a businessman, lives in Westbridge with his rich parents, Herbert and Doris (Ransom Sherman, Lurene Tuttle), and is not Stanley's idea of the perfect man for Kay (he believes Buckley is a smooth talker and sweet-talked Kay into marrying him). Stanley, a Dartmouth Graduate, wants a man who will make Kay happy, support her and make a home for her (as time passed, "I got used to him" says Stanley).

Stanley, at age 25, married Ellie when she was 18. "Now it was time for me to give up my little girl. She'll always love us, but not in the old ways." Stanley and Ellie have always lived simply and within their means. The next shock to Stanley is the wedding and its associated cost when a simple affair turns into an extravagant expense (his only consolation is Tommy—whom he'll present to the father of the bride as his one and only contribution). It was at the wedding that Stanley "realized what I was doing. I was giving up Kay. What is it going to be like when I come home and she's not there to say 'it's Pops'? You know what they say. My son's my son until he gets a wife, but my daughter's my daughter all of her life, our life."

The newlyweds establish a home in a small apartment at 324 Adams Street and, shortly before the series ended, become the parents of a boy they name Stanley Banks Dunston. Based on the films *Father of the Bride* (1950) and *Father's Little Dividend* (1951). Jerry Fielding composed the theme.

47. The Flying Nun ABC, 1967–1970

Sister Bertrille (Sally Field) is a nun with the Order of the Sisters of San Tanco and assigned to the Convent San Tanco in San Juan, Puerto Rico. San Tanco is a small town with a population of 3,956. The convent was built in 1572 on land given to the sisters by King Philip of Spain. Their rent is one dollar a year. To the children of working mothers, the convent is a day-care center.

Sister Bertrille is actually Elsie Ethrington, a once typical teenage American girl who was so impressed by her aunt's work as a missionary that she too decided to devote her life to helping the less fortunate. Elsie attended Westside High School in California (where she was voted "Most Far-Out Girl of 1965") and was a member of a rock band called the Gorries (all of which are references to Sally Field's earlier series, *Gidget*). During the summer of 1966, Elsie worked as a counselor at Camp Laughing Water.

Shortly after being assigned to the convent, Sister Bertrille discovers she has the ability to fly. Her white coronets (headgear) have sides that resemble wings. Sister Bertrille weighs only 90 pounds and San Juan is an area affected by trade winds. A strong gale wind enables her to soar above the ground and, by manipulating her coronets, she acquires some control over flight but landings are difficult (she often crashes into things).

Every time Carlos Ramirez (Alejandro Rey) sees a nun, especially Sister Bertrille, he believes they want him to make a donation to their convent. Carlos is a playboy who owns the Casino Carlos, a disco in San Juan. He is wealthy and considers himself an excellent pool player ("The Minnesota Fats of San Tanco"). His niece, Linda Shapiro (Pamelyn Ferdin), is a young girl who idolizes Sister Bertrille and wants to become a nun "when I grow up" (she is nicknamed the "Little Nun"). Madeleine Sherwood plays Sister Bertrille's superior, the Reverend Mother Plaseato; Marge Redmond, Linda Dangcil and Shelley Morrison are Sisters Jacqueline, Ana and Sixto. Warren Barker composed *The Flying Nun* theme.

48. The Gale Storm Show: Oh! Susanna CBS, 1956– 1959; ABC, 1959–1960

Susanna Pomeroy (Gale Storm) is the social director aboard the *SS Ocean Queen*, a luxury liner owned by the Reardon Steamship Lines. It sets sail from the port of Southampton and docks at New York Harbor. Susanna and her friend Elvira "Nugey" Nugent (ZaSu Pitts) look forward to each cruise as a way to meet handsome bachelors. Nugey is first a manicurist, then a salesgirl in the souvenir shop. Simon Huxley (Roy Roberts) is the ship's captain, a former Navy man who was awarded a bust of John Paul Jones for his work by the Anglo Globetrotters. In the opening theme, the ship sounds its horn once; the ship's bell sounds four times and *The Gale Storm Show: Oh! Susanna* is spelled out by the ship's flags.

49. The George Burns and Gracie Allen Show CBS, 1950–1958

George Burns and his wife, Gracie Allen (Themselves), live at 312 Maple Street in Beverly Hills, California, with their son, Ronnie (Ronnie Burns). George is a straightman and Gracie, a scatterbrained comedienne who has a knack for confusing people.

George met Gracie while they were performing in vaudeville during the 1920s. On their first date, George gave Gracie flowers (which she pressed between the pages of the book *A Report on the Sheep Herding Industry*). In 1927 they eloped and were married in Cleveland (George's friend, Jack Benny, was a witness). They lived at the Edison Hotel in New York City for three years before buying their home in California.

In early episodes, George delivers monologues, introduces songs by the Skylarks vocal group (backed by the Leith Stevens Orchestra) and comments on Gracie's activities from the side of the stage. In later episodes, George's upstairs den becomes his base of operations; he watches TV and comments on the situations that develop. George claims "that in order to have a successful TV show you have to have something special. I do. Gracie." Without her, he says "I'd be selling ties." Gracie sews up the button holes on George's shirts "so no one will know the buttons are missing," sometimes has to watch a movie twice "so my popcorn and the movie finish at the same time," and believes that her father is younger than her husband ("I met my husband when he was 30; I first saw my father when he was 24").

"My Life with George Burns" is the 1952 article Gracie wrote for *Look* magazine (she had to type two copies; she tried using carbon paper "but it's black and you can't see what you type on it"). Gracie also has a system for avoiding misspelled words: she never uses that word again ("That way I don't make the same mistake twice").

Carnation Evaporated Milk sponsored the series (cans of the product can be seen in kitchen shots) and Gracie was constantly confused by the product: "How can they get milk from carnations?" George tries to discourage salesmen from coming to the house: "You heard of the play *Death of a Salesman*? Well, trying to sell Gracie something is what killed him." Gracie has a collection of hats visitors leave behind when they try to talk with her but become so confused that they rush to get out.

George believes he is a great singer (a baritone) but nobody else apparently does (the only way he can sing with the Skylarks, for example, is to tell them about "this other group I'm thinking of hiring"). George is a member of the Friars Club, and is famous for smoking cigars and the "pause" (which he developed for Gracie's responses to his questions).

Many episodes feature George and Gracie relaxing in the living room where Gracie either talks about or reads letters from her mother. (The letters are about her wacky family, especially her mother and her Uncle Harvey. Gracie's mother lives in San Francisco and Market 1-0048 is her phone number. According to Gracie, she attended the wedding but cried through the entire ceremony because she had to miss the premiere of *The Sheik* with Rudolph Valentino. Uncle Harvey is a forger who spends much of his time in the San Quentin Prison.) Ronnie, a teenage ladies' man, attends UCLA.

"I just came in and I'm already confused," can be heard after George's announcer, Harry Von Zell (Himself), first greets Gracie. George often uses Harry as a pawn to add to or resolve the problems that arise from Gracie's antics. George's original announcer, Bill Goodwin (Himself), was a ladies' man and flying enthusiast (he owned "a twin seater yellow plane").

Blanche Morton (Bea Benaderet) and her husband, Harry (Hal March, John Brown, Bob Sweeney, Fred Clark, Larry Keating), are George and Gracie's neighbors at 314 Maple Street. They have been married for 13 years and George's neighbors for 12 years. Harry attended Dartmouth and will drink only one alcoholic beverage—blackberry cordial. He was first an insurance salesman, then real estate broker and finally a CPA. Harry often says "Why do I live here?" after an encounter with Gracie. When he comes home from work, he insists that Blanche have his dinner ready.

The hedge seen in the front windowbox was planted by Gracie (she trims it with George's electric razor); in New York episodes, George and Gracie stayed at the St. Moritz Hotel (Suite 2216). In 1958, when Gracie Allen retired from show business, George continued the series (as *The George Burns Show*) on NBC (1958–1959). George was now a theatrical producer and Ronnie Burns, Bea Benaderet, Larry Keating and Harry Von Zell recreated their roles from the prior series. *The George Burns and Gracie Allen Show* is based on George and Gracie's long-running radio series of the same title.

50. Get Smart NBC, 1965–1969; CBS, 1969—1970

A vulture standing on top of the world is the symbol for KAOS, an evil, international organization seeking to dominate the world. Its leader, Conrad Siegfried (Bernie Kopell), believes that only one man stands between him and global domination—Maxwell Smart (Don Adams), an agent for an organization of good called CONTROL. To accomplish his goals, the German-accented Siegfried has made stopping Maxwell his top priority and has put out the word to all his operatives—"Get Schmart."

CONTROL is a supposedly secret U.S. government agency located at 123 Main Street in Washington, D.C. (555-3734 is its phone number and it is accessed by using the public telephone booth in front of the building. The floor lowers and agents pass through a series of iron security gates before entering headquarters.) Admiral Harold Harmon Hargrade (William Schallert) was the original head of CONTROL. He has retired when the series begins and has been replaced by a man identified only as Thaddeus but who is called the "Chief" (Edward Platt).

Maxwell Smart, the agency's top operative, has the code name Agent

86. He works with a beautiful operative identified only as Agent 99 (Barbara Feldon). Max is, in reality, a bumbling klutz whose foul-ups manage to foil the enemy. Agent 99, on the other hand, is bright, often covers for Max, and uses various aliases to protect her true identity (even after she and Max marry, Max continues to call her 99 and her mother "99's mother" and "Mrs. 99"). To protect his agent's identity, Max uses the cover of Maxwell Smart, salesman for the Pontiac Greeting Card Company; the Chief poses as his boss, Howard Clark. Max and 99 were voted "Spy Couple of the Year" in 1968. While 99 relies on her intuition and training as a spy to battle the enemy, Max believes his weapons are his constant vigilance and his razor-sharp instincts. He wears a size 40 regular jacket and has a standard issue shoe phone (the Chief's means of contacting Max in the field). Max drives a red sports car (plate 6A7-379) and has to use the voice-activated password *Bismark* for safe entry into his booby-trapped apartment. "Sorry about that, Chief," "Would you believe..." and "I asked you not to tell me that" are Max's catchphrases. "Oh Max" is what 99 usually says when Max does what he does best—bumble.

The seldom working Cone of Silence is the agency's antibugging device. Hymie (Dick Gautier) is a former KAOS robot that has been reprogrammed for good for CONTROL. He is often assigned to assist Max and 99 but suffers from one flaw—he takes what he is told to do literally (for example, if Max wants to shake Hymie's hand and says "Shake," Hymie shakes). Agent 13 (Dave Ketchum) is a top-notch undercover agent (hiding in places one would never suspect—like a washing machine, desk drawer or mail box). Agent Charlie Watkins (Angelique Pettyjohn) is a stunning blonde Max has a hard time believing is a man in drag; and Fang is the agency's lone dog agent. The dim-witted Larabee (Robert Karvelas) assists the Chief while the bumbling Schtarker (King Moody) aides Siegfried. Irving Szathmary composed the *Get Smart* theme.

Updates

1. *Get Smart, Again*, ABC TV Movie, 2/26/89. In 1974, CONTROL is deactivated and its records stored in a warehouse at 96427 43rd Street in Washington. In 1989, when KAOS threatens the world with a stolen weather machine, Commander Drury (Ken Mars), the head of U.S. intelligence, reactivates CONTROL to again battle KAOS. Maxwell Smart (Don Adams) is now a protocol officer for the State Department; 99 (Barbara Feldon) is writing her memoirs in a book called *Out of Control*; Hymie (Dick Gautier) has been working as a crash dummy for the National Car Testing Institute; and Agent 13 (Dave Ketchum) has been doing various undercover assignments for the government. Hover Cover (agents meeting on a roof with the noise from three helicopters preventing them from being overheard) and the Hall of Hush (where one's words can be seen as one speaks) have replaced the Cone of Silence. Drury's phone number is 555-3931.

2. *Get Smart*, Fox, 1/8/95–2/19/95. Maxwell Smart (Don Adams) is now the Chief of CONTROL. His wife, 99 (Barbara Feldon), is a congress-woman and still uses her agent's number ("I don't like to be called Mrs. Smart. That makes me feel like 100. Call me 99"). Max is still a bumbler and his son, Zack (Andy Dick), is following in his footsteps. Zack uses the cover of executive vice president of the Western Hemisphere for the Pontiac Greeting Card Company. His hobby is collecting mahogany boats from the 1930s.

Assisting Zack is Agent 66 (Elaine Hendrix) a beautiful agent without a real name ("It's tattooed on my body somewhere but nobody is seeing it"). Agent 66 wears a "Bullet Bra" (a round in each cup) that doubles as her "Bra Phone" (Zack has a sneaker phone; Max still uses the shoe phone). To relax, Agent 66 lets loose with several hundred rounds on the firing range. She uses her beauty to manipulate men ("I do it every day").

Siegfried (Bernie Kopell), the head of KAOS, is still seeking to "Get Schmart" and is assisted by his beautiful daughter Gretchen (Leah Lail). They have set their goal to rule the world via total world economic domination. Siegfried's headquarters are in the KAOS Tower Building.

Getting Together *see* **The Partridge Family**

51.   **The Ghost and Mrs. Muir** NBC, 1968–1969; ABC, 1969–1970

Gull Cottage is a charming little home in Schooner Bay, New England, that is occupied by Carolyn Muir (Hope Lange), her children, Candy and Jonathan (Kellie Flanagan, Harlen Carraher), her housekeeper, Martha Grant (Reta Shaw) and the ghost of Captain Daniel Gregg (Edward Mulhare), the former owner who has returned to watch over his beloved home. Carolyn is a free-lance magazine writer and lived previously in Philadelphia. She is a widow and sleeps in the captain's former bedroom, "The Captain's Cabin," which houses his beloved telescope. Daniel, who calls Carolyn "Madame," resides in the attic and each night stands watch on the porch above the bedroom. In his youth, the captain was a ladies' man and had a girl in every port. He died accidentally one cold night while sleeping "when I kicked the blasted gas heater with my blasted foot." The fumes escaped and killed him. Claymore Gregg (Charles Nelson Reilly) is the captain's wimpy descendant. He runs Claymore Gregg Real Estate Sales and Services and is also the town's notary public and justice of the peace. Candy and Jonathan attend the Schooner Bay School, the family has a dog named Scruffy, and Martha calls the captain the "Old Barnacle." Dave Grusin composed *The Ghost and Mrs. Muir* theme.

52. Gidget ABC, 1965–1966

Frances Lawrence (Sally Field) is a 15½-year-old girl who lives at 803 North Dutton Drive in Santa Monica, California, with her widowed father, Russell (Don Porter), a college professor. Frances was a typical American girl until June 23, 1965, "The day I fell in love with two things: My Moondoggie and surfing." Her Moondoggie, as he is known, is Jeff Matthews (Stephen Mines), a student at Princeton University; he and his surfer friends have nicknamed Frances "Gidget" ("A girl who is neither tall nor a midget — a Gidget").

Gidget attends Westside High School (where she is president of the civic club and author of the "Helpful Hannah" advice column for its newspaper, the *Westside Jester*).

Gidget is the only one who is aware of a viewing audience. She speaks directly to the camera and relates her feelings as the story progresses. She is very philosophical and, for one so young, wonders "why we can't be born with maturity and lose it as we grow older and don't need it." Gidget cherishes her privacy and has a pink Princess phone in her room (GRanite 5-5099, later 477-0599, is her phone number). She applies Perpetual Emotion pink polish to her toe nails and has an understanding with her father: if either of them has a problem, they can turn to the other for help. When Gidget hears "Frances" from her father, she knows she is in trouble. Russ teaches English at UCLA.

The other girls at the beach wonder why "Gidget hangs around with an ox like that." That "ox" is a very pretty and shapely girl named Larue (Lynette Winter). Gidget loves to wear two-piece bathing suits at Malibu Beach while Larue, who is allergic to direct sunlight, has to wear "cover-up clothes" (like large hats) and hence her "ox" reputation. Larue is also allergic to roses and Gidget feels that her friend is hiding her beauty "in the unflattering clothes she wears." She wants to "blast that wall, demolish it and blow it out of existence." Gidget tries makeovers, improving Larue's appearance, but the awkward girl still thinks she is a "Limpnick" ("a left-footed, lopsided jerk. I can't walk right, talk right or even sit right"). Deep down Larue really doesn't care "because when the people I like are happy, I'm happy. I really don't care what other people think." Russ thinks Larue "is a nice kid and [we're] always glad to have her around. You're a rare bird," he tells her, "a genuinely happy, unselfish person." Larue's passion is horses and she has an old gelding named Snowball.

Gidget and Larue's hangouts are the Shaggy Dog, the Shake Shop and Pop's (all hamburger and soda shops). They performed with a rock group called the Young People (later called Gidget and the Gorries) and they see movies at the Spring Street Theater. When Gidget has a dire emergency, she calls Larue. Gidget says "Tootles" for goodbye and when she is on the phone and her father enters her room she says "Gotta hang up, visit from the parent." Gidget and Larue like to have a snack before dinner; Russ sometimes calls Gidget "Gidge."

Anne "Annie" Cooper (Betty Conner) is Gidget's older sister. She is married to John (Peter Deuel) and they live in Apartment 17 (address not given). Anne thinks Russ is too permissive with Gidget and worries so much about "my little sister" that she has taken on the role of parent ("I know Annie means well," says Gidget, "but I wish she would stop being my mother"). John is a graduate student pursuing his master's degree in psychology. Gidget thinks John is a bit "whacko and it is going to be a contest to see whether they'll let him practice or put him away."

The series is based on the feature film *Gidget* starring Sandra Dee. Johnny Tillotson sings the *Gidget* theme.

Updates

1. Gidget Grows Up, ABC, 12/30/69. An unsold pilot with Karen Valentine (Gidget Lawrence), Bob Cummings (Russ Lawrence) and Paul Petersen (Jeff Griffin—not Matthews as in the series). Gidget begins work as a tour guide for the United Nations in New York City.

2. Gidget Gets Married, ABC, 1/4/72. A second pilot with Monie Ellis (Gidget Lawrence), Macdonald Carey (Russ Lawrence) and Michael Burns (now called Jeff Stevens). Gidget marries Jeff, becomes a housewife and sets out to change the social caste system in Jeff's company.

3. Gidget Makes the Wrong Connection, ABC, 9/22/73. An animated pilot that returns Gidget (voice of Kathi Gori) to teenage status and relates her beach adventures with friends Rink and Steve (Denny Evans) and Gorgeous Cat (Don Messick). The story finds Gidget trying to expose a gold-smuggling ring.

4. Gidget's Summer Reunion, Syn., 6/85. The pilot for *The New Gid-*

get (see number 5, below). Gidget (Caryn Richman), now 27, is married to Jeff Griffin (Dean Butler). Russ (William Schallert), Gidget's father, is retired (he now has the last name of Hoover). Gidget also cares for Kim (Allison Barron), her sister Annie's daughter (Anne and her husband, John, are away on business). Larue Powell (Anne Lockhart) is Gidget's partner in the Gidget Travel Agency. Jeff works for the Bedford Construction Company.

5. *The New Gidget*, Syn., 1986–1988. Gidget is now Gidget Griffin (Caryn Richman), the owner of Gidget Travel in Los Angeles. She is married to her Moondoggie, Jeff Griffin (Dean Butler), a city planner for the city of Los Angeles. Living with them at 656 Glendale Avenue is Danni Collins (Sydney Penny), the daughter of Gidget's unseen sister, Anne (not Kim as in the pilot; Anne and John are in Europe on business). Gidget's business associate is now Larue Powell (Jill Jacobson) and Gidget's father is still retired, but has his original name of Russell Lawrence (William Schallert).

When Gidget first learned to surf she was teased about needing training wheels on her surfboard. She turned her love of surfing into a home video called "Gidget's Guide to Surfing." As a kid, Gidget was called a "Perky Doo-Bee" when she appeared on the *Romper Room* TV show. She is also a fan of Lawrence Welk. She first drives a Dodge van, then a Volkswagen Rabbit (both with the plate GIDG TVL); her phone number is 555-1385 (later 555-9099).

Here, Gidget and Jeff met at Westside High School. Jeff was taught to surf by the legendary Great Kahuna and did a commercial for Wipeout Deodorant.

Danni, tall, slender and attractive, inherited Gidget's love for surfing. She and her friend Gail Baker (Lili Haydn) attend Westside High School and listen to radio station K-Gold. Danni likes strawberry fruit facials and Gail has a low threshold for fright ("I freak out on spooky nights"). Danni calls Gidget "Aunt Gidget" and carries her Uncle Jeff's credit card "for emergency use only." Gidget and Danni eat Ghost Busters cereal for breakfast and were models in the Passion for Fashion P.T.A. show. Danni was also a contestant in the Young Debs Pageant.

Jeff Vilinsky, Craig Snyder and Marek Norman composed the theme, "One in a Million."

53. Gilligan's Island CBS, 1964–1967

An uncharted island about 300 miles southeast of Hawaii was once inhabited by a tribe of headhunters called the Kubikai. It is now home to the seven survivors of the shipwrecked *SS Minnow*, a small sightseeing boat that ran aground on the island after encountering a tropical storm at heading 062. Jonas Grumby (Alan Hale, Jr.), called the "Skipper," captained the *Minnow*. He was assisted by his first mate, Gilligan (Bob Denver). Ginger Grant (Tina Louise), Thurston Howell III and his wife, Lovey (Jim Backus, Natalie Schafer), Mary Ann Summers (Dawn Wells) and Roy Hinkley (Russell Johnson) are the stranded passengers.

The *Minnow*, which ferries passengers between the various Hawaiian islands, is thought to have sunk and the Coast Guard has given up its search, forcing the castaways to make the island their home and find a means by which to escape. They hope to be spotted by a plane or passing ship.

The Skipper lost everything when the *Minnow* was beached. He is a Navy man, loves the sea, and plans to use the insurance money to start over again. It was the Skipper's quick thinking that saved his crew and passengers; it was Gilligan's bumbling that helped beach the *Minnow* (I.D. number GG1200). The Skipper hates it when Gilligan reminds him "that I'm your crew."

Gilligan has no first name (producer Sherwood Schwartz wanted to call him Willie). He was born in Pennsylvania and met Jonas while serving a hitch in the Navy. Gilligan has a pet duck (Gretchen) and carries a not-so-lucky rabbit's foot. He likes coconut, papaya and tuna fish pie and is called "Little Buddy" by the Skipper (who also hits him with his captain's cap when Gilligan annoys him). Skinny Mulligan was Gilligan's stateside friend. Gilligan's image is carved in wood on top of a totem pole (natives believe he is their reincarnated chief).

Ginger, a movie actress, broke into show business as an assistant to Merlin the Mind Reader. She measures 38-27-35 (36-25-36 in another episode) and bases her appearance on Marilyn Monroe. She was voted "Miss Hour Glass" ("They said I had all the sand in the right places") and starred in the following movies: *Belly Dancers from Bali Bali*, *Mohawk Over the Moon*, *The Rain Dancers of Rango Rango*, *San Quentin Blues* and *Sing a Song of Sing Sing*.

While Ginger has virtually no wardrobe (she made her almost skin-tight dress from the *Minnow*'s sail), the Howells have a fabulous wardrobe (and considerable cash) that, for unexplained reasons, they brought with them "for a three-hour tour." Thurston, called the "Wolf of Wall Street," is a multimillionaire who heads Howell Industries (he later says he is retired and doesn't work—"Dear Dad left me everything"). He married the former (and wealthy) Lovey Wentworth and they are members of the Newport Country Club. Amalgamated is Thurston's favorite stock and he has a teddy bear (his security blanket) named Teddy. The New York Stock Exchange is his favorite club and the *Social Register* his favorite reading matter. He attended SMU (Super Millionaires University) and has a practice polo pony (made of bamboo) named Bruce. Lovey holds the title "Queen of the Pitted Prune Bowl Parade" and they have dinner at 8 P.M. sharp. (In another episode, Thurston says that his bath must occur at 8:05 P.M. with a water temperature of 79 degrees.)

Mary Ann is a pretty farm girl whose knowledge of planting and crops added greatly to the castaways' diet of fish and fruit. She worked as a clerk and was said to be born in Horners Corners, Kansas (later Winfield, Kansas). Shorts and stomach-revealing blouses comprise most of Mary Ann's wardrobe. She, Ginger and Lovey formed the Honeybees, a singing group, in a failed attempt to get a vocal group visiting the island, the Mosquitos, to take them off the island. The Wellingtons, who sing the show's theme, "The Ballad of Gilligan's Island," played Mosquitos Bingo, Bango and Bongo; musician Les Brown, Jr. was their leader, Irving.

Roy Hinkley, called the "Professor," is a high school science teacher and scout troop leader. He discovered five different mutations of ragweed on the island and his knowledge and inventions make life tolerable. Halibut with kumquat sauce is his favorite dessert. He has his own living quarters (hut) while Gilligan and the Skipper, Ginger and Mary Ann, and the Howells share huts.

The castaways are called the "Shipwrecked Seven" in news reports and Gilligan always manages to spoil attempts at escape. Thurston left Gilligan an oil well in his will. He gave the Skipper 40 acres of land in downtown Denver, Colorado; Ginger, a diamond mine; Mary Ann, a plantation; and the Professor, the Transcontinental Railroad. The tallest coconut tree serves as their observation post (with Gilligan as the lookout). Gilligan does the fishing (offshore with a pole; a large marlin was the first fish he caught). The castaways have a portable radio. The Skipper and Professor listen for weather reports; Mr. Howell, the stock market reports; Ginger and Mary Ann, exercise shows; and Gilligan, kid shows.

Origins

Gilligan's Island, TBS, 10/16/92. Although produced in 1964, the original series pilot aired for the first time in 1992. The characters of the Skipper, Gilligan and the Howells are played by the same actors. John Gabriel was the Professor and Kit Smith was Ginger, a bright, pretty secretary (not a movie star). There was no Mary Ann. Instead, Nancy McCarthy played Bunny, a blonde, slightly dizzy secretary. Johnny Williams provided the music.

A different, uncredited theme is used (it tells of "a six-hour ride" and Lovey is called "Mrs. Millionaire").

TV Movie Updates

1. ***Rescue from Gilligan's Island***, NBC, 10/14 and 10/21/78. The original cast, with the exception of Ginger (now played by Judith Baldwin) are rescued from the island by the Coast Guard after they become stranded on a raft made by the Professor. The Skipper purchases the *Minnow II* and the seven gather for a reunion cruise—only to again become shipwrecked on the same island when they are caught in a tropical storm at sea.

2. ***The Castaways on Gilligan's Island***, NBC, 5/3/79. The prior cast reprise their roles. Here the Professor salvages the parts from two World War II airplanes which enables the castaways to escape and again be rescued by the Coast Guard when their plane crashes into the sea. Thurston turns the island into a tropical resort ("The Castaways") with each castaway as a partner.

3. ***The Harlem Globetrotters on Gilligan's Island***, NBC, 5/11/81. Constance Forslund is now Ginger. The castaways team with basketball legends the Harlem Globetrotters to stop J.J. Pierson (Martin Landau), an evil billionaire from mining Supermium, a rare energy source on the island.

54.   Gimme a Break NBC, 1981–1987

Carl Kanisky (Dolph Sweet) is a widower who lives at 2938 Maple Lane in Glenlawn, California (555-8162; later 555-2932 is his phone number). He is the father of Katie (Kari Michaelsen), Julie (Lauri Hendler) and Samantha (Lara Jill Miller) and receives help in raising his daughters from Nell Ruth Harper (Nell Carter), a promising night club singer. Nell gave up her career to keep a promise: help Carl care for the children if anything should happen to her best friend, their mother, Margaret (played in a flashback by Sharon Spelman). The series begins five years after Margaret's death.

Nell was born in Alabama on April 3, 1950. She grew up on Erickson Road and attended Etchfield High School. She took singing and dancing lessons at the Joyce Landis Academy and held a number of jobs—from waitress to salesgirl—while waiting for her big break. She performed in a number of clubs—from the Silver Spoon in Manhattan to Mr. Funky's and the Tierra Club in California—before putting her career on hold. Nell is a Democrat and a newspaper food coupon clipper.

Carl is a no-nonsense police chief with the Glenlawn Police Department. He was born and raised in Glenlawn and worked his way up from foot patrolman to his present status. He attended the McDougal School for boys and Glenlawn Junior College.

Katie, the oldest and prettiest of the girls, attended Glenlawn High School (later called Lincoln High) and was a member of a club called the Silver Slippers. With her girlfriends Doris (Bonnie Urseth), Kelly (Crystal Bernard) and C.C. (Alexa Kenin), Katie formed a rock band called the Hot Muffins. They performed their first song, "I Can't Stop the Fire," at the Impromptu Club. While Katie could not bowl ("the first time she tried," says Carl, "she threw herself down the alley"), she had a flair for fashion and started her own business, Katie's, a clothing store in the Glenlawn Mall. She later moved to San Francisco to become a buyer for the Chadwick Department Store.

Julie, the middle child, collects coins, has an I.Q. of 160 and enjoys watching TV with Nell. She is pretty but not sure of herself. She wears glasses and feels comfortable with being plain and simple. Although she will not admit it, she is jealous of Katie and wishes she could be like her. She jokes about the Silver Slipper Club ("The biggest thing those girls have going for them is their bras") but wishes she could become one of them (she was nominated but rejected). Katie feels Julie dresses like "an awning on a pizza shop" and has no taste in clothes (Samantha thinks Julie buys her clothes at a garage sale). Julie can "hold my breath for two whole minutes underwater" and attended Lincoln High. Julie married Jonathan Silverman (Jonathan Maxwell), a delivery boy for Luigi's Pizza Parlor. They moved to San Diego where Julie gave birth to a daughter she named Little Nell.

Samantha, the youngest of the girls, wears braces and likes Katie's group ("they make my braces vibrate"; Carl feels they are too loud—"I can't hear my Rice Krispies"). Sam, called "Baby" by Nell, loves sports, especially hockey, and enjoys accompanying her father to sporting events (the more violent and bloody the sport the better for her). Samantha likes horror movies (although she roots for the monsters) and attended Glenlawn Elementary, Lincoln High and Littlefield College in New Jersey. As a kid she had an imaginary friend named Debbie Jo.

Also living with the family is their pet goldfish, Gertrude; Carl's father, "Grandpa" Stanley Kanisky (John Hoyt); and Joey Donovan (Joey Lawrence), an orphan Nell later adopts. Stanley came to America from Poland in 1924 on a ship called *Karkov*. Joey is a member of the fourth grade Dodgers baseball team. The station house dog is named Rex. In the opening theme, two poplar trees are seen in planters on each side of the front door of their white house. In the series, when an outdoor shot is required, an evergreen is seen on the left side of the front door.

Carl passes away in 1986. The girls have moved out and Nell, who had been taking child psychology classes at Glenlawn Junior College, decides to move to New York City. She and Joey find a home at 609 East 29th Street; Nell acquired a job as an editor at the McDutton and Leod publishing house. Also in the cast is Nell's friend, Addie Wilson (Telma Hopkins), a Phi Beta Kappa who teaches at Littlefield College (she previously taught at Glenlawn Junior College). Nell Carter sings the theme, "Gimme a Break."

55.   The Girl with Something Extra NBC, 1973–1974

Sally and John Burton (Sally Field, John Davidson) are a happily married couple who live at 10 Havilland Drive in Los Angeles. John is a lawyer with the firm of Metcalf, Klein and Associates, and Sally and her girlfriend Annie (Zohra Lambert) run a variety shop called the Store. Sally, whose favorite color is yellow, possesses a form of ESP that allows her to read minds—"Some people some of the time, some people most of the time and a very few people all of the time." John, a private person, falls into the last category. Dave Grusin composed "The Girl with Something Extra Theme."

56.   Glynis CBS, 1963

Murder Takes the Bus, *Murder at Martha's Inn* and *Murder Aboard Ship* are three of the novels written by Glynis Granville (Glynis Johns), a pretty, British, middle-aged mystery writer and amateur sleuth whose stories evolve from the situations she encounters. She lives in an apartment at 9800 Wilshire in San Diego and is married to Keith Granville (Keith Andes), a private-practice criminal attorney. Glynis keeps her shower cap in the car, buys Keith pajamas with three snappers ("in case you gain weight") and when she needs to get Keith out of a sound sleep she says "Keith, you're gonna be late for your golf game." Glynis says "I dream about murders" and a relaxing bath gives her the inspiration to write. Keith's license plate reads CCL 4. In the original pilot, *Hide and Seek* (CBS, 8/5/63), Keith Andes played Glynis's husband as John. George Duning composed the theme, "Glynis."

57.   Gomer Pyle, U.S.M.C. CBS, 1964–1969

The character of Gomer Pyle (Jim Nabors) was first seen as a naive gas station attendant on *The Andy Griffith Show*. He works at Wally's Filling Station in Mayberry, North Carolina, and is saving his money for college (hoping to become a doctor). That was in 1962 when he lived in a room in the back of the gas station. In 1964, when he learns he is expected to serve a term of military duty, he enlists in the Marines. He is proud of the fact that he knows all the words to the *Marine Hymn* ("From the Halls of Montezuma to the shores of Tripoli ..."), which he learned from the back of a calendar put out by Nelson's Funeral Parlor. Gomer had a dog named Spot as a kid. He likes Limburger and onion sandwiches and says "Shazam" when something goes wrong. When he leaves, he says "Lots of luck to you and yours."

Gomer is first stationed at Camp Wilson at the Wilmington Naval Base in North Carolina. Here he meets his superior, Vincent "Vince" Carter (Frank Sutton), the hot-headed gunnery sergeant ("It will do you well to remember that name because it is the only name that is going to matter from now on"). Gomer was late for reporting on his first day. He was given four weeks K.P. and two additional weeks of kitchen patrol for trying to explain that a leaky air valve on his car's tire made him late.

Following basic training, Gomer Pyle, now a private, is transferred to Camp Henderson in Los Angeles (Second Platoon, B Company). Sergeant Carter, who was also transferred, again becomes his superior. Gomer wants to become the best Marine that he can, but he unconsciously breaks the rules of the system and complicates matters; Carter relentlessly struggles to resolve the chaos that results from Gomer's antics.

When something fascinates Gomer he says "Gol-ly"; "Hey" is his greeting (for example, "Tell the captain Gomer says hey") and "Surprise, surprise, surprise" is another of Gomer's catchphrases. When Carter asks his squad something and they fail to reply in a loud enough voice, Carter responds with "I can't hear you!"

Gomer buys his suits from Friendly Freddy, the Gentleman's Tailor (Sid Melton played Freddy, the shady one-man discount store). Gomer had an old horse named Polly (whom he bought to save from the glue factory). He was called "Crazy Legs Gomer" when he ran in the platoon's foot race. When Gomer and Vince appeared on the TV show *Win a Date*, Gomer won a free trip to Hawaii with starlet Wendy Sparks (Jeannine Riley). Carter appeared in the Marine documentary *A Day in the Life of a Sergeant*. The local dance club is the Way Out a Go-Go; the platoon's booby prize is the lead combat boot; Gomer was promoted to Pfc (private, first class) in 1968.

Lou Ann Poovie (Elizabeth MacRae) is Gomer's girlfriend, a singer at the Blue Bird Cafe; Bunny Olson (Barbara Stuart) is Vince's patient girlfriend. Other members of B Company are privates Duke Slater (Ronnie Schell) and Frankie Lombari (Ted Bessell). Corporal Charles Boyle (Roy Stuart) is Vince's aide; Colonel Edward Gray (Forrest Compton) is the commanding officer. Earle Hagen composed the theme.

58.   Good Morning, World CBS, 1967–1968

Music by such "classic" groups as the Four Dropouts and Murray, Billy and the Bing Bongs, the Daydreamers and the Tijuana Symphony Orchestra can be heard on *The Lewis and Clark Show*, a daily 6:00 A.M. to 10:00 A.M. Los Angeles radio program hosted by Dave Lewis and Larry Clark (Joby Baker, Ronnie Schell). Dave and Larry, friends since working for station KOUA in Honolulu, broadcast from studio B and buy their morning snacks from Mrs. Jelly Donuts. Crestview 6-7399 is the unidentified station's phone number. Dave and his wife, Linda (Julie Parrish), live at 63 Court Plaza, Apartment 1B. Larry, a swinging bachelor, lives at 3126 Orion Place. Dave builds model airplanes as a hobby and clams oregano and garlic bread are his favorite foods. Linda, called "Pumpkin" by Dave, was born in San Francisco and worked as a receptionist before marrying Dave a year ago. Rolland B. Hutton, Jr. (Billy DeWolfe), the station owner, worked in vaudeville under the name Billy Jones. He lives in a magnificent house that was featured in *Home and Terrace* magazine (pages 9–16) and has a bust of himself in the master bedroom. Sandy Kramer (Goldie Hawn) is Larry's girlfriend, a dancer "with the craziest legs in town," who hopes to one year win the Pillsbury Bake-Off. Dave Grusin composed the theme.

59.   Good Times CBS, 1974–1979

Florida Evans (Esther Rolle) originally worked as a maid in the Findlay household in Tuckahoe, New York (on the series *Maude*). When her husband, Henry (John Amos), objected to her working as a maid, Florida quit and moved to the south side of Chicago. Florida, her husband (now called James) and their children, J.J. (Jimmie Walker), Thelma (BernNadette Stanis) and Michael (Ralph Carter) live at 963 North Gilbert (Apartment 17C of the Cabrini Housing Project). Their rent is $104.50 a month; 555-8264 is their phone number. In some episodes their address is mentioned as 763 North Gilbert.

James is totally dedicated to Florida and a loving but stern father to his children. The times are bad and James struggles to provide a decent life for his family by taking what work he can get. In an attempt to improve himself, James enrolled in a trade school. Shortly after graduating, he acquired a job in rural Mississippi working at a garage. The family had prepared to move but before doing so they received word that James had been killed in a car accident. Florida, now head of the house, acquired a job as a school bus driver for the Roadway Bus Company. As a kid, she had the nickname of "Pookie Poo."

In 1977, a year after James's death, Florida meets and falls in love with Carl Dixon (Moses Gunn), the owner of a small appliance shop. They are married in an unseen wedding in the summer of 1977. When John Amos and the producers could not solve contractual differences, his character of James had been killed off; when Esther Rolle complained about the stereotyped images *Good Times* was portraying (especially with the character of J.J.), Florida was written out (first she was said to be on her honeymoon, then in Arizona with Carl for her health). Esther eventually returned to the series when the image of the 18-year-old J.J. "who doesn't work, can't read or write and doesn't think" was toned down. In Florida's absence, Wilona Woods (Ja'net DuBois) was brought on to care for the Evans children. She worked in a beauty parlor, department store and finally George's Fashion Boutique. Wilona was also the adoptive mother of Penny Gordon (Janet Jackson), a battered child.

J.J. (James, Jr.) is a ladies' man who considers himself the "Ebony Prince." He is a hopeful artist and later works as an art director for the Dynamite Greeting Card Company. J.J. was originally a delivery boy for the Chicken Shack, a fast food store. At age 12, he painted a naked lady eating grits on an elevator wall ("I didn't know how to draw clothes then"). "Dyn-O-Mite" is J.J.'s catchphrase and he hides his money "in that sock in his dresser drawer" (although when he needs money, he borrows it from Sweet Daddy [Teddy Wilson], a loan shark who charges 25 percent a week interest). Artist Ernie Banks produced the pictures J.J. paints.

Thelma, the middle child, was born on June 15, 1957. She and J.J. attend an unnamed high school. While J.J. sees Thelma as having "a face whose mold could make gorilla cookies" (Thelma sees J.J. as "Beanpole"), Thelma is very pretty and has aspirations of becoming an actress. She attended classes at the Community Workshop and married her boyfriend, Keith Anderson (Ben Powers), a former football player who now drives a taxi for the Windy City Cab Company.

Michael, the smartest of the children, attends Harding Elementary School and is dedicated to the black movement. While his high school is not named, he is a member of the Junior War Lords Gang. Wilona calls him "Gramps."

Nathan Bookman (Johnny Brown) is the overweight building super (called "Buffalo Butt" by J.J. and Wilona). His middle name is Millhouse and he is a member of the Jolly Janitors Club. Dave Grusin, Alan Bergman and Marilyn Bergman composed the *Good Times* theme.

60.   Goodnight, Beantown CBS, 1983–1984

Jennifer Barnes and Matt Cassidy (Mariette Hartley, Bill Bixby) are coanchors of *The Six O'Clock Report*, a news program on WYN-TV, Channel 11 in Boston. Matt, a graduate of Boston University, signs off with "That's the news. I'm Matt Cassidy. Goodnight, Beantown." He is a bachelor and lives at 321 Waverly Place, Apartment 1. Jennifer, born in California, previously worked as a special features reporter for KRF-TV. She lives in Apartment 2 at 321 Waverly. She is divorced and the mother of Susan (Tracey Gold), a pretty 13 year old who attends Ridgefield Junior High. Matt reads the *Boston Tribune* and he and Jennifer have drinks at Kelly's Bar and Grill; 555-NEWS is the station's phone number. Dennis McCarthy composed the theme.

61.   The Governor and J.J. CBS, 1969–1972

William R. Drinkwater (Dan Dailey) is described as "a man of integrity, a man who dedicates himself to the services of the people." He is the governor of an unidentified Midwestern state and resides in the Governor's Mansion at 1103 Madison Lane with his 23-year-old daughter Jennifer Jo (Julie Sommars), called J.J. William is a widower and was previously a lawyer with the firm of Saunders and Drinkwater. When J.J. was five, William was urged by his wife of 30 years to enter politics. His press secretary, George Callison (James Callahan), worked previously for the attorney general; William's secretary, Maggie McCloud (Neva Patterson), has been with him for 19 years. J.J., curator of the local (unnamed) children's zoo, attended Central City High School. She starts eating breakfast and reading the newspaper before she sits down at the table. In the opening theme, William is seen reading a copy of *World* magazine in a cover story about himself. Jerry Fielding composed the theme.

62.   The Great Gildersleeve Syn., 1954–1955

The house at 217 Elm Street in the town of Sommerfield is owned by Throckmorton P. "Gildy" Gildersleeve (Willard Waterman), the former owner of the Gildersleeve Girdle Works Company turned water commissioner. He is also the guardian of Marjorie and Leroy Forrester (Stephanie Griffin, Ronald Keith), his orphaned niece and nephew (their parents were killed in a car accident). Marjorie, who attends Sommerfield High School, calls Gildy "Unkie" and Leroy, who attends Sommerfield Elementary School, calls him "Unk." Gildy likes to putter around the house. He is a ladies' man and president of the Jolly Boys Club ("All for one, one for all"; weekly meetings are called "Jolly Boys Night"). The Southern belle Leila Ransom (Shirley Mitchell) and Kathryn Milford (Carole Matthews), a maternity nurse at Sommerfield Hospital, are the women seeking Gildy's hand in marriage. Jack Meakin composed the theme. Based on the radio series *The Great Gildersleeve* (NBC, 1941–58) with Hal Peary and then Willard Waterman as Gildersleeve, Louise Erickson and then Marylee Robb as Marjorie, and Walter Tetley as Leroy.

63.   Green Acres CBS, 1965–1971

Oliver Wendell Douglas (Eddie Albert) has a dream: "To buy a farm, move away from the city, plow my own fields, get my hands dirty, sweat and strain to make things grow. To join with other farmers, the backbone of the American economy." One day Oliver makes that dream come true. He purchases, sight unseen, the 160-acre Haney farm in Hooterville from an ad he sees in a seed catalogue (Oliver grows crops in his office desk drawer and on the patio of his Penthouse at 255 Park Avenue in Manhattan). Oliver, however, has a problem—his beautiful and sophisticated wife, Lisa (Eva Gabor), who is reluctant to relinquish her life of luxury in New York City. After realizing how much farming means to Oliver, she agrees to try "farm living" for six months; if she feels she cannot become a farmer's wife, Oliver has promised to move back to the city.

Hooterville has an elevation of 1,427 feet (its zip code is 40516½) and its neighboring communities are Pixley and Crabtree Corners. The area is serviced by the C.F. & W. railroad's Cannonball Express, an 1890s steam engine that carries a coal tender and a mail/baggage/passenger coach. Green Acres, the farm Oliver purchased, is located four miles outside of town. The land appears to be rocky and barren and the house is in a shambles, although it is a historic landmark—the birthplace and home of Rutherford B. Skrug, "the founder of the great state of Hooterville." Water has to be hand-pumped, the floors, walls and roof need repairing and there is no inside telephone (the phone company ran out of wire and had to place the phone on the top of the nearby pole). Despite the problems, Oliver is determined to become a farmer.

Oliver had his own law practice in Manhattan. He is a graduate of Harvard Law School and was a fighter pilot during World War II (his biggest regret was having to bomb farm lands). Oliver does his chores in a suit and tie and plows with an ancient, run-down Hoyt-Clagwell tractor. Oliver is a member of the Hooterville Volunteer Fire Department band and likes his coffee black with sugar.

Lisa, a socialite, eventually agrees to live in Hooterville. She is the only person who hears a fife playing when Oliver talks about his dream of farming. She calls the town "Hootersville," has a milk cow (Eleanor) and a group of chickens she calls the "Girls" (Alice is her favorite). Eleanor gives Lisa just the amount of milk she requires (she places a glass under the cow and says "One cup, please"); the chickens also oblige Lisa by giving her the exact amount of eggs she needs. Lisa enjoys her coffee with cream and sugar.

Eb Dawson (Tom Lester) is Oliver's hired hand. He calls Oliver "Dad" and has a poster of his hero, western film star Hoot Gibson on his bedroom wall (which is in the barn). Eb claims he has a second job—standing in for Stuffy, Oliver's cornfield scarecrow, when he goes to Pixley for lunch. Sam Drucker (Frank Cady), the postmaster, owns the general store (called Sam Drucker's) and publishes the newspaper, the *Hooterville World Guardian*.

Eustace Haney (Pat Buttram) is the valley's con artist. He is always called Mr. Haney and is a member of the Hooterville Chamber of Commerce. He sells merchandise (junk) from the back of his pickup truck and is chairman of the Bringing Outside Money Into Hooterville Committee. He has a wooden Indian he calls Irving Two Smokes.

Oliver is not the only one with phone trouble. Farmer Fred Ziffel (Hank Patterson) and his wife, Doris (Fran Ryan, Barbara Pepper), have no receiver (Fred uses a hammer to represent one and can only talk to people, not hear them). Fred and Doris are the "parents" of Arnold, an intelligent pig they raised as their own son. His official name is Arnold Ziffel and he is in the third grade at Hooterville Elementary School. Arnold has tea with Lisa, enjoys lime soda and can predict the weather with his tail. He has an orange bedroom (which he painted himself), plays cricket (has his own bat) and becomes shy in the presence of beautiful women. His favorite TV show is *The CBS Evening News with Walter Cronkite*. Eddie Albert and Eva Gabor sing the theme, "Green Acres" (composed by Vic Mizzy).

Origins

Granby's Green Acres, NBC Radio 1950. Gale Gordon portrayed John Granby, a bank clerk who leaves the hassle of the big city for the life of a farmer in Doverville. He is reluctantly joined by his wife, Martha (Bea Benaderet), and daughter, Janice (Louise Erickson). Parley Baer plays Eb, the hired hand.

TV Movie Update

Return to Green Acres, CBS, 5/18/90. Oliver calls on his skills as a lawyer to save Hooterville from a company (Armstrong Development) planning to turn the town into a modern development. The original cast reprised their roles with the exception of Fred and Doris Ziffel. After the Ziffels' passing, their niece, Daisy Ziffel (Mary Tanner), inherited their farm as well as Arnold (Frank Welker is credited as "Arnold's voice"). Mr. Haney runs a hotel called Haney's House of Hospitality; Eb has married a girl named Flo (Lucy Lee Flippen) and is the father of a teenage son named Jeb (Mark Ballou).

64.   Guestward Ho ABC, 1960–1961

Guestward Ho is a dude ranch in New Mexico that is owned by Bill Hooten (Mark Miller), a New York advertising executive who left the rat race of the big city for a quieter life out west. His wife Babs (Joanne Dru) and son Brook (Flip Mark) assist him in running the ranch (rates are $25 a day). Santa Fe is the nearest town and the Flying Horse Dude Ranch is their competition. Bill purchased the ranch from Hawkeye (J. Carrol Naish), a scheming Indian chief who runs the local trading post and souvenir stand opposite the reservations desk at Guestward Ho. (He buys his "genuine" bows and arrows from Hong Kong.) Pink Cloud (Jolene Brand), a gorgeous Indian princess, assists him. Arthur Hamilton composed the theme, "Guestward Ho."

65.   The Halls of Ivy CBS, 1954–1955

Dr. William Todhunter Hall (Ronald Colman) is the president of Ivy College, the prestigious, mythical university in Ivy, U.S.A. He is married to Vickie (Benita Hume) and they reside at One Faculty Row, the house that is reserved for the president of Ivy College; Ivy 4-0042 is their phone number.

Dr. Hall was originally a student at Ivy. He became an instructor when he graduated and lived in the boarding house across the street from Faculty Row. When he was appointed an assistant professor, he moved to the opposite side of Faculty Row. When William became a full professor, he vacationed in England and fell in love with and married Victoria "Vickie" Cromwell, a celebrated London stage star (William first saw her in the play "Give Them Tears" and returned to see it 25 times before he had the nerve to approach her). Victoria began her show business career at age 15 in a variety act called "Pinarro and Cromwell—Those Funny People." They worked in a variety of clubs in the East End of London and got more boos than laughs. Victoria never ate before a performance and was always ravenous at the final curtain. Victoria calls William "Toddie" and his pride and joy is coming out ahead with the finances. The students call his home the "Power House."

Professor Warren (Arthur Q. Bryan) is one of the dedicated instructors at Ivy. "Teaching hardly ever pays off in money," he says, "and it hardly ever pays off in glory .... it's pride in the job that makes us stick with it." It is also a good bet not to accept an invitation to coffee from Professor Warren: "In all the world no one concocts as nauseating a cup of coffee as I do." Clarence Wellman (Herb Butterfield) is the chairman of the board of Ivy College (he was editor of the school's newspaper, *The Ivy Bulletin*, in 1907). Clarence is after Dr. Hall's job, and Victoria calls him a "Stinker" and "chairman of the board of governors and spark plug of the let's drive Dr. Hall to an early grave campaign."

Ivy is a small college. It is a school rich in tradition and dedicated to giving its students the best education possible. It also has a century-old Christmas tradition: at this time of the year, if a reasonable amount of snow has fallen, students build a snowman in the front of the home of each faculty member. The more affection the students have for a professor, the larger the snowman they build. Of all the faculty at Ivy, only Professor Bessemer (the president in 1900), who was nicknamed "Old Pinch Face Bessemer," never got a snowman. Les Baxter composed the theme adaptation of the song "The Halls of Ivy."

66. **Happy Days** ABC, 1974–1984

The Cunninghams are a family of five who live in Milwaukee, Wisconsin, during the 1950s. Howard and Marion (Tom Bosley, Marion Ross), the parents, married in 1936 and set up housekeeping at 618 Bridge Street. Richie (Ron Howard), Joanie (Erin Moran) and Chuck (Ric Carrott, Gavan O'Herlihy, Randolph Roberts) are their children.

When Howard was a young man he went to a hardware store on 8th Street to buy a plunger. When he saw the various items lining the shelves he became hooked. He began working there as a stockboy and by 1946 he owned that store, which he renamed Cunningham Hardware. (The store offers free color paint mixing and Howard buys his merchandise from Ernie's Hardware Supplies.)

Howard also worked as a hot dog vendor at Yankee Stadium and served a hitch in the Army during World War II (where he was called "Cookie"). Howard, a Republican, is a member of the Leopard Lodge (Local 462) and drives a black DeSoto (plate F-3680). He likes the color blue and omelets are his favorite breakfast. His back goes out if he has an irritating day at work and he gets a headache if he doesn't have dinner by 7 P.M. Howard claims that the saddest day of his life occurred when he could no longer hold Joanie in his arms ("It was the day I knew she was no longer my little girl").

Marion and Howard danced to the song "Moonlight in Vermont" on their wedding night. They honeymooned at the Holiday Shore Lodge in Lake Geneva and stayed in Suite 325. Howard called Marion "Baby Cakes"; she called him "Snookems." Marion worked as a secretary before marrying Howard. She is a member of the Milwaukee Women's Club and Howard's bowling team, The Ten Pins (she bowls 119). *As the World Turns, The Edge of Night* and *The Secret Storm* are Marion's favorite TV soap operas. She is allergic to cayenne pepper and her favorite drinking glass has a picture of movie star Rudolph Valentino on it. Her mother (Mother Kelp) calls Howard "Fatso."

Richie, the middle child, first attended Jefferson High School, then the University of Wisconsin. He weighs 135 pounds, is five feet nine inches tall, has red hair and blue eyes. He was called "Freckles" as a child and was said to resemble "Howdy Doody." The song "Blueberry Hill" became his trademark (he frequently sang the first line, "I found my thrill on Blueberry Hill").

Richie received a medal for reading comprehension in grammar school and enjoys blueberry pancakes and fresh-squeezed orange juice for breakfast; meatloaf is his favorite dinner. His first car, a 1952 Ford he called the "Love Bandit," had the license plate F-7193. Richie, a reporter for the school newspaper, the Jefferson *Bugle*, was also a member of the French Club, the basketball team (jersey 17) and an ROTC 3rd Squadron leader. He earned $25 a week as a disc jockey at radio station WOW and appeared on the TV game show *Big Money*. He was later a cub reporter for the *Milwaukee Journal*. He married Lori Beth Allen (Lynda Goodfriend), the girl who called him "Sizzle Lips," and had a son, Richie, Jr. (Bo Sharron). Richie left the series when he joined the army and was transferred to Greenland.

Joanie Louise, the youngest child, attends an unnamed grammar school and later Jefferson High. She has a hamster (Gertrude), was a member of the Junior Chipmunks and is called "Shortcake" and "Pumpkin." Joanie's first word as a baby was *hardware*, and baked macaroni and applesauce is her favorite meal. Joanie was a member of the singing group the Suedes, backup vocalists for singer Leather Tuscadero (Suzy Quatro).

When Joanie became romantically involved with schoolmate Charles "Chachi" Arcola (Scott Baio), the spinoff series *Joanie Loves Chachi* evolved (ABC, 1982–1983). In the latter series, Chachi, a former member of a band called The Velvet Clouds (playing drums), moves to Chicago with his mother, Louisa (Ellen Travolta), when she marries Al Delvecchio (Al Molinaro) and they open Delvecchio's Family Restaurant at 1632 Palmer Street. Chachi joins a band (as a singer); Joanie, who leaves home (with permission), joins him and they form a duo. The series failed. Joanie and Chachi return to Milwaukee and marry shortly after.

Chuck, the eldest son, appeared in early episodes only and appeared to do nothing but bounce a basketball. He was written out (he was said to be attending college).

Arthur Herbert Fonzarelli (Henry Winkler) is the cool high school dropout known as "Fonzie" and the "Fonz." Girls flock to him and he commands attention by snapping his fingers. He wears a leather jacket, rides a motorcycle and has been associated with the Falcons and Demons gangs. He worked as a mechanic at Otto's Auto Orphanage, Herb's Auto Repairs and Bronco's Auto Repairs and returned to Jefferson High to get his diploma. He first taught auto shop at Jefferson, then became the dean of boys at the rowdy George S. Patton High School. Fonzie has a Lone Ranger toothbrush, a bathrobe and toolbox that say "Sweetums" on them (a gift from a girl), and a dog named Spunky. He uses Mr. Musk after shave lotion and lives in a $50 a month apartment over the Cunningham's garage (he previously lived in a small apartment, number 154, where he parked his motorcycle in the living room). He gives a "thumbs up" when he agrees with someone and "Aaayh" and "Whoooa" are his catchphrases. Fonzie has an autograph from Annette Funicello ("She gave me hers and I gave her mine") and is plagued by the "Fonzarelli Curse" (bad luck occurs if he is asked to be best man at a wedding). Fonzie was most notably involved with Pinky Tuscadero (Roz Kelly), a biker who dressed in pink, and Ashly Pfister (Linda Purl), a widow with a young daughter named Heather (Heather O'Rourke).

Richie's best friends are Warren Weber (Anson Williams) and Ralph Malph (Donny Most). As a kid, Warren would make things out of clay; his mother nicknamed him "Potsie." Together with Richie, Ralph and Potsie started a business called "Cheap Work" ("any job for money") and formed a band called Happy Days (later called the Velvet Clouds). Richie played sax; Potsie sang; Ralph played keyboard. Potsie performed professionally at the Vogue Terrace Club and he, Richie and Ralph, were members of the Alpha Tau Omega fraternity at college (also given as Pi Kappa Nu). Their favorite makeout spot is Inspiration Point.

Jennifer "Jenny" Piccolo (Cathy Silvers) is Joanie's sexy best friend (she considers herself "the object of mad desire"). She reads *Passionate Romance* magazine and calls Joanie "Joans." She memorized the entire Milwaukee phone book to join the Rondells, the "cool" girls club at Jefferson High, and invested $29.95 in the Ajax Bust Developer to enlarge her breasts and attract boys. Her phone number is 555-4242.

Arnold's Drive-In is the local hangout (at 2815 Lake Avenue; it was originally called Arthur's Drive-In). Arnold Takahasi (Pat Morita) and later Al Delvecchio (Al Molinaro) own it. When Arnold's burns down, Fonzie and Al become partners in "Arnold's—Fonzie and Big Al, Proprietors." College banners at the drive-in represent Indiana, Iona, Purdue, State and Yale. The vending machine dispenses Spring Time Cola and when Fonzie appeared on the TV show *You Wanted to See It*, he was called "Fearless Fonzarelli" as he attempted but failed to jump over 14 garbage cans with his motorcycle in Arnold's parking lot (he crashed into Arnold's Milwaukee Fried Chicken stand). The "Guy's Room" in the drive-in doubles as Fonzie's office.

During the opening theme, the record seen playing on the Seebring 100 Selecto-Matic jukebox at Arnold's reads: "'Happy Days,' lyrics by Norman Gimbel, music composed by Charles Fox." While this song is heard as the closing theme (later the opening theme), "Rock Around the Clock" by Bill Haley and the Comets is actually heard as the record plays.

Note: In the original pilot, *New Family in Town*, Harold Gould played Howard and Susan Neher was Joanie; Fonzie did not appear. The story finds Richie trying to impress a girl as their family prepares for a big event—their first television set. The pilot was retitled *Love and the Happy Days* and aired on *Love, American Style* on 2/25/72. See also *Laverne and Shirley*, the spin-off series.

Animated Extension Series

Fonz and the Happy Days Gang, ABC, 1980–1982. When Cup Cake, a girl from the 25th century, lands in 1957 Milwaukee, she befriends Fonzie, Richie and Ralph and takes them aboard her slightly defective time machine. During a demonstration, they become lost in time. Stories follow their adventures as they seek the way back to their own time. *Voices:* Didi Conn (Cup Cake), Henry Winkler (Fonzie), Ron Howard (Richie), Donny Most (Ralph). Frank Welker is the voice of Mr. Cool, Fonzie's dog.

67. Harper Valley NBC, 1981–1982

Stella Johnson (Barbara Eden) and her daughter Dee (Jenn Thompson) live at 769 Oakwood Street in Harper Valley, Ohio. Stella is a beautiful, outspoken widow who sells Angel Glow Cosmetics; Dee attends Harper Valley Junior High School. First season episodes find Stella battling the P.T.A., a group of prudes who believe she is a bad influence and should leave town (the plot of the movie *Harper Valley P.T.A.*, on which the series is based). Second-season episodes drop the P.T.A. aspect and focus on Stella as the executive assistant to Otis Harper (George Gobel), the intoxicated town mayor. Stella's friend Cassie Bowman (Fannie Flagg) is first owner of the La Modene Beauty Shop then publisher of the Harper Valley *Sentinel*. She lives at 675 Pine Valley Lane. Jeannie C. Riley sings the original theme, "Harper Valley P.T.A."; Carol Chase sings the revised theme, "Harper Valley, U.S.A."

68.   The Hathaways ABC, 1961–1962

Walter and Elinor Hathaway (Jack Weston, Peggy Cass) are a happily married couple who live at 148 Magnolia Drive in Los Angeles. Walter owns the Hathaway Realty Company and Elinor manages the Hathaway Chimps, three talented theatrical chimpanzees she adopted and trained. The Marquis Chimps play Charlie, Enoch and Candy (Walter calls them the "Children"; Elinor refers to them as the "Kids"). Charlie, the oldest, is mischievous; Enoch copies Walter's mannerisms; Candy is the baby and clings to Enoch for comfort. The chimps have appeared on the *Jack Benny* and *Ed Sullivan* shows and have their own comedy segment on *Barney Holt's Merchandise Showcase*. Walter drives a car with the plate 0846249 and has a development called Desert Charm Estates ("Home Sights for People with Foresight") that he can't unload. Herbert Spencer composed "The Hathaways Theme."

69.   Hazel NBC, 1961–1965; CBS, 1965–1966

George Baxter (Don DeFore), his wife, Dorothy (Whitney Blake), and their son, Harold (Bobby Buntrock), live at 123 Marshall Road in an unspecified Eastern city. Their phone number is Klondike 5-8372; later 555-8372. Also living with them is Hazel Burke (Shirley Booth), their maid.

George is a lawyer with the firm of Butterworth, Hatch, Noll, and Baxter (located in the Arcade Building). He attended Dartmouth and is a member of the board of regents of the university law school (he delivers the Oliver Wendell Holmes Memorial Lectures). George, who has been practicing law since 1949, is also counsel for the Symphony Association. George reads the *Daily Chronicle*, and chocolate fudge cake is his favorite dessert. He first drives a convertible (plate 49-753) then a red sedan (plate J2R 2855; later 53-859). Harvey ("Call Me Harv") Griffin (Howard Smith) is the firm's biggest client (owner of Griffin Enterprises).

Dorothy is a freelance interior decorator (no business name given). She is a member of the I.D.S. (Interior Decorator's Society) and her local neighborhood women's club. She buys her lingerie at Blackstone's Department Store (she wears a size eight negligee) and her dresses at Montague's Boutique.

Hazel has been working for the Baxters since 1950. She is a member of the Sunshine Girls (a society of neighborhood maids) and was voted "Maid of the Month" by *American Elegance* magazine. She loves bowling (she has an insurance policy to cover her back) and owns 11 shares of stock in the Davidson Vacuum Cleaner Company. Hazel is famous for her fudge brownies and was the spokesgirl for Aunt Nora's Instant Cake Mix. She owned a 1920 Model-T Ford (plate 306-579) that she bought for $25 (and later sold to a collector for $1,250). Hazel mentioned that her only true love was Gus Jenkins (Patrick McVey), a merchant marine she met in the Empire State Building's observation tower. He called her "Brown Eyes" and she would have married him if he'd asked her. He never did.

Hazel calls George "Mr. B," Dorothy "Missy" and Harold "Sport." She keeps her government bonds in her footlocker and has an account at the Commerce Trust Bank. Thursday is Hazel's day off and she takes time off on Sunday to attend mass. Hazel serves breakfast at 7:00 A.M., lunch at 12:15 P.M. and dinner at 6:30 P.M. Hazel usually gives George a handkerchief for his birthday and says "Everything is just peachy keen, Mr. B" when George asks her something. George calls Hazel's brownies "Hazel's peachy keen pecan brownies" and is constantly nagged by Hazel to stay on his diet. George says that Hazel will never tell a lie ("She has George Washington heroics") and is the only person who knows the true meaning of Christmas ("She makes her own presents"). Hazel says "Just dustin' the cobwebs off Mr. B's law books makes me feel smart." Hazel likes to help out where she can and George often regrets telling Hazel about his clients, as she always butts in and tries to help. ("Two years of pre-law training, four years of law school and 12 years of successful practice and I still haven't learned to keep my mouth shut around Hazel," says George.)

Harold has a dog named Smiley. Harold attends an unnamed grammar school and calls Hazel's brownies "the good stuff." Pancakes are his favorite breakfast.

At 325 Sycamore Road, an hour's drive from George's home, lives George's brother, Steve Baxter (Ray Fulmore), his wife, Barbara (Lynn Borden), and their daughter, Susie (Julia Benjamin). When George is transferred to the middle East to handle an oil deal for Mr. Griffin, the CBS episodes begin. Dorothy leaves with George to live in Baghdad and Hazel and Harold move in with Steve.

Steve owns the Baxter Realty Company and is called "Mr. Steve" by Hazel (who also joins him and his friends for their Friday night poker game). Barbara, a housewife, and Hazel tried to make money by marketing "Aunt Hazel's Chili Sauce" for Richie's Supermarket (they made it for 15 cents a jar and sold it for 98 cents). Susie and Harold attend an unnamed grammar school; Steve and Barbara are in bed by 10:00 P.M. Millie Ballard (Ann Jillian) is Steve's secretary, a pretty teenager who works after school and on Saturday's. Fred and Mona Williams (Charles Bateman, Mala Powers) are Steve and Barbara's friends (and neighbors). Helen Miller and Howard Greenfield composed the first *Hazel* theme; Sammy Cahn and Jimmy Van Heusen composed the revised *Hazel* theme.

70.   He and She CBS, 1967–1968

Marrieds Richard and Paula Hollister (Richard Benjamin, Paula Prentiss) live at 365 East 84th Street in Manhattan. Richard is the creator of the comic strip turned television series *Jetman*; Paula works for the Manhattan Tourist Aid Society. Richard's favorite watering hole is Hammond's Bar.

Oscar North (Jack Cassidy) is the egotistical star of *Jetman* (a superhero with a jet-shaped helmet and two power packs on the back of his vest for flying). *Jetman* is filmed on Stage 2; Oscar arrives at the studio at 5:30 A.M. and makeup takes 4½ hours. Jerry Fielding composed the *He and She* theme.

71.   Heaven for Betsy CBS, 1952

Peter and Betsy Bell (real life husband and wife Jack Lemmon and Cynthia Stone) are a happily married couple who live at 136 Oak Tree Lane in New York. Peter is shy and timid and easily taken advantage of. He works as an apprentice executive at the Wilmott Department Store and earns $42.50 a week (although he says "I'm a combination salesman, floor walker, buyer, accountant, store detective, complaint bureau and errand boy").

Betsy, a former secretary, is strong and forceful and hoping to instill her traits in Peter so he can become successful and stand up to his overpowering boss, Alonzo Wilmott (Cliff Hall). Floor walker inspection is at 10:30 A.M.

72.   Hello, Larry NBC, 1979–1981

The Larry Adler Show, originally called *Hello, Larry*, is a call-in talk radio program on Trans-Allied, Inc., radio station KLOW-AM in Portland, Oregon (555-3567 is its phone number). Larry Adler (McLean Stevenson) is the host, a widower who lives with his daughters, Diane (Donna Wilkes, Krista Errickson) and Ruthie (Kim Richards) in Apartment 2B of an unnamed building (555-4521 is their phone number); Diane and Ruthie attend Portland High School. Larry's producer, Morgan Winslow (Joanna Gleason), lives at 67543 Baker Avenue; 555-0098 is her phone number. John LaSalle and Tom Smith composed the theme.

73.   Here We Go Again ABC, 1973

Richard Evans (Larry Hagman), owner of Evans Architecture, Inc., and his new wife, Susan (Diane Baker), live at 1450 North Valley Lane in Encino, California. Jerry Standish (Dick Gautier), Susan's ex-husband, a former Rams quarterback, now owner of the Polynesia Paradise Cafe, lives one block away at 1490 North Valley Lane. Judy Evans (Nita Talbot), Richard's ex-wife, the editor of *Screen World* magazine, lives a half mile away at 361 Oak Tree Drive. Richard and Susan attempt to start a new life while constantly being plagued by the intrusion of their exes. Carol Sager and Peter Allen sing the theme, "Here We Go Again."

Here's Lucy *see* I Love Lucy

74.   Hey Landlord! NBC, 1966–1967

Woody Banner (Will Hutchins) is an aspiring writer who lives at 140 West 41st Street in Manhattan in an old brownstone that he has converted into a ten-room apartment house. He shares the ground floor apartment with his friend Chuck Hookstratten (Sandy Baron), a hopeful comedian. Woody grew up on a farm in Ohio, was a boy scout (member of the Skunk Troop) and attended Fillmore High School in Toledo (where he was on the football and swim teams). Woody inherited the brownstone from a late uncle. Chuck was born in New York City and says "I was a rotten kid." He wrote on the school walls and once tried to burn down the school. He and Woody met at Ohio State University where, after graduating, they decided to pursue their goals in New York. Commercial photographer Jack Ellenhorn (Michael Constantine) is the easily exasperated, ulcer-ridden tenant who feels that the antics of Woody (whom he calls "The Boy Landlord") and Chuck ("Chuckula") are tied with the aggravation of his job in a competition to kill him. Jack enjoys a drink at the Elegant Palace Bar and Chuck appeared in one of his ads for Sedgewick Socks. Quincy Jones composed the *Hey Landlord!* theme.

75.   Hey, Mulligan NBC, 1954–1955

Mickey Mulligan (Mickey Rooney) is a page at the fictional I.B.C. (International Broadcasting Company) in Los Angeles. His official title is guest relations staff and he earns $47.62 a week after taxes. Mickey calls himself "the tallest short man you'll ever meet" and feels that his lack of height (at 5 feet) prevents him from becoming a success. He takes acting classes at the Academy of Dramatic Arts and is looking for that big break. Mickey lives at home with his father, Joe (Regis Toomey), a retired policeman (with the 23rd Precinct of the L.A.P.D.), and his mother, Nell (Claire Carleton), a former vaudeville actress. Mickey's girlfriend, Pat Harding (Carla Balinda), is a secretary at I.B.C. (which broadcasts such shows as *True to Life Tim*, *The Trials and Tribulations of Auntie Julia*, *The Saturday Night Super Dooper Special*, *Breakout* and *Macaroni and His Enchanted Piano*). Van Alexander composed the theme.

76.   Hogan's Heroes CBS, 1965–1971

Robert Hogan (Bob Crane), a U.S. Army Air Corps Colonel (with the 504th Bomber Squadron), is a World War II prisoner of war. His plane was shot down and he is now confined to Stalag 13, a camp outside Hammelburg, Germany, commanded by Colonel Wilhelm Klink (Werner Klemperer) and his bumbling assistant, Sergeant Hans Schultz (John Banner). Also residing with Hogan in Barracks 2 are Captain Peter Newkirk (Richard Dawson), Corporal Louis LeBeau (Robert Clary), Sergeant Andrew Carter (Larry Hovis) and Sergeant James Kinchloe (Ivan Dixon), Allied prisoners who have banded together to help fellow prisoners escape the Nazi high command and secure German secrets for their superiors. (In last-season episodes, Kinchloe was replaced by Kenneth Washington as Sergeant Richard Baker.)

Hogan, voted "Most likely to become a troublemaker" in school, was born in New Jersey and frequented Garlotti's Pizzeria. He plots to outwit his captors and leads his squadron of four "heroes" on various missions to achieve his goals. They have a secret radio receiver (disguised as a coffee pot), a series of tunnels (entrances are under the guard dog doghouse in the kennel, the tree stump in the woods outside the camp, a lower bunk in the barracks, and under the stove in Klink's quarters), a hidden microphone (behind the picture of Hitler in Klink's office), and a submarine (code-named Mama Bear). Hogan's first code name was Goldilocks and Papa Bear was the code for London. Later, Papa Bear became Hogan's code name while Mama Bear (and sometimes Goldilocks) became the code for London. Hogan also used disguises to fool Klink and Schultz: Frank Dirken, Colonel Klink, Major Hoganborg, Captain Gruber and Major Hoople.

Peter Newkirk, the British prisoner, was given several aliases to fool Klink: a London fire warden, a talent scout, and a barrister. He was actually a master pickpocket with a talent for impersonation.

Andrew Carter ran a drugstore in Muncie, Indiana, and hopes to become a pharmacist when he returns home. He first mentions that he enlisted in the Army; he later says he was drafted. He is an explosives expert and Hogan passed him off as an interior decorator and business school graduate (so he can control the distribution of supplies to the area's stalags). In the pilot, Carter is a lieutenant and escapes from Stalag 13; for the series he is returned as a sergeant.

Louis LeBeau, the French POW, is a jack-of-all-trades—from cooking to sewing. To help him pull off schemes, Hogan has passed LeBeau off as a big-game hunter; expert marksman; "Yvette of Paris," a fashion designer; a chemist known as "Mr. Test Tube"; a descendant of Gypsies; "Madame LaGrange," the owner of a Paris dance studio; and "Le Smoke," a fire brigade champion. LeBeau's weekly assignment is to visit Wilhelmina, the underground contact (Celeste Yarnell), a beautiful woman he loved but described as "a mean old lady" to his fellow prisoners.

James Kinchloe (later called Ivan Kinchloe) was nicknamed "Kinch" and was a former Golden Gloves boxer. He and Baker ran the underground communications center; Kinch was also a radio and electronics expert.

Colonel Klink and Sergeant Schultz are members of the Luftwaffe (the German Air Force). They opposed Hitler and hated the war. They performed as soldiers because it was their job (their fear of the Gestapo and combat duty led Hogan to manipulate them for his own benefit). Klink was born in Leipzig and received military training in Potsdam. Before the war he worked as a bookkeeper and mentioned he once played Peter Pan in a play. Hogan's men have nicknamed him "Klink the Fink" (the "Fink" standing for "Firm Impartial Nazi Kommandant"). He is hoping to perform his job as kommandant without incident so he can get a promotion.

Schultz was the owner of a toy company before the war. He is a bumbling klutz and rather naive and easily manipulated by Hogan. He wants only to come home from the war alive and often looks the other way when he feels Hogan is up to something. His catchphrase became "I know nothing, I see nothing."

Bruno, Hans, Heidi and Wolfgang are the guard dogs at Stalag 13. Helga (Cynthia Lewis) was Klink's first secretary; she was replaced by Sigrid Valdis as Hilda. Marya (Nita Talbot) was the beautiful Russian spy who helped Hogan (and was fond of him). The real villains were General Albert Burkhalter (Leon Askin) and Major Wolfgang Hochstetter (Howard Caine). Burkhalter, Klink's superior, was a stern Gestapo agent with a weakness for pretty women. Hochstetter was devoted to Hitler's cause and intent on destroying the enemy. He constantly threatened to send Klink to the Russian front if he didn't do his job.

Jerry Fielding composed the *Hogan's Heroes* theme.

NBC attempted to copy the success of *Hogan's Heroes* with an unrealized series called *Campo 44* (about the activities of the American and British captives in an Italian POW camp as they manipulate their captors to help the Allied cause). The pilot aired on 9/9/67 and starred Philip Abbott, Jim Dawson, Dino Fazio, Vito Scotti and Fred Smoot.

77. **The Honeymooners** CBS, 1955–1956

The apartment house at 728 Chauncey Street in Bensonhurst, Brooklyn, New York, is home to Ralph and Alice Kramden (Jackie Gleason, Audrey Meadows) and their upstairs neighbors Ed and Trixie Norton (Art Carney, Joyce Randolph). The address is also given as 328 and 358 Chauncey Street; Ralph's phone number is BEnsonhurst 0-7741; Ed's is BEnsonhurst 5-6698 (also as 6-0098).

Ralph attended P.S. 73 grammar school and at age 14 worked as a newspaper delivery boy. He had high hopes of playing the cornet in a band but couldn't afford the price of lessons. Ralph took his future wife, Alice Gibson, dancing at the Hotel New Yorker on their first date, but three versions were given as to how he met her. It is first said that Ralph noticed Alice in a diner when she yelled to the waiter "Hey Mac, a hot frank and a small orange drink." Next, it is a snowy winter day when Ralph, assigned by the WPA to shovel snow, meets Alice, a WPA employee who is handing out the shovels. Finally, Ralph mentions that he met Alice in a restaurant called Angie's when they both ordered spaghetti and meatballs. A marriage took place in 1941 and the newlywed Kramdens moved in with Alice's mother (whom Ralph calls "Blabbermouth"). They rented their first (and only) apartment when Ralph became a bus driver for the Gotham Bus Company. He drives bus number 247 (also given as 2969) along Madison Avenue in Manhattan. Over the course of his

14 years with the company (at 225 River Street), Ralph has been robbed six times (five times the crooks got nothing; the sixth time they got $45). Ralph's astrological sign is Taurus and he owns two suits (one black, one blue). He has type A blood and is thought of as cheap (his electric bill is 39 cents a month and he refuses to buy Alice a TV "until they invent 3-D TV").

Alice was also said to have worked in a laundromat before meeting Ralph. To help pay the bills, Alice held two part time jobs: donut jelly stuffer at Krausmeyer's Bakery (later promoted to doughnut taster) and secretary to a man named Tony Amico. Alice, whose birthsign is Aquarius (born February 8), was also chosen "Cleaning Lady of the Month" by Glow Worm Cleanser. She and Ralph dine most often at the Hong Kong Gardens restaurant and attend dances at the Sons of Italy Hall. When they first married Ralph called Alice "Bunny"; she called him "Old Buttercup."

"Homina, homina, homina" is what Ralph says when he doesn't know what to say. He says "Baby, you're the greatest" to Alice to show her he loves her, but when he gets upset with her he waves his fist and says "You're going to the moon Alice" or "Pow! Right in the kisser." When Ralph realizes he has said something he shouldn't have, he yells "I've got a big mouth." Ralph is also easily aggravated. To help him overcome his anger, he tried saying (without success) "Pins and needles, needles and pins. A happy man is a man who grins." Ralph also believes he is the head of the house—"I give the orders, I make the decisions" or so he thinks.

Edward L. Norton works as an "Engineer in Subterranean Sanitation" (a sewer worker for the department of sanitation). He says the *L* in his name stands for Lilywhite (his mother's maiden name) and that he majored in arithmetic at vocational school (in another episode he mentions attending P.S. 31 in Oyster Bay, Brooklyn). As a kid Ed had a dog named Lulu (although in another episode he is allergic to dogs) and did a hitch in the Navy (he later took up typing on the G.I. Bill). He found that he couldn't stand being cooped up in an office, so he took the job in the sewer (which he started in 1938). Ed's astrological sign was given as both Capricorn and Pisces. *Captain Video* is his favorite TV show (he is a ranger third class in the Captain Video Fan Club) and his hero is Pierre Francois de la Brioski (who Ed thought designed the sewers of France; in reality, he condemned them). Ed can play the piano, but before he goes into the actual song, he warms up with "Swanee River." Ed shops with Trixie on Saturday afternoons and Trixie claims "Ed can't look into an empty refrigerator. It makes him cry." Ed coaches the Cougars stickball team and calls Ralph "Ralphie Boy." While Ralph most often calls Ed "Norton," he also says "You're a mental case" when Ed upsets him and "Out, get out" when he throws Ed out of the apartment. It is mentioned that when Ed came down to invite Ralph and Alice to dinner they became instant friends.

Ralph and Ed are members of the Raccoon Lodge (also called the International Order of the Friendly Sons of Raccoons and the International Loyal Order of Friendly Raccoons. In some episodes, raccoon is spelled as racoon). Ralph is the treasurer; Alice and Trixie are members of the Ladies' Auxiliary of the lodge. A lodge uniform costs $35 and to become a member one must comply with section two of the rules: "Applicants must have earned a public school diploma; applicants must have resided in the U.S. for at least six months; applicants must pay a $1.50 initiation fee." An executive meeting of the lodge means a poker game.

In 1949, when the bus company put on a play, Ralph starred in its production of "The 1949 Bus Drivers Follies." When the lodge put on a play (untitled), Ralph was the rich Frederick and Ed his rival, Hamilton, for the affections of Rachel (Alice).

Ralph and Norton enjoy playing pool and bowling (they are members of the Hurricanes and use alley 3 at the Acme Bowling Alley on 8th and Montgomery).

Ralph has a dream of making it big. He ventured into a number of moneymaking schemes that all failed: low-cal pizza, a uranium mine in Asbury Park, glow-in-the-dark wallpaper, Kran-Mars Delicious Mystery Appetizer (Ralph mistook dog food for an appetizer Alice made and approached his boss, Mr. Marshall, with a plan to market it) and paying 10 cents each for 2,000 Handy Housewife Helpers (a combination peeler, can opener and apple corer) that they tried to sell for one dollar each in a "Chef of the Future" commercial (during the third break in a Charlie Chan movie). Ralph got stage fright and ruined the commercial. Ralph also started the Ralph Kramden Corporation (where, for $20, Ed got 35 percent of everything Ralph made above his salary, which was first $42.50, then $60 and $62 a week). Ed also had an idea for making money—Pablum on pizza for babies. Ralph appeared on the TV game shows *Beat the Clock* and *The $99,000 answer* (his category was popular songs, but he failed to answer the first question correctly: "Who wrote Swanee River?" He answered "Ed Norton"). Ralph also did a commercial for Chewsey Chews Candy bars (for *The Chewsey Chews Musical Hour* on TV).

Together Ralph and Ed wrote a hit song called "Love on a Bus" (dedicated to Alice) that was later made into a movie, and won a radio contest with the song "Friendship." Jackie Gleason and Bill Templeton composed the theme, "You're My Greatest Love."

Origins

Jackie Gleason first played Ralph Kramden on DuMont's *Cavalcade of Stars* from 1950 to 1952. Art Carney was Ed Norton, Pert Kelton was Alice Kramden, and Elaine Stritch was Trixie Norton. A series of "Honeymooners" segments appeared on *The Jackie Gleason Show* (CBS, 1952–1955) featuring the same cast as the 1955 series. The same cast returned to a new *Jackie Gleason Show* (CBS, 1956–1961) wherein additional "Honeymooners" segments were produced. These segments are syndicated as *The Lost Honeymooners*.

Updates

On *Jackie Gleason and His American Scene Magazine* (CBS, 1962–1966), Jackie Gleason and Art Carney reprised their roles as Ralph and Ed with Sue Ane Langdon and Patricia Wilson as Alice and Trixie in short "Honeymooners" segments. Jackie and Art reprised their roles of Ralph and Ed with Sheila MacRae and Jane Kean as Alice and Trixie in short and then full-hour episodes of "The Honeymooners" on *The Jackie Gleason Show* (CBS, 1966–1970). The hour segments produced in 1970 are syndicated as *The Honeymooners European Vacation*. This cast repeated their roles on two *Jackie Gleason Specials* (CBS, 12/12/70 and 11/11/73).

Four additional ABC specials aired with Jackie Gleason, Art Carney, Sheila MacRae and Jane Kean reprising their roles:

1. *The Honeymooners Second Honeymoon* (2/2/76). The Nortons join Ralph and Alice as they celebrate their 25th wedding anniversary.

2. *The Honeymooners Christmas* (11/28/77). Ralph directs the play *A Christmas Carol* for the Raccoon Lodge.

3. *The Honeymooners Valentine Special* (2/13/78). Alice attempts to surprise Ralph with a new suit for Valentine's Day.

4. *The Honeymooners Christmas Special* (12/10/78). Ralph and Ed attempt to win a million dollars by investing in lottery tickets.

78.   How to Marry a Millionaire Syn., 1958–1960

Penthouse G on the 22nd floor of the Tower Apartment House on Park Avenue in New York City is home to Michele "Mike" McCall (Merry Anders), Loco Jones (Barbara Eden) and Greta Hanson (Lori Nelson), three beautiful girls seeking millionaire husbands. Plaza 3-5099 is their phone number and their rent is due on the tenth of each month. The girls have taken a pledge ("On my honor I promise to do my best to help one of us marry a millionaire. So help me, Fort Knox"). After an exhausting date, the girls massage each other's feet.

Mike, Loco and Greta were each renting a small apartment on Amsterdam Avenue before Mike convinced them to pool their resources ("You gotta spend money to make money") and rent a swank penthouse ("We have something to sell—ourselves—and we have to surround ourselves in the best possible surroundings"). While each seeks to help the other find a millionaire, virtually every cent they make goes toward paying the rent. When Mike spots a potential prospect, she sees dollar signs (as does the viewer—when a moneybag is superimposed over the subject); her credo is "Have money, will marry." The girls shop at Burke's Department Store and eat at Nate's Deli.

Mike, the schemer of the group, works as an analyst for the Wall Street firm of Hammersmith, Cavanaugh and Hammersmith. She believes that "the only way for a girl to be smart is to be dumb." Mike reads the financial section of the newspaper and uses *Dunn and Bradstreet* for her research material. She feels that "one of these days we're gonna hit it big" and knows that women have to put on airs—"Men go for either the sophisticated Tallulah [Bankhead] type or the slinky Marilyn Monroe type."

Greta is a hostess on the TV game show *Go for Broke*, a takeoff of *The $64,000 Question* (it airs at 9:00 P.M. but no network affiliation is given). She reads *Who's Who in America* (her research material) and the drama and TV section of the newspaper. Greta borrows Mike and Loco's nylons, doesn't make her bed and enjoys soaking in a bubble bath. She hopes that if there is a millionaire out there for her that "he comes along before he has to whisper sweet nothings in my ear trumpet."

Loco (her given name) was born in North Platte, Nebraska, on February 25. She was voted "The one most likely to go further with less than anyone" at North Platte High School. She is a bit naive when it comes to current events but has acquired encyclopedic knowledge of comic strips by reading *Super Comics* magazine. Loco is nearsighted and needs to wear eyeglasses but feels men will not find her attractive if she does. The resulting chaos often costs the girls a prospective husband ("Loco has cost us more millionaires than the 1929 stock crash" says Greta).

Loco, a fashion model for the Travis (later Talbot) Modeling Agency, is called "a fabulous blonde with an hourglass figure." She has photos taken at Marachi's Photography Studio and reads *Fashion Preview* magazine. While always fashionably dressed, Loco worries about short skirts that show her legs. Greta assures her that this is okay "because a man can't appreciate the flower of womanhood unless he can see the stems."

At the start of the second season it is learned that Greta married and moved to California ("Greta wanted to marry an oil man," said Mike, "but she married a man who owns a gas station"). Mike and Loco acquire new roommate Gwen Kirby (Lisa Gaye) when she responds to their *Journal News* newspaper ad. Gwen, born in Illinois, was a girl scout and had been working on a small magazine before coming to New York. She now works as an editor for *Manhattan Magazine* and is almost a clone of Greta: Marilyn Monroe figure, lover of bubble baths and a borrower (of Mike and Loco's nylons).

In the original, unaired 1957 pilot, Greta Lindquist (Lori Nelson), Loco Jones (Charlotte Austin) and Mike Page (Doe Avedon) are the women seeking millionaire husbands (they share a 13th floor Manhattan penthouse apartment). Loco is a brunette in this version but just as vain about wearing her glasses. She mentions that her real name is Rita Marlene Gloria Claudette Jones and that Loco is her nickname. She is a model but no agency name is given.

Greta, a blonde who majored in psychology at college, is hostess on the TV game show *The Dunlap Quiz Show*. Mike is a stockbroker for the firm of Hammersmith, Cavanaugh and Hammersmith. Both versions are based on the feature film of the same title.

79.   I Dream of Jeannie NBC, 1965–1970

The modest house at 1030 Palm Drive in Cocoa Beach, Florida, is owned by Captain (later Major) Anthony Nelson (Larry Hagman), an astronaut with the NASA Space Center at Cape Kennedy. Also living with him is Jeannie (Barbara Eden), a beautiful genie he found after a rocket he was testing malfunctioned and crash-landed on a deserted island in the South Pacific.

Jeannie was born in Baghdad on April 1, 64 B.C., at a time when the planet Neptune was in Scorpio. When she became of age, the Blue Djin (Michael Ansara), the most powerful and most feared of all genies, asked for her hand in marriage. When she refused, he turned her into a genie, placed her in a bottle and sentenced her to a life of loneliness on a deserted island. Centuries later Anthony, called Tony by Jeannie, found her green bottle (while making an S.O.S. signal), opened it, set her free and became her master. Jeannie wears a pink harem costume that is designed to conceal her navel. (Although it was considered indecent to show a girl's navel on TV at the time, occasional "sneak peaks" of Barbara Eden's can be seen—especially when the extrawide waist band she wears slips to reveal what one is not supposed to see. Strangely, it was all right for Barbara to show ample cleavage when wearing her harem outfit.) By NASA's scales, Jeannie weighs 109 pounds (but she insists "I have never weighed over 107 pounds"; a later episode establishes Jeannie's weight at 127 pounds). Jeannie crosses her hands over her chest and blinks her eyes to invoke her powers. She appears and disappears in a pink smoke.

When Jeannie becomes unhappy, her powers weaken; if she becomes very sad, she begins to vanish. She has green blood (green corpuscles give her envy), and Pip Chicks is her favorite homemade candy (it has a bad side effect of bringing out people's hidden fantasies). Jeannie wrote a book (under Tony's name) called *How to Be a Fantastic Mother* (published by Woodhouse Publishers in New York) and tried to make Tony rich by marketing Cousin Tony's Texas Chili.

Tony was born on July 15 in Fowlers Corners, Ohio, and attended Fowlers Corners High School (where he was called "Bunky Nelson"). Tony weights 181½ pounds and 555-7231 is his phone number. His address was also given as 811 Pine Street and 1137 Oak Grove Street. He has piloted "Apollo 14" and "Apollo 15," "Stardust I" (the ship that misfired in the pilot), the "X-14," the "Trail Blazer" and the "T-38" (the first fully automated plane).

Tony's main goal is to keep Jeannie's presence a secret—especially from NASA officials (he fears the Air Force will discharge him for having a genie). Tony has forbidden Jeannie to use her powers. She rarely listens and Tony often winds up in trouble (at which time she always says "How do you get yourself into these things, Master?" Tony always responds with "Jeannie!").

Captain (then Major) Roger Healey (Bill Daily) is Tony's best friend and the only other person who knows about Jeannie. He is a swinging bachelor and lives in Apartment 217 (also seen as 213). It was said that he attended Horace Mann High School and Tony, Horace Mann Elementary School. Thanks to Jeannie, Tony and Roger contracted the Persian Flu, making them the only known cases in 2,000 years.

Dr. Alfred Bellows (Hayden Rorke) is the base psychiatrist who, after meeting Tony, has set two goals for himself: to prove to someone else that something strange is going on, and to figure out what it is (Dr. Bellows most often experiences the aftereffects of Jeannie's magic). Dr. Bellows, an opera buff, is married to Amanda (Emmaline Henry). Amanda becomes Jeannie's close friend in later episodes but is unaware of Jeannie's true identity. (In Hawaiian episode segments set on the beach, one can clearly see Amanda's navel while Jeannie's is concealed).

Jeannie becomes excited if Tony asks her for a favor. She first mentions that "if a mortal marries a genie only then will she lose her powers." She later says "Only the power of Hadji can take away the power of a genie." It was also said that a genie cannot be photographed; this was contradicted when Jeannie's picture appeared in a newspaper after she won a rodeo queen title.

A recurring aspect of the series was the efforts of Jeannie's evil sister, Jeannie II (Barbara Eden), to steal Tony away from Jeannie and marry him. This failed when Tony and Jeannie wed in 1969. Jeannie II wears a green harem outfit and has been married 47 times.

Gin Gin is Jeannie's genie dog (she was mistreated by palace guards as a puppy and hates uniforms—thus she wreaks havoc at NASA). General Martin Peterson (Barton MacLane) and General Winfield Schaefer (Vinton Hayworth) are the base commanders. Schaefer has a dog named Jupiter. Hugo Montenegro, Buddy Kaye and Richard Wells composed the *I Dream of Jeannie* theme.

TV Movie Updates

1. *I Dream of Jeannie: 15 Years Later*, NBC, 10/20/85. Jeannie (Barbara Eden) and Tony (Wayne Rogers), now a colonel, have a teenage son, T.J. (for Tony, Jr.) (Mackenzie Astin). Major Roger Healey (Bill Daily) and Dr. Alfred Bellows (Hayden Rorke) have retired. The locale has changed to Houston, Texas. The story finds Jeannie II (Barbara Eden) attempting to make the content-as-a-housewife Jeannie independent when Tony decides to forsake retirement and continue with the space program.

2. *I Still Dream of Jeannie*, NBC, 10/20/91. The setting is the Lyndon B. Johnson Space Center in Houston, Texas. Jeannie (Barbara Eden) is still married to Tony (not seen) and the mother of Tony Nelson, Jr. (Christopher Bolton). Jeannie's past was also changed. She was born in Mesopotamia 4,233 years ago and attended genie school to learn her craft. She was said to have had many masters over the centuries. Roger (Bill Daily) is now a colonel and Jeannie II (Barbara Eden) was said to have never had a master; hence she is bound to remain in Mesopotamia forever (she can only leave for a period of 24 hours at a time and has to return to maintain her beauty and powers). Tony is away on a top secret mission and Jeannie cannot remain in Houston without a master (she will be exiled to Mesopotamia forever if Tony does not return in three months). The story finds Jeannie choosing high school guidance counselor Bob Simpson (Ken Kercheval) as a temporary master until the return of Tony (who is left in unknown space as the movie-pilot ends).

80. I Love Lucy CBS, 1951–1957

The converted Brownstone at 623 East 68th Street in Manhattan is owned by Fred and Ethel Mertz (William Frawley, Vivian Vance). Lucy and

Ricky Ricardo (Lucille Ball, Desi Arnaz) are tenants who occupy Apartment 3B (later 3D). They pay $125 a month in rent and moved into the building on August 6, 1948 (at which time they lived on the fourth floor). Murray Hill 5-9975 (later 5-9099) is their phone number.

Lucille "Lucy" Esmerelda McGillicuddy was born in Jamestown, New York, on August 6, 1921 (another episode claims she was born in West Jamestown in May 1921 and Taurus is her astrological sign). She has been juggling her age for so long "that I kinda lost track of how old I am." In grade school, Lucy was called "Bird Legs" and played Juliet in her Jamestown High School production of *Romeo and Juliet* (another episode claims she attended Celeron High School). She also played the sax in the school band ("Glow Worm" was the only song she ever learned to play).

Lucy met Ricky Ricardo Alberto Fernando Acha (a.k.a Ricky Alberto Ricardo IV) in New York City in 1941 when her friend Marian Strong arranged a blind date for her with Ricky. They fell in love and Ricky proposed to Lucy at the Byrum River Beagle Club in Connecticut.

Ricky, a Cuban drummer who later has his own rumba band, performs at the Tropicana Club in Manhattan. In 1956 Ricky buys a controlling interest in the Tropicana and renames it the Club Babalu, after his favorite song. (The club is also called the Ricky Ricardo Babalu Club and the Babalu Club, and Bob Hope was the opening night guest. Plaza 3-2099 is the club's phone number.) Ricky plays the conga drums, and roast pig is his favorite meal. Lucy claims she married Ricky when she was 22 years old and weighed 110 pounds at the time (she now weighs 132 pounds).

Lucy gets the hiccups when she cries ("It's happened since I was a little girl") and is famous for her "spider noise" ("Eeeuuuuu") when something doesn't go her way. Many episodes relate Lucy's efforts to defy Ricky and break into show business. Lucy loves to read murder-mystery novels and has a hard time managing the family budget. Lucy appeared on the TV game show *Females Are Fabulous* ("Any woman is idiotic enough to win a prize") to win $1,000 when Ricky took away her credit cards. She also tried to market her Aunt Martha's recipe for salad dressing as "Aunt Martha's Old Fashioned Salad Dressing" (which sold for 40 cents a jar). When Lucy upsets Ricky, he takes her over his knee and spanks her.

Lucy wrote a play for her women's club, the Wednesday Afternoon Fine Arts League, and said she studied ballet in high school for four years. She also worked in a chocolate factory and did the infamous Vitameatavegamin TV commercial on *Your Saturday Night Variety Show* (the vitamin product contained meat, vegetables, minerals and 23 percent alcohol; Lucy became intoxicated during rehearsals).

Lucy and Ricky were interviewed on the TV program *Face to Face* and were hosts of a morning TV show called *Breakfast with Ricky and Lucy* (sponsored by Phipps Drug Store). They also did a TV benefit for the Heart Fund and Lucy wrote an article for *Photoplay* magazine called "What It Is Really Like to Be Married to Ricky Ricardo."

In 1953 Lucy and Ricky become parents with the birth of Ricky Ricardo, Jr., better known as Little Ricky (James John Gauzer, Richard Lee Simmons, the Mayer Twins, Richard Keith). Little Ricky, who is learning to play the drums, has the following pets: Fred (dog), Alice and Phil (parakeets), Tommy and Jimmy (turtles), Hopalong (frog), and Mildred and Charles (fish). In his first school play, *The Enchanted Forest*, Little Ricky played the lead; Lucy, the witch; Ricky, the hollow tree; Fred, a frog; and Ethel, the Fairy Princess.

Ricky made a TV pilot for an unrealized musical series called *Tropical Rhythms* and traveled to Hollywood to star in a movie called *Don Juan*. The movie is shelved and the film that Ricky eventually makes is never revealed.

Ethel was born in Albuquerque, New Mexico, and called "Little Ethel" by her Aunt Martha and Uncle Elmo. Her maiden name is Potter and her middle name was given as Louise, Roberta and Mae. She can play the piano and has been married to cheapskate Fred Mertz for 18 years (in 1951; in 1952, they mention they have been married for 25 years). Fred, born in Steubenville, Ohio, is a member (with Ricky) of the Recreation Club. He met Ethel (both of them are performers) in vaudeville (Fred gave up the stage in 1925). When Ethel gets upset, Fred slips her a sedative. Ethel claims that Fred once came up with an idea to make money "but is mad at Edison for coming up with the idea of the light bulb before him." Fred claims that "the only way for Ethel to keep a secret is if she doesn't hear it." In one episode, "The Diet," Fred and Ethel are seen with a dog (Butch); the dog is never seen or mentioned again. The Mertzes' phone number is Plaza 5-6098.

Lucy's habit of loudly stirring her coffee (hitting the spoon against the side of the cup) most annoys Ricky (his habit of tapping annoys Lucy). Ethel's "chewing like a cow" most annoys Fred; his habit of jiggling his keys annoys Ethel. In the European-based episodes (12/55–6/56), Fred becomes Ricky's band manager and the quartet books passage on the oceanliner *SS Constitution*.

While visiting friends in Connecticut, Lucy falls in love with an Early American–style house for sale. She convinces Ricky to move. When they find the cost of living higher than expected, they decide to raise chickens and take on boarders—Fred and Ethel Mertz.

Lucy, Ricky, Fred and Ethel appeared on the TV game show *Be a Good Neighbor* (attempting to win a trip to Hawaii) and opened a diner called A

Little Bit of Cuba (with Ricky as the maître'd, Fred, the cook, Lucy and Ethel, waitresses). When they had a squabble, Fred and Ethel used their half of the diner to open A Big Hunk of America.

Origins

The series is based on the 1948–51 radio series *My Favorite Husband*. Lucille Ball played Liz Cooper and Richard Denning her husband, George. A TV pilot, called *I Love Lucy*, was produced in 1951 (it aired in 1990 after being lost for 39 years) that cast Lucille Ball and Desi Arnaz as Lucy and Ricky Ricardo (not Lucy and Larry Lopez as reported in *TV Guide*). Here, Lucy and Ricky live in a seventh-floor Manhattan apartment. Fred and Ethel are not a part of the concept (although Lucy's efforts to break into show business are).

Updates

The Lucille Ball–Desi Arnaz Show, CBS, 1957–1960 (titled *The Lucy-Desi Comedy Hour* for syndication). Thirteen episodes were produced as specials and continued to relate events in the lives of Lucy, Ricky, Fred and Ethel. The first episode, "Lucy Takes a Cruise to Havana" (11/16/57), changes how Lucy and Ricky met. Here Lucy and her friend Susie McNamara (Ann Sothern) are in Havana when Lucy meets Ricky and falls in love with him. Also aboard ship are Fred and Ethel, celebrating their tenth anniversary second honeymoon. The remaining episodes are "The Celebrity Next Door" (12/3/57), "Lucy Hunts Uranium" (1/3/58), "Lucy Wins a Racehorse" (2/3/58), "Lucy Goes to Sun Valley" (4/14/58), "Lucy Goes to Mexico" (10/6/58), "Lucy Makes Room for Danny" (12/11/58; Danny Thomas guests), "Lucy Goes to Alaska" (2/9/59), "Lucy Wants a Career" (4/13/59), "Lucy's Summer Vacation" (6/8/59), "Milton Berle Hides Out at the Ricardos" (9/25/59), "The Ricardos Go to Japan" (11/27/59) and "Lucy Meets the Moustache" (4/1/60); Ernie Kovacs guests).

Other Lucille Ball Series

1. *The Lucy Show*, CBS, 1961–1968. Lucy Carmichael (Lucille Ball) is a widow with two children, Chris (Candy Moore) and Jerry (Jimmy Garrett), who lives at 132 Post Road in Danfield, a town in New York State. She shares the house with her divorced friend Vivian Bagley (Vivian Vance) and her son, Sherman (Ralph Hart). Lucy and Vivian are former Navy WAVES who met during World War II. They are volunteers for the Danfield Fire Department and members of the Volunteer Fireman's Barbershop Quartet.

Vivian has claustrophobia, complains and compulsively eats. She is also arrogant, vain and proud and famous for her homemade caramel corn. Lucy is disorganized and desperate for money (she lives off a trust fund established for her by her late husband at the Danfield First National Bank). Lucy's maiden name is Taylor and she worked at a number of different jobs (hospital candy striper, meter maid, police department decoy to catch a lover's lane thief, and vacuum cleaner salesperson). When Lucy has to cut the grass on her front lawn, she rents a sheep named Clementine to eat it down.

Chris is 14 years old and had her first job at the Ice Cream Shoppe to earn $40 for a drum majorette uniform for a parade. Eight-year-old Jerry is a member of the YMCA football team; nine-year-old Sherman is a member of the cub scouts.

Theodore J. Mooney (Gale Gordon) is the bank president plagued by Lucy's efforts to get her hands on her money. He collects stamps and coins and enjoys singing and dancing. He is a wine connoisseur and has a dog (Nelson) and a parakeet (Greenback).

On September 13, 1963, Lucy moves to Hollywood and into a new house at 700 Grover Street. Her trust fund is transferred to the Westland Bank where Mr. Mooney is the vice president. Chris is said to be in college and Jerry has been sent to a military school. Vivian had married prior to the format change (she appeared several times as Vivian Bunson). Mary Jane Croft as Mary Jane Lewis becomes Lucy's best friend.

Lucy first works as a secretary at a recording studio; several episodes later she is working part time as Mr. Mooney's secretary, then full time a few weeks later. Lucy also worked as a temporary flight attendant for Trans Global Airways and as Iron Man Carmichael, a famous Hollywood stuntman.

2. Here's Lucy, CBS, 1968–1974. Lucille Ball is Lucille Carter, a widow who works as a secretary to her brother-in-law, Harrison Otis Carter (Gale Gordon), the owner of the Unique Employment Agency ("Unusual Jobs for Unusual People"). Lucy lives at 4863 Valley Lawn Drive in Encino, California (in the San Fernando Valley). She is a widow and the mother of 17-year-old Kim (Lucie Arnaz) and 15-year-old Craig (Desi Arnaz, Jr.). The employment agency is located in a high-rise building on Wilshire Boulevard in Los Angeles. Lucy is a Leo and her maiden name is McGillicuddy. Kim and Craig attend Angeles High School (what the *A* on Kim's cheerleading jersey stands for). Kim worked as Lucy's assistant, as a salesgirl in a dress shop, and as a pet shop salesgirl. Kim has a cat, a female she calls Harry, and banks at the Weststate Bank (as does Lucy). When Kim moved out, she acquired a job with a talent agency. This episode, "Kim Finally Cuts You Know Whose

Apron Strings" (2/21/72), was an unsold pilot for the Lucie Arnaz series "Kim."

Craig first worked as a supermarket box boy and then in a hobby shop. He plays the drums and has an unnamed band (in which Kim sang); he wrote the song "Country Magic."

Harrison, called "Uncle Harry," is president of the Beverly Hills Chamber of Commerce. He attended Bullwinkle University (Class of 1928) and was a naval photographer during World War II. He has a side business called Harry's Canine Boutique and can't resist a certain quality in a woman—"She's loaded."

Lucy and her best friend, Mary Jane Lewis (Mary Jane Croft), dine at the Villa Roma restaurant. Mary Jane is an Aquarius and she and Lucy invested in a franchise called the Proud Penguin (where they made five cents on each frozen custard they sold).

3. *Life with Lucy*, ABC, 1986. Lucille Barker (Lucille Ball) and Curtis MacGibbon (Gale Gordon) are co-owners of the M&B Hardware Store at 1027 Hill Street in Pasadena, California. Lucy, a widow, lives with her married daughter, Margo MacGibbon (Ann Dusenberry), and her family: Ted (Larry Anderson), her husband, and her children, Becky and Kevin (Jenny Lewis, Philip J. Amelio).

Lucy's late husband was named Sam and her maiden name is Everett. She is a health food nut and financially well-off. Curtis was on vacation in Hawaii when Lucy took half interest in the business (Sam and Curtis were partners). When he returned and found his life plagued by Lucy's antics, he also moves in with Ted (his son) so he can keep an eye on Lucy (whom he doesn't trust around his grandchildren). Ted's job is not revealed; nor is Margo's line of work. Ted and Margo have been married for nine years; Kevin has a teddy bear named Charley.

81.   I Married Joan   NBC, 1952–1955

Joan and Bradley Stevens (Joan Davis, Jim Backus) are a married couple who live at 345 Laurel Drive in Los Angeles (also given as 133 Stone Drive); Dunbar 3-1232 is their phone number. Joan is scatterbrained and often complicates Brad's life with her antics. She is president of the local women's club (meetings are held every other Monday to play bridge) and is a member of the Women's Welfare League. *Two Hearts Against the Wind* is her favorite TV show and Guy Lombardo is her favorite orchestra leader. Bradley is a domestic relations court judge for the County of Los Angeles. He is level-headed and loves Joan ("How else could I put up with all her shenanigans"). He collects stamps, enjoys hunting and playing golf; pot roast is his favorite dinner; hot cakes with melted butter and coffee his favorite breakfast. The Roger Wagner Chorale sings the theme, "I Married Joan."

82.   Ichabod and Me CBS, 1961–1962

Bob Major (Robert Sterling), a former editor for the *New York Times*, now publishes the *Bulletin*, the daily newspaper of Phippsboro, a small New Hampshire town. Bob is a widower and lives with his son Benjie (Jimmy Mathers) at 432 Maple Lane. Bob is assisted by the paper's former owner, Ichabod Adams (George Chandler), the town's mayor and traffic commissioner. Bob dates Ichabod's daughter, Abby Adams (Christine White), and eats lunch at Bailey's Drug Store. Ichabod and Abby reside at R.F.D. Number 6. Ichabod grows petunias as a hobby; Abby is a member of the Garden Club. Pete Rugolo composed the theme. The original pilot, *Adams Apples* (4/24/60), found advertising executive Terry Major (Fred Beir) moving to Phippsboro to run an apple farm (which he rents for $125 a month from Ichabod Adams, played by George Chandler).

83.   I'm Dickens ... He's Fenster ABC, 1962–1963

Harry Dickens and Arch Fenster (John Astin, Marty Ingels) are friends who work as carpenters for the Bannister Construction Company in Los Angeles. Harry is married to the former Kate Conway (Emmaline Henry) and they live at 285 South Lakehurst (555-3438 is their phone number). Kate, a stunning blonde, eats Diet Krisp cereal for breakfast. Harry, the shop foreman, is a bit of a klutz and not very handy when it comes to making home repairs. Arch is a swinging bachelor and famous for his "little black book" (a six- by nine-inch 300-page softcover). He lives in an apartment at 366 Brockhurst and dines at Fontano's Restaurant. Arch can make dolls out of bread and likes to date ditzy girls (he loses confidence around brainy girls). Myron Bannister (Frank DeVol) is their boss; Mel Warshaw and Bob Mulligan (Dave Ketchum, Henry Becman) are fellow carpenters. Irving Szathmary composed the theme, "The Dickens and Fenster March."

84.   It's a Living ABC, 1980–1982; Syn., 1985–1989

Above the Top, a 13th floor Los Angeles restaurant that features "Sky High Dining," is owned by Pacific Continental Properties. Nancy Beebee (Marian Mercer) is the hostess, a snob who takes her work seriously and demands respect from her waitresses (Cassie, Lois, Jan, Dot, Vickie, Amy, Ginger and Maggie; they wear black and white uniforms). Before acquiring her job as hostess, Nancy was a ballerina for 15 years. She tells her waitresses "I'm in charge and that spells B-O-S-S." When Nancy hears a "please" from one of them she knows that they want something from her. Nancy was born in South Philadelphia and married the restaurant's chef, Howard Miller (Richard Stahl). Howard was born in Trenton, New Jersey, has a dog (Bluto) and two fish (Ike and Mamie). He enjoys fishing on the Rogue River in Oregon.

Katie Lou "Cassie" Cranston (Ann Jillian) is the prettiest and sexiest of the waitresses. She flaunts her sexuality (especially her breasts) to attract men and is looking to marry money. Although Cassie cannot cook (she keeps clothes in her kitchen) she tells men "I'm a terrific cook" (she also mentioned that her cooking "abilities" were less extensive when she said, "I can make toast"). Cassie was born in Kansas and dropped the "Katie Lou" so people would not think of her as a hick. She lives in Los Angeles at the Sun Palace Condominium Complex; on her only night off devotes time to reading to senior citizens at the Willow Glen Rest Home. While Cassie appears to be self centered, she is there for any of her friends who need her.

Lois Adams (Susan Sullivan) lives at 8713 Mercer Street in Los Angeles. She is the most sophisticated of the waitresses and married to the never-seen Bill. She is also the mother of Amy and Joey (Tricia Cast, Keith Mitchell) and is struggling to make ends meet (Bill is a salesman). Lois was born in Minnesota and worked as a secretary before marrying. She loves art and reading and rejoined the work force when a night position opened up at the restaurant (Bill cares for the kids while she is at work). Amy and Joey attend the Gramacey Street Elementary School.

Jan Hoffmeyer (Barrie Youngfellow) is divorced and the mother of Ellen (Lili Haydn, Virginia Keehne). She remarried in 1985 (Richard Grey, played by Richard Kline) when the series first began its syndicated run. Jan's maiden name is Frankel and she was born in Philadelphia. She attended Templar High School (class of '66) and during her college years at Berkeley, she was arrested during a demonstration for mooning a cop. Jan has a cat (Ralph) and is attending night classes at North Los Angeles Law School ("I plan to do more with my life than hand out menus"). Ellen takes ballet lessons (at Madam LaSonia's School of Dance), and to pay for her continuing the classes, Jan took a second job hand-writing invitations.

Margaret "Maggie" McBirney (Louise Lasser) is a widow and the most insecure member of the group. (She had been pampered by her late husband, Joseph, a salesman for Kitchen Help dishwashers. Since his death, she has retreated, somewhat, into a shell and is afraid to take a chance.) She lives alone in a spacious house at 1417 Brooke Avenue and while she involves herself with the waitresses and their problems, she pretty much keeps her life private. She was born in Ohio and attended Fernwood High School. Her one regret is that she and Joseph never had children.

Dorothy "Dot" Higgins (Gail Edwards) is a hopeful actress (although Nancy believes "she is hopelessly irresponsible"). Dot was born in Detroit and majored in theater at Baxter College. She made her TV debut in a commercial for Autumn Years dog food and also did a commercial for Le Stif hair spray. She played triplets on the TV soap opera *All My Sorrows* and appeared in three stage plays: *Bye Bye Birdie* (as Kim), *The Garden of Countess Natasha* (as Natasha) and *Esmerelda* (a play about the history of the Philippine Islands). Dot appeared on the *Adopt a Pet Telethon* (where she sang "My Buddy" to a dog) and her likeness appeared as "Betty Spaghetti, the Waitress" in the comic strip "Billy Bonkers." Dot lives at the Dunhill Apartments and has several pets: Mr. Puss (cat), Pardon (dog, whom she rescued from the pound) and a mouse (Mouse).

Amy Tompkins (Crystal Bernard) was born in Snyder, Texas, and is the most outrageous of the waitresses. She is a member of the American Gun Owners Association and owns a chrome-plated .357 Magnum with a six-inch barrel. She keeps the gun "in my pink jammy bunny with a zipper in its tummy" and left home with these words from her father: "Keep your chin up and your skirt down." Amy lives at the Carrie Nation Hotel for Women in Los Angeles and has a plush rabbit she calls Snuggle Bunny.

Virginia "Ginger" St. James (Sheryl Lee Ralph) shares an apartment with Amy. Ginger, the only black waitress, was born in Buffalo, New York, and attended Buffalo High School (where she was called "Booby Soxer" for stuffing her bra with socks). Ginger has a flair for fashion designing and hopes to parlay that talent into an occupation. Like Cassie, Ginger has many boyfriends and uses her sexuality to attract men (one named a boat after her— "Ginger Snaps").

Victoria "Vickie" Allen (Wendy Schaal) is the most sensitive of the waitresses. She was born in Pocatello, Idaho, and now lives at 102 North Brewster Place in Los Angeles, with her parakeet, Squeaky. She attended Pocatello High School and worked as a waitress in the local diner after school and on weekends. She came to Los Angeles to better her life and has set no immediate goals for herself.

"Run quick" are the two words that come to Cassie's mind when she sees Sonny Mann (Paul Kreppel), the restaurant's one-man entertainment center who thinks of himself as the "Singing Sex Symbol." Sonny was born in Reno, Nevada, and his real last name is Manischevitz. He has aspirations of becoming a rich and famous singer and puts on elaborate shows when record producers dine at Above the Top. His idol is singer Jack Jones and he has a Franklin Mint All Nations doll collection. Sonny's favorite TV show is *Rocky and His Friends* (he is a charter member of the Bullwinkle the Moose Fan Club). Sonny first performed at Vinnie's Romper Room, then in the Play Pen Lounge at Chuck's Game Room in Las Vegas. As a kid Sonny had a dog named Buster and wrote the book *Mann to Mann* (a guide for picking up girls) that he had printed himself (750 copies when no publisher would touch it).

The program was originally titled *It's a Living* (1980–81) with waitresses Lois, Jan, Cassie, Vickie and Dot. It became *Making a Living* (1982) with waitresses Cassie, Jan, Maggie and Dot, and *It's a Living* again (1985–89) with waitresses Jan, Cassie, Dot, Amy and Ginger. Nancy and Sonny were a part of each version and the entire package is titled *It's a Living* for repeats in syndication. Leslie Bricusse sings the theme, "It's a Living."

85.   **It's Always Jan** CBS, 1955–1956

Jan Stewart (Janis Paige) is a talented but relatively unknown singer represented by the Harry Cooper Talent Agency. She is a widow and lives with her daughter, Josie (Jeri Lou James), at 46 East 50th Street in Manhattan. Jan shares the apartment with Valerie Marlow (Merry Anders), a model, and Patricia Murphy (Patricia Bright), a secretary. Jan performs regularly at Tony's Cellar, a Greenwich Village night club, and dreams of starring on Broadway and performing at the Sky Room of the Sherry-Waldorf Hotel. Sid Melton plays Harry Cooper, Jan's agent. Earle Hagen and Herbert Spencer composed the *It's Always Jan* theme.

86.   **The Jack Benny Program** CBS, 1950–1964; NBC, 1964–1965

Jack Benny (Himself) is an entertainer who stands five feet, 11 inches tall and weighs 158 pounds. He was born in Waukegan, Illinois, and claims to be only 39 years old ("I've been 39 for so long I've forgotten how old I really am"). Jack felt he was born with show business in his blood but before he could test that theory, he joined the Navy. After his discharge in 1921, he broke into vaudeville. Audiences seemed to despise him, but Jack pushed on and teamed with a comedian named George Burns when they met in Philadelphia. They formed their own comedy team (Benny and Burns) but with Jack as the foil and George as the straight man, the act bombed and broke up. George teamed with a girl named Gracie Allen (forming "Burns and Allen") and Jack became famous when he went into radio and began his own show, *The Jack Benny Program*. When television began to take hold, Jack transformed his radio program into a visual treat for his audience.

Like his radio program, Jack's TV series is a glimpse into his life at home and at the studio. Jack lives at 366 North Camden Drive in Beverly Hills, California. Eddie "Rochester" Anderson (Himself), his ever-faithful valet, lives with him (he calls Jack "Boss" or "Mr. Benny"). Jack has an image for being cheap; he blames this on his writers, who thought making him stingy would be funny. Although Jack has an account at the California Bank, he rarely withdraws money; he enjoys visiting it. When he decides to make a withdrawal, people fear the economy is in trouble and rush to withdraw their money. While Jack trusts banks, he feels safer storing most of his money in a large vault in the dungeon beneath his home. To access the vault, one must overcome a mine field, poison gas, a rickety bridge, an alligator pool and flame throwers.

Jack has a laundry business on the side and enjoys attending parties (he has a Yellow Pages listing for "Available for Parties"). Jack wrote the song "When You Say I Beg Your Pardon, Then I'll Come Back to You" and is proud of his "ability" to play the violin (which everyone hears off key except him). Professor Pierre LeBlanc (Mel Blanc) is Jack's long-suffering violin teacher.

Mary Livingston (Herself) is Jack's girlfriend, a salesgirl at the May Company department store (where Jack does his Christmas shopping). Mary was born in Plainfield, New Jersey, and for her and Jack, a night at the movies is going over to her house "because her TV screen is bigger than mine." Jack buys his suits at the Fenchel and Gordon Men's Shop. Jack also mentioned living at 904 Santa Monica and that he was in a vaudeville act with Bing Crosby and George Burns.

Dennis Day (Himself) is Jack's vocalist. Jack wanted "a nice cheap Morton Downey–like singer for $35 a week who had comedy potential." Jack's agent, Steve Burke (Jesse White), recommended Dennis, an unknown singer slinging hash at the Lotus Blossom Inn. When Jack heard him sing, but most importantly when Dennis agreed to $35 a week, Jack hired him. Dennis is a member of the Elks Club and has to sometimes take outside jobs to survive ("I can't survive on what Mr. Benny pays me").

Don Wilson (Himself) is Jack's overweight announcer; Lois Corbett plays Don's wife, Lois; and Dale White is his overweight son, Harlow (whom Don is grooming to become a TV announcer). Don lives at 4946 West End in Beverly Hills and it was mentioned that when Jack first hired Don, he paid him $5 a week plus meals. Mel Blanc also provides the voice for Jack's car, a run-down Maxwell, and plays Si, the Mexican who confuses Jack with the "See and Si" routine. Mahlon Merrick performs Jack's theme, "Love in Bloom."

87. **Jackson and Jill** Syn., 1949

Jackson and Jill Jones (Todd Karns, Helen Chapman) are a married couple who live in a one-room apartment (1A) at 167 Oak Street in Manhattan (Main 6421 is their phone number). Jackson, an accountant for the Gimmling Company (Main 6244 is his office phone number), has a short-wave radio with the call letters W10GEC. Jill is a beautiful housewife who believes she is "mean, suspicious and narrow-minded" (Jackson says she isn't—"You're sweet, lovely and wonderful"). Jackson served with the Marines during World War II and believes you can tell a man's character by the coat he wears. Jill believes Jackson is forgetful "because he has something else on his mind" and always asks Jackson "if he prefers a girl with looks or a girl with brains." Jackson's answer, "Neither one darling, I prefer you," causes Jill to give a puzzled look to the camera. Jill does have a suspicious mind and constantly believes Jackson is seeing other women (each episode finds Jill threatening to leave Jackson). She ultimately learns she has jumped to the wrong conclusions. Each episode opens and closes with Jill writing an entry in her diary (which we see as a flashback). Only a cast is credited. The program closes with "Watch for another 'Jackson and Jill' on this station soon."

88. **Jamie** ABC, 1953–1954

Jamison John Francis McHummer, Jamie for short (Brandon DeWilde), is a young boy who comes to live with his grandfather, Frank M. Dimmer (Ernest Truex), Frank's daughter, Laurie (Polly Rowles), and Laurie's daughter, Liz (Kathleen Nolan), after the death of his parents. Jamie has an allowance of 50 cents a week and earns $3 a week as a bicycle delivery boy for Briggs Hardware Store. If there are chores to be done, Jamie takes his time coming home from school. Frank, called "Grandpa," owns Dimmer's Drug Store. Laurie earns money through a catering business she runs with her friend Annie (Alice Pearce). Eva Marie Saint played Liz in the pilot episode.

89.   The Jean Arthur Show CBS, 1966

While the theme song invites viewers to ride "on our merry merry-go-round," it shows attorneys Patricia Marshall and her son Paul (Jean Arthur, Ron Harper) riding a carousel. In a more serious light they are the owners of Marshall and Marshall, a prestigious law firm at 100 West Beverly Boulevard in Beverly Hills. Patricia, a widow, and her 30-year-old son are graduates of Harvard Law School. Patricia lives at 367 South Oak Street and is a brilliant corporate attorney; she enjoys looking for sea shells on the beach. Paul, a by-the-books attorney, lives in an apartment at 360 Etchfield Road, and seeks only the high-paying, important clients—not the frivolous clients his mother makes a habit of helping. Paul has spunk; Patricia makes things happen—a combination their clients want. Johnny Keating, Richard Kennedy and Richard Quine composed the theme, "Merry-Go-Round."

90.   The Jeffersons CBS, 1975–1985

The Jeffersons were originally Archie Bunker's well-to-do black neighbors on *All in the Family* from 1971 to 1975. The family consisted of Louise (Isabel Sanford), her son, Lionel (Mike Evans), and Louise's brother-in-law, Henry (Mel Stewart). Louise's husband, George, was mentioned but did not appear until 1973 when Sherman Hemsley appeared in the role. Two years later, *The Jeffersons* was born when George, Louise and Lionel moved to Manhattan (from Queens, New York) and into a luxurious high-rise apartment (12-D).

George is the wealthy, snobbish owner of the successful Jefferson Cleaners (stores in Manhattan, the Bronx, Brooklyn, Harlem and Queens). He and his long-suffering wife have been married for 25 years (George claims that their marriage lasts because "I put up with all her faults"). George opened his first store in Queens. Before marrying George, Louise lived on 13th Street and Amsterdam Avenue. Louise, called "Weezie" and "Weez" by George, has type O blood. She is the den mother to the Red Robins, a girl scout troop, and her maiden name is Mills.

George was born in Georgia and served time in the galley of a Navy aircraft carrier. He is always thought of as cheap. This comes from his youth when he was growing up in poverty (Apartment 5C at 984 West 125th Street in Harlem). Christmas was always a bad time for him. He made a promise that if he ever made it big, he would do something for the people who moved into that apartment. Each month he anonymously sends them $100. Feldway Cleaners is George's competition.

Tom and Helen Willis (Franklin Cover, Roxie Roker) are TV's first interracial couple. Tom (who is white) is an editor for the Pelham Publishing Company. He has been married to Helen (who is black) for 23 years. Their daughter, Jenny (Berlinda Tolbert), is engaged to Lionel (also played by Damon Evans). Lionel, who had the street name "Diver" when they lived in Harlem, calls Jenny "Honey Babes." Lionel and Jenny married and became the parents of a girl they name Jessica (Ebonie Smith).

On *All in the Family*, Lionel was Mike and Gloria's best friend. It was an established fact that Archie didn't like blacks but he liked Lionel (a lot of the humor comes when Archie makes remarks against black people in front of Lionel without being aware of what he is doing). Lionel likes Archie and realizes he isn't a vicious man. Archie calls people names and gives them stereotyped labels. Archie just doesn't know any better and Lionel understands this.

Harry Bentley (Paul Benedict) is George's across-the-hall neighbor (Apartment 12E). He was born in England, attended Oxford University, and works as an interpreter at the United Nations.

Florence Johnston (Marla Gibbs) is George's sassy maid. This character was spun off into a series called *Checking In* (1981) wherein Florence takes a leave of absence to work as the executive housekeeper for Lyle Block (Larry Linville), the manager of the St. Frederick Hotel in Manhattan. Jeff Barry and Ja'net DuBois composed the *Jeffersons* theme, "Movin' on Up."

91.   Jennifer Slept Here NBC, 1983–1984

Jennifer Farrell (Ann Jillian) was a beautiful actress who died suddenly in 1978. She attended Pinehurst Elementary and, after three years at Lanford High School in Illinois, she dropped out to pursue her dream of acting. She held a job as a waitress at Danny's Diner in Hollywood and made her TV debut as a banana in the audience of *Let's Make a Deal*. At age 18 she posed nude for a girlie calendar and had a small role in the film *Desire*. She achieved stardom in the movie *Stairway to Paradise*. In 1983 Jennifer returns as a ghost to help guide the life of Joey Elliot (John P. Navin, Jr.), the son of lawyer George Elliot (Brandon Maggert), when his family moves into Jennifer's mansion at 32 Rexford Drive in Beverly Hills. Georgia Engel is Joey's mother, Susan, and Mya Akerling is his sister, Marilyn. The theme is sung by Joey Scarbury.

92.   Joe and Mabel CBS, 1955–1956

Joe Sparton (Larry Blyden) is an independent cab driver (plate T124T) who lives at 764 Chauncey Street in Brooklyn, New York (cab rates are 25 cents for the first fifth of a mile; five cents for each additional fifth of a mile). He is dating the marriage-minded Mabel Spooner (Nita Talbot), a manicurist at the Westside Beauty Shop in Manhattan (934-3114 is its phone number). Mabel lives at 2314 Bushwick Avenue (Apartment 3H) in Brooklyn with her mother, Adele (Luella Gear), and 14-year-old brother, Sherman (Michael Mann). Mabel mentioned that in 1950 she worked at the Beverly Hills Hotel; Joe's favorite eatery is Mac's Coffee Shop; and he and Mabel met on a blind date. Wilbur Hatch composed the theme. Based on the radio series (NBC, 1941–42) with Ted de Crosia (as Joe Spartan) and Ann Thomas (as Mabel Stooler).

93.   The Joey Bishop Show NBC, 1961–1964; CBS, 1964–1965

The original format, 1961–62, finds Joey Barnes (Joey Bishop) employed by the public relations firm of Wellington, Willoughby and Jones (originally the J.P. Willoughby Company). He is a bachelor and lives on Wilshire Boulevard with his mother (Madge Blake), sister Stella (Marlo Thomas) and brother Larry (Warren Berlinger). Joey, a former boy scout and Army sergeant (82nd Airborne Division, Abel Company), gives his mother $300 a month to run the house. Stella is studying to become an actress; Larry is attending medical school (he has a $60 used skeleton called "Mr. Bones"). Joey's catchphrase is "Son of a gun" and 257-7934 is his phone number. In the revised version, Joey is a former night club comedian who hosts *The Joey Barnes Show*, a daily talk-variety series. He lives at the Carlton Arms Apartments in New York City, is married to Ellie (Abby Dalton) and the father of Joey Barnes, Jr. (Matthew David Smith). Larry Corbett (Corbett Monica) is Joey's writer, winner of the 1963 TV Critics "Writer of the Year Award." Prior to this role, Corbett played Johnny Edwards, a comedian at the Purple Pussycat Club who substituted for Joey when he went on vacation. Herbert Spencer composed the original theme; Sammy Cahn and James Van Heusen the revised theme with lyrics.

94.   Karen NBC, 1964–1965

Karen Scott (Debbie Watson) is a 16-year-old sophomore at Beverly High School. She lives with her parents, Steve and Barbara (Richard Denning, Mary LaRoche), and sister, Mimi (Gina Gillespie), in southern California at 90 Bristol Court; later at 437 Maple Lane in Los Angeles. Karen has aspirations to be an actress and has the trust of her parents (who do not want to overprotect her). Her friends' parents feel she is dependable and her girlfriends believe Karen "has a natural beauty that attracts boys." Mimi attends Beverly Junior High, has a 9:00 P.M. curfew and calls her parents disciplining Karen "being mean to her." Steve, a lawyer, calls it "being fair." Originally broadcast as a segment of *90 Bristol Court*. The Beach Boys sing the theme, "Karen."

95.   Karen ABC, 1975

Karen Angelo (Karen Valentine) is an idealistic staff worker for Open America, a Capitol Hill citizens lobby in Washington, D.C. Dale W. Bush (Denver Pyle, Charles Lane) is the stern, no-nonsense founder of Open America and demands results when his people lobby. Karen, a graduate of Berkeley, lives at 1460 Cambridge Street in Jamestown. Benny Golson composed the theme.

96.   Kate and Allie CBS, 1984–1989

An unspecified apartment in New York's Greenwich Village is home to childhood friends Katherine "Kate" Elizabeth Ann McArdle (Susan Saint James) and Allison "Allie" Julie Charlotte Adams Lowell (Jane Curtin). Kate, divorced, is the mother of Emma (Ari Meyers) and works for the Sloane Travel Agency. She has an account (375-70-60-572) at the Holland Savings Bank and during the 1960s, when she attended Berkeley, Kate went to Woodstock, burned her bra in protest and participated in sit-ins. Allie, a divorcee, is the mother of Jennie and Chip (Allison Smith, Frederick Koehler). Allie attends night classes at Washington Square College and worked at Manhattan Cable Station G before she and Kate formed their own company, Kate and Allie Caterers. In 1987, Allie marries Bob Barsky (Sam Freed), a sportscaster for WNTD-TV, Channel 10 in Washington, D.C. Bob commutes and he and Allie relocate to Apartment 21C at West 55th Street. Jennie and Emma attend an unnamed high school. Emma later attends UCLA; Jennie, Columbia University. Chip has two cats (Iggie and Triston) and a Sunday morning job delivering bagels to the neighbors. John Leffler sings the theme, "Along Comes a Friend."

97.   Laverne and Shirley ABC, 1976–1983

Laverne DeFazio (Penny Marshall) and Shirley Feeney (Cindy Williams) are best friends who share Apartment A at 730 Knapp Street in Milwaukee, Wisconsin, during the 1960s (address also given as 730 Hampton Street). The characters, who first appeared on *Happy Days*, work together in the beer bottle capping division of the Shotz Brewery (at $1.35 an hour) and shop at Slotnick's Supermarket. They are graduates of Fillmore High School and served a hitch in the Army. (They trained at Camp McClellan and played prostitutes in the Army training film *This Can Happen to You*. Shirley wrote of her military experiences under the pen name S. Wilhelmina Feeney.) In high school, they were members of the group the Angora Debs. Their superior in the Army was Sergeant Alvinia Plout (Vicki Lawrence) who was called "The Frog."

Laverne, an Italian Catholic, wears a large capital *L* on all her clothes, including her lingerie. She has a fear of small places and her favorite foods are milk mixed with Pepsi, Scooter Pies, and sauerkraut on raisin bread sandwiches. As a little girl, Laverne had the nickname "Messy Pants." Laverne dated Randolph Carpenter (Ted Danson), a fireman who was ready to propose but lost his life in the line of duty.

Shirley is an Irish Protestant and has a plush cat named Boo Boo Kitty. She greets people with "Hi-Yooo" and says "Bye-Yooo" for goodbye. She is famous "for my Shirley Feeney scarfdance" and never orders chicken with extra barbecue sauce ("It's too messy and gets under my nails"). She drives Laverne crazy with the "Ringo Dream" (wherein Shirley imagines that her idol, Ringo Starr, is in love with her) and her memories of kindergarten are of Candy Zarvarkes who made her eat a box of Crayola crayons.

After being stuck in a rut for five years, the girls decide to move to California. They now live at 113½ Laurel Vista Drive and work as gift wrappers at Bardwell's Department Store. A year later Shirley marries Dr. Walter Meeney and Laverne finds work at the Ajax Aerospace Company. Shirley's original boyfriend was Carmine Ragusa (Eddie Mekka), a singing messenger who was called the "Big Ragu" (he called Shirley "Angel Face"). His phone number was Klondike 5-1321.

Leonard "Lenny" Kosnoski (Michael McKean) and Andrew "Squiggy" Squigman (David L. Lander) are Laverne and Shirley's counterparts. They live above the girls in Milwaukee and work as beer truck drivers for the Shotz Brewery. In California, they are ice cream vendors with a truck (Squignoski's Ice Cream) and co-owners of the Squignoski Talent Agency of Burbank (where they seek young starlets to appear in a movie they have written called *Blood Orgy of the Amazon*). Their favorite food is Bosco—which they put on everything.

Lenny had one toy and one pet turtle as a kid. The toy was sauerkraut and the turtle killed itself when it tried to scratch Lenny's name off its back. Lenny likes horror movies and was co-owner with Squiggy of a restaurant they called Dead Lazlo's Place, after its late owner, Lenny's Uncle Lazlo. (Shirley worked there as Betty the waitress; Laverne did the cooking.) Squiggy's prized possession is his moth collection. He is a Lutheran and collects old sandwiches and toe nail clippings. He boasts of being blessed with "The Squigman Birthmark" (a large red blotch shaped like Abraham Lincoln).

Laverne's father, Frank DeFazio (Phil Foster), was owner of the Milwaukee-based Pizza Bowl (a pizzeria and bowling alley). In California episodes, he owns a Cowboy Bill's Western Grub fast food store ("Stuff Your Face the Western Way"). As a child, Frank called Laverne "Muffin." Frank is married to Edna Babbish (Betty Garrett), Laverne and Shirley's landlady. Edna had been married five times before. Each time the wedding had to be postponed and each marriage ended in divorce. She originally lived in Madison, Wisconsin, and is the mother of a retarded daughter named Amy (Linda Gillin). Cyndi Grecco sings the theme, "Make Our Dreams Come True."

Animated Extension Series

1. *Laverne and Shirley in the Army*, ABC, 1981–1982. Laverne and Shirley's antics as army privates stationed at Camp Fillmore. Their superior is Sergeant Squeely, the U.S. Army's only talking pig. *Voices:* Penny Marshall (Laverne), Cindy Williams (Shirley), Ron Palillo (Sgt. Squeely).

2. *Laverne and Shirley with the Fonz*, ABC, 1982–1983. The further antics of Camp Fillmore Army privates Laverne and Shirley and their friend the Fonz, a private in charge of the motor pool. Their superior is Sgt. Squeely, a talking pig. *Voices:* Julie McWhirter (Laverne), Lynne Stewart (Shirley), Henry Winkler (Fonzie), Ron Palillo (Sgt. Squeely).

98.   Leave It to Beaver CBS, 1957–1958; ABC, 1958–1963

Ward and June Cleaver (Hugh Beaumont, Barbara Billingsley) and their children, Wally and Theodore (Tony Dow, Jerry Mathers), live at 211 Pine Street in the small town of Mayfield. Before the Cleavers move to a new home at 211 Lakewood Avenue, their address was also given as 211 Maple Street and 211 Pine Avenue. Their phone number is KL5-4763. Madison is the neighboring town and the boys play ball at Metzger's Field. In the first episode only, the Cleavers have a maid named Minerva.

Ward enjoys fishing and reading the *Mayfield Press*. He grew up on Shannon Avenue (in the Shaker Heights section of town) and was a member of the 4H Club. He was on the shotput team in high school and studied engineering in college. He was also an engineer with the Seabees during World War II but his current profession (other than being a businessman) is not revealed. He drives a sedan with the license plate WJG 865 (later KJG 865). He and June are strict but not stern parents. They never spank their sons but when it comes to punishing or disciplining them, Wally and Theodore know what to face: a lecture by their father in the study (Ward often asks his sons what their punishment should be). June rarely disagrees with Ward's decisions. She is an excellent cook and loves to wear jewelry. (During filming it was noticed that Barbara Billingsley photographed with a brown spot on her neck. This was due to her muscle tone and she wore pearls to hide it.) June, maiden name Bronson, was educated in a boarding school (where she received a letter in basketball).

Wallace, nicknamed Wally, is the older brother. He is in the eighth grade at the Grant Avenue School when the series begins. He later attends Mayfield High School then State College. In high school Wally becomes a three-letter man. He is captain of the varsity football team and 53.2 seconds is his best time on the Mayfield High swim team. He wears Arabian Knights aftershave lotion and has locker 221 (its combination lock is 10-30-11). Wally drives a car with the plate JHJ 335 and he and his girlfriend, Julie Foster (Cheryl Holdridge), had their first date at the White Fox Restaurant.

Theodore is named after June's Aunt Martha's brother. He acquired the nickname of "Beaver" when Wally couldn't pronounce Theodore and said "Tweder." Ward and June thought "Beaver" sounded better. Beaver, also called the "Beave," attends the Grant Avenue School and then Mayfield High. He wears a green baseball cap, hates "mushy stuff" and likes "to mess around with junk." He would "rather smell a skunk than see a girl" and Miller's Pond is his favorite "fishin' hole." The most challenging thing Beaver does is walk half on the curb and half in the street on his way home from school. He played a tree in a kindergarten play and Hans in his fifth grade production of *The Little Dutch Boy*. Beaver had a teddy bear named Billy and tried playing the clarinet for the second grade school orchestra. Mary Margaret Matthews (Lori Martin) was the first girl Beaver found attractive (she called him "Teddy"). The first mishap Wally and Beaver encountered was buying an alligator for $2.50 from an ad in the comic book *Robot Man of Mars*.

Edward W. Haskell (Ken Osmond), better known as Eddie, is Wally's wisecracking friend (he and Wally met in the second grade). Eddie is extremely polite to adults (he fears their authority) but mean to everyone else, especially Beaver (whom he calls "Squirt"; he calls Wally "Sam," "Gertrude" and "Ellwood"). Eddie attends the same schools as Wally and lives at 175 Grant Avenue. *Woody Woodpecker* is his favorite TV show and he is allergic to mayonnaise. Eddie, who claims his middle name is Clark in another episode, was the first to get a credit card (number 06212312) from the Universal Gas and Oil Company.

Clarence Rutherford (Frank Bank), the overweight friend of Wally and Eddie, is nicknamed "Lumpy." He takes tuba lessons and drives "a sickly green car" with the plate PZR 342; his phone number is 433-6733 and his father, Fred (Richard Deacon), is Ward's boss. Fred calls Ward "Lord of the Manor." He is married to Geraldine (Helen Parrish); his wife in later episodes is named Gwen and is played by Majel Barrett and Margaret Stewart. Fred originally talked about having three children: a girl, Violet (Wendy Winkelman), and two boys who were offered football scholarships. Later, he has only two children, Lumpy and Violet (Veronica Cartwright).

Beaver's friends were Larry Mondello (Rusty Stevens), Gilbert Grover (Stephen Talbot) and Hubert "Whitey" Whitney (Stanley Fafara). Larry was first credited as Robert Stevens; Gilbert was first introduced as Gilbert Harrison, then Gilbert Gates and finally Gilbert Bates. Judy Hessler (Jeri Weil) is the obnoxious girl who kisses up to teachers and annoys Beaver and his friends with her smug attitude. She was replaced by Penny Woods (Karen Sue Trent), a similar character, in last-season episodes.

Cornelia Raeburn (Doris Packer) is the principal of the Grant Avenue School, Alice Landers (Sue Randall) is Beaver's caring teacher, and Gus (Burt Mustin) is the old fire chief Beaver visits at Fire Station Number 5. Michael Johnson and Melvyn Lenard composed the theme, "The Toy Parade."

Origins

It's a Small World, Syn. 1957 (as a segment of *Studio '57*). The original pilot starred Barbara Billingsley (June Cleaver), Casey Adams (Ward Cleaver), Paul Sullivan (Wally), Jerry Mathers (Beaver), Richard Deacon (Mr. Baxter) and Harry Shearer (Frankie). The character of Mr. Baxter would become Fred Rutherford and the Frankie character, Eddie Haskell. The pilot story finds Wally and Beaver attempting to collect 1,000 Franklin Milk Company bottle caps to win a free bicycle.

Updates

1. *Still the Beaver*, CBS, 3/19/83. A TV movie that is set in Mayfield 20 years later. June (Barbara Billingsley) is now a widow. Wally (Tony Dow) is a lawyer and married to Mary Ellen (Janice Kent). Beaver (Jerry Mathers) is married to Kimberly (Joanna Gleason) and is the father of Corey and

Oliver (Corey Feldman, John Snee). Eddie Haskell (Ken Osmond), owner of the Eddie Haskell Construction Company, is married to Gert (not seen) and the father of Eddie Haskell, Jr. (Eric Osmond). The story finds Theodore, now 33 years old, attempting to turn his life around (he feels he is "Still the Beaver" and plagued by life's misfortune).

2. *The New Leave It to Beaver*, TBS, 1986–1989. June (Barbara Billingsley) lives in the original series house at 211 Pine Street with Beaver (Jerry Mathers) and his sons, Kip and Oliver (Kipp Marcus, John Snee). Beaver and Kimberly (Joanna Gleason) are now divorced. Wally (Tony Dow) lives at 213 Pine Street with his wife, Mary Ellen (Janice Kent), and daughter, Kelly (Kaleena Kiff). Eddie Haskell (Ken Osmond) and his wife, Gert (Ellen Maxted), are the parents of Freddie and Bomber (Eric Osmond, Christian Osmond). Lumpy Rutherford (Frank Bank) is married and the father of J.J. (Keri Houlihan).

Beaver and Lumpy are partners in the Cleaver and Rutherford Company (exactly what they do is not revealed). Wally is a private-practice attorney and Eddie runs the somewhat shady Eddie Haskell Construction Company. Pop Tarts and beer is Eddie's favorite breakfast and chocolate pudding his favorite dessert. His son, the wisecracking Freddie, attends Mayfield High School while the mischievous Bomber is enrolled in the Vicksburg Military School.

Kip attends Mayfield High while Oliver and Kelly attend the Grant Avenue School. Kelly is a member of the Junior Chipmunks and the Mayfield Youth Soccer Team. Kip's first job was attendant at Vince's Full Service Gas Station. Oliver, called "Ollie" by Beaver, has a pet dove (Wilma) and finds the clothes hamper the perfect place to hide. He and Kelly hang out at the Soda Shop.

The population of Mayfield was given as 18,240. June's license plate reads NO. 1 MOM (she is a member of the Mayfield City Council); Beaver's license plate is G 102; Lumpy's Mercedes plate is 20 3056.

99. The Life of Riley DuMont, 1949–1950; NBC, 1953–1958

Chester A. Riley (Jackie Gleason), his wife, Peg (Rosemary DeCamp), and his children, Babs and Junior (Gloria Winters, Lanny Rees), live at 1313 Blue View Terrace in Los Angeles. Riley, as he is called, and his neighbor Jim Gillis (Sid Tomack) earn $59 a week as riveters for Stevenson Aircraft and Associates. Jim and his wife, Olive (Maxine Semon), whom he calls "Honeybee," were married with Chester and Peg in a double wedding ceremony in Brooklyn in 1932. Babs attends North Hollywood High; Junior and Jim's son, Egbert (George McDonald), attend the John J. Boskowitz Junior High School. Lou Kosloff composed the theme.

The revised NBC version finds Chester A. Riley (William Bendix), his wife, Peg (Marjorie Reynolds), and their children, Babs and Junior (Lugene Sanders, Wesley Morgan), living first at 1313 Blue View Terrace then at 5412 Grove Street and finally 3412 Del Mar Vista in Los Angeles. Riley and his friend Jim Gillis (Tom D'Andrea) work as riveters for the Cunningham Aircraft Company. Jim's wife Olive, nicknamed "Honeybee," is played by Veda Ann Borg, Marie Brown, and Gloria Blondell; their son, Egbert, by George Mitchell. Babs married Don Marshall (Martin Milner) and set up housekeeping at 1451 Blue View Terrace. Riley's catchphrase is "What a revoltin' development this is." Jerry Fielding composed the theme. Based on the radio series (CBS, 1941; ABC, 1944–45; NBC, 1945–51) that starred Lionel Stander and William Bendix as Riley. There is also a 1948 NBC pilot (4/13) with Herb Vigran (Riley), Alice Drake (Peg), Lou Krugman (Jim), Jo Gilbert (Honeybee).

Life with Lucy *see* I Love Lucy

100.   Life with Luigi CBS, 1952–1953

Luigi Basco (J. Carroll Naish, Vito Scotti) is an Italian immigrant who owns Luigi Basco Antiques at 21 North Halstead Street in Chicago's Little Italy (he lives in the back of the store and Circle 2-0742 is his phone number). His most cherished possession is a bust of George Washington that was made in 1833. Pasquale (Alan Reed, Thomas Gomez), the owner of Pasquale's Spaghetti Palace at 19 North Halstead Street, brought Luigi here from Italy in a plan for him to marry his overweight daughter, Rosa (Jody Gilbert, Muriel Landers). Pasquale calls Luigi "Cabbage Puss" and "Little Banana Nose." Luigi has an account at the Chase National Bank (he pays Pasquale $40 a month rent) and wears a size 38 suit. Pasquale wears a size 54 suit; Rosa a size 50 dress. Each episode opens and closes with Luigi writing of his experiences to his Mama Basco in Italy. Lud Gluskin performs the "Oh Marie" theme. Based on the radio series (CBS, 1948–53) with J. Carrol Naish, Alan Reed and Jody Gilbert in the same roles.

101.   Love That Bob NBC, 1955; 1957–1959; CBS, 1955–1957

Bob Collins (Bob Cummings) is a photographer whose job requires him to capture the world's most beautiful women on film. He owns his own business (Bob Collins—Photography) in downtown Hollywood, and lives at 804 Grummond Road with his widowed sister, Margaret (Rosemary De-Camp), and her teenage son, Chuck MacDonald (Dwayne Hickman).

Bob was born in Joplin, Missouri, and is descended from Scottish ancestors. He claims his fascination for girls began at the age of four when he started playing post office (Margaret says "Bob is now the Post Master General"). He served a hitch in the Air Force during World War II and his hobby is flying (he has a rarely seen twin-engine Beechcraft). Bob, "The Casanova of the Camera" (as Margaret calls him) says "I'm a confirmed bachelor" but "I'm married to my camera. Any other type of marriage is a serious commitment and I need time before settling down. I need time to find the right person—no matter how many girls I have to date to find her." Margaret says "All the Collins men are confirmed bachelors until something snaps and they suddenly get married."

Bob wears a cologne called Moustache ("That drives girls crazy") and considers his models "lumps of clay" that "I mold into bright, shimmering butterflies. I give them grace, style and charm." Bob's work is seen in the various fashion magazines and his swimsuit models cannot have a waist larger than 23 inches. His worst month is June—when girls are the most marriage-minded and he finds it difficult to remain single.

When Bob does decide to get married there is someone waiting for him—Charmaine Schultz (Ann B. Davis), Bob's plain-looking girl Friday. Schultzy, as she is called, is totally dedicated to Bob and in love with him—"I can't compete with the models on the sofa, but give me the kitchen and food and I'll land him." Bob feels comfortable with Schultzy (who calls him "Boss") because "before Schultzy I would train girls only to lose them to marriage."

Also seeking Bob's hand in marriage is Shirley Swanson (Joi Lansing), a gorgeous model whom Bob calls "Wild Flower" (Schultzy calls her "Blondie"). Shirley measures 38-26-36 and wears a perfume called Bachelor's Doom. Although she does not have that 23-inch waist, Bob lets her model bathing suits ("I may be strict but I'm not crazy"). Shirley has some talent in the kitchen ("I can make ham and eggs") and mentioned she lived opposite Bob's studio in a large white building with a red tile roof.

Margaret takes care of the house. She cooks, cleans and does the shopping and Bob feels she should marry again. Margaret, however, feels she is not ready to settle down, and is dating Paul Fonda (Lyle Talbot), Bob's World War II Air Force buddy (now an airline pilot).

"Bob is a kind man," say Margaret. "He lets us share his house and is putting Chuck through school." But Margaret also worries about Bob's influence on Chuck as he has been raised in "an atmosphere of girls, girls, girls." Chuck has no complaints and hopes that whatever his Uncle Bob has "it can be inherited by a nephew." Bob feels Margaret is overprotective and worries too much about Chuck. "It all started when Chuck was an infant," he says. "She put him in a highchair and he cried. She called the pediatrician to see if he had the colic, then a child psychologist to see if he had acrophobia. She finally called the upholsterer to pad the highchair. Altogether it cost $150 to find out the kid needed changing."

Chuck first attended Hollywood High School and was a member of the R.O.T.C. drill team. He joined the National Guard after graduation and later enrolled in Gridley College (where he majored in premed). Chuck originally dated Francine Williams (Diane Jergens). College episodes find him dating Carol Henning (Olive Sturgess), a coed at nearby Beaumont University.

Photography runs in the Collins family. Bob's father was in the business as is his elderly but young-at-heart grandfather Joshua "Josh" Collins (Bob Cummings in a dual role). Josh owns Josh Collins—Photography in Joplin, Missouri, and lives in a drafty old house that his father built (and died from pneumonia in). Josh is a member of the Joplin Globetrotters basketball team and like Bob, has an eye for the girls and can guess their measurements. His favorite song is "Some Enchanted Evening" and he calls Bob "Young Rooster," Chuck "Chuckie Boy" and Margaret "Mag Pie."

Harvey Helm (King Donovan) is Bob's friend (his copilot during the war). He is a henpecked wholesale furniture salesman for the Gravener Furniture Company and married to Ruthie (Mary Lawrence), a former swimsuit model of Bob's. Bob, called "Bobby Boy" by Harvey, says "Harvey brings home the bacon, but his wife decides how to slice it." Pamela Livingston (Nancy Kulp) is Bob's friend, a member of the Bird Watchers' Society, and Frank Crenshaw (Dick Wesson) is the sailor with a crush on Schultzy.

Marie DiPaola (Donna Martel) is the Italian model Bob calls "My Little Venutian Ambassador of Loveliness" (she calls him Roberto, and her kitchen specialty is meatballs and spaghetti). Collette DuBois (Lisa Gaye) is the French model Bob calls "Sly Little Thief"; her culinary expertise is pancakes. The series was originally called *The Bob Cummings Show*, but titled *Love That Bob* for syndication. Both versions open with Bob pointing a camera at the screen and saying "Hold it, I think you're gonna like this picture." Mahlon Merrick composed the theme.

102.   Love That Jill ABC, 1958

Jill Johnson (Anne Jeffreys) and Jack Gibson (Robert Sterling) are the rival owners of all-girl modeling agencies in New York City. Jill owns Model Girls, Inc., at 670 Madison Avenue and lives at 1064 Park Avenue, Apartment 14A; Plaza 6-7017 is her phone number. Jack owns the Gibson Girls (at 540 Madison Avenue) and lives at 1360 West 63rd Street (*TV Guide* incorrectly lists Jack's agency as the House That Jacques Built). Both agencies cater to TV, film and print ads and neither Jack nor Jill will readily admit that they love each other. Lud Gluskin composed the theme.

The Lucy Show *see* I Love Lucy

103.   Madame's Place Syn. 1982–1983

The theme tells us that "at Madame's Place, she's a prime-time queen; she struts her stuff on the TV screen; her outlandish charm fills this funny farm we call Madame's Place." The "she" being referred to is Madame (a puppet controlled by Wayland Flowers), the host of *Madame's Place*, a talk show broadcast from her Hollywood mansion. Madame, whose antique Roll Royce license plate reads MADAME, began her show business career as a comedian and starred in such films as *Ride the Wild Surf, Trampoline Honeymoon* and *A Woman Named Hey You*. She reads the *Enquiring Star*, has been married six times and is a member of the Fetish of the Month Club. She orders her body lotion, Me Tarzan—You Jane, from the House of Pleasure catalogue. Sara Joy Pitts (Judy Landers) is Madame's stunning blonde niece. She measures 37-24-36 and is hoping to become an actress "like my Auntie Madame." Sara Joy wears cleavage-revealing blouses and short shorts and loves the TV soap opera *The Young and the Stupid*. Walter Pinkerton (Johnny Haymer), called "Pinky" by Madame, is Madame's butler. Larry Lunch (John Moschitta, Jr.), owner of the Lunch Agency, is Madame's exasperating, super-fast-talking agent, and Rollin Espinoza (Hector Elias) leads the Madame's Place All-Divorced Orchestra. Lynn LaVecque (Barbara Cason) is Madame's competition, the host of *Naked All-Star Bowling*. Denise DeCaro sings the theme, "Here at Madame's Place."

104.   Make Room for Daddy ABC, 1953–1957; CBS, 1957–1964

Danny Williams (Danny Thomas), his wife, Margaret (Jean Hagen), and their children, Terry (Sherry Jackson, Penny Parker) and Rusty (Rusty

Hamer), live at the Parkside Apartments (Apartment 1204) in Manhattan. Danny is a night club entertainer who performs at the Copa Club in New York City. He was born in Toledo, Ohio, and attended Ursuline Academy (a Catholic school run by the nuns of the Ursuline Order; in another episode, Danny mentions he was born in Deerfield, Michigan, raised in Toledo, and attended Woodward High School). He enjoys reading the magazine, *The Saturday Evening Post.*

Danny, 24, met his future wife, Margaret Summers, when she was 17 years old. He was a struggling young stand-up comedian; she worked as a part-time waitress and piano player (in another episode, Margaret mentions she and Danny have known each other since they were children). Margaret was born in Baraboo, Wisconsin, and was cared for by Mom and Pop Finch while her parents were on the road in vaudeville. The family has a pet dog named Laddie.

Actress Jean Hagen wanted to leave the series. The 1955 season ended with Danny's emotional talk with Terry and Rusty that their mother "had gone to Heaven." The following season found Danny as a widower struggling to raise two children with the help of his maid, Louise (Louise Beavers, Amanda Randolph). Various actresses were brought on to date Danny and win over the affections of his children. At the close of the 1956–57 season, Danny hires Kathleen "Kathy" O'Hara (Marjorie Lord), a widowed nurse, to care for Rusty, who had come down with a case of the measles. Kathy, the mother of a young daughter named Patty (Lelani Sorenson), soon catches the measles and is quarantined in the Williams apartment. A romance develops and Danny proposes to Kathy (ending the ABC series). When the CBS series begins (now called *The Danny Thomas Show*) Danny and Kathy are married and Kathy's daughter is now Linda (Angela Cartwright). When Danny was courting Kathy he would bring her roses and candy.

Kathy was born in Peoria, Illinois. She and Danny honeymooned in Las Vegas (Room 504 of the Sands Hotel). The CBS episodes find the Williams family now living at 505 East 56th Street (Apartment 542; also given as 781) in Manhattan. Their phone number is Plaza 3-1098; also given as Plaza 3-0198. Danny calls Kathy "Clancy" and her maiden name is also given as Daly. Although they have a maid, Kathy can be seen cleaning the apartment in many episodes.

Teresa (Terry) is Danny's oldest child. She attended West Side High School then goes to an unnamed college (where she is a member of the Alpha Beta Chi sorority). At this point Terry was written out but returned to marry Pat Hannigan (Pat Harrington, Jr.), a night club performer.

Russell (Rusty) was born on February 15, 1947. He attended P.S. 54,

Claremont Junior High School and then West Side High. He is a member of Scout Troop 44 and in 1956 called himself Elvis Earp (combining his favorite singer, Elvis Presley, with his favorite TV show, *The Life and Legend of Wyatt Earp*). He also ran away from home and began a career as an orphan at Miss Martin's Home for Children. His first crush was on a girl named Sylvia Watkins (Pamela Beaird) and he felt the best part of school was recess, lunch and holidays. (He is the best speller in his class and won several spelling bees. He always seems to get "a leaky old fountain pen.")

Linda attends P.S. 54 and has milk and cookies when she comes home from school. She believes in the Tooth Fairy and Santa Claus and has an "imaginary" friend who nobody believes exists, called Mr. Jumbo. (He is ten feet tall and wears a red coat. He did actually exist—as the doorman at the Drake Hotel.)

In Terry's absence, Danny sponsored Italian high school exchange student Gina Minelli (Annette Funicello). She attends West Side High and tutors the school's star football players, Buck Weaver and Bronco Lewis (Mr. Inside and Mr. Outside on the team). Frankie Laine is her favorite singer and she had a dream become a reality when Danny arranged for Frankie to sing at her bedside when she came down with the measles and couldn't attend his performance at school.

Danny's Uncle Tonoose (Hans Conried) is the self-proclaimed head of the family. He is nicknamed "Hashush-al-kabaar" (Lebanese for "The man who made a monkey out of a camel") and loves goat cheese and grape leaves. He claims the family ancestors include King Achmed the Unwashed. Prior to his role as Uncle Tonoose, Hans Conried played Margaret's Cousin Carl, who "drank and traveled with jugs of wine." Charlie Halper (Sid Melton) is Danny's boss, the owner of the Copa Club; Pat Carroll plays his wife, Bunny.

Updates

1. *The Danny Thomas TV Family Reunion*, NBC, 2/14/65. A special that reunites the cast of *The Danny Thomas Show* for a series of skits that continues to depict events in the lives of the Williams family: Danny (Danny Thomas), Kathy (Marjorie Lord), Rusty (Rusty Hamer), Linda (Angela Cartwright), Louise (Amanda Randolph) and Uncle Tonoose (Hans Conried).

2. *Make More Room for Daddy*, NBC, 11/6/67. A segment of *The Danny Thomas Hour* that reunites Danny Thomas (as Danny Williams) with his former costars: Marjorie Lord (Kathy), Rusty Hamer (Rusty), Angela Cartwright (Linda), and Sid Melton (Charlie Halper). Linda is now in college and Rusty has enlisted in the Army. It is here that Rusty falls in love with Susan MacAdams (Jana Taylor), the daughter of Colonel MacAdams (Edward Andrews).

3. ***Make Room for Granddaddy***, CBS, 9/14/69. The pilot for the ABC series of the same title (1970–1971). The story finds Danny and Kathy (Danny Thomas, Marjorie Lord) becoming grandparents when Rusty's (Rusty Hamer) wife, Susan (Jana Taylor), gives birth to a boy they name Michael. The series, however, changes key aspects of the pilot. Michael is advanced to the age of six (Michael Hughes) and is now the son of Terry (Sherry Jackson). Terry is married to Bill Johnson (who is not seen; no explanation is given as to what happened to her original husband, Pat Hannegan). In order for Terry to join Bill, a serviceman stationed in Japan, Terry leaves Michael in Danny and Kathy's care (hence the title). Linda (Angela Cartwright) is attending a boarding school in Connecticut and Rusty and Susan (Rusty Hamer, Jana Taylor) are struggling newlyweds. Sid Melton and Hans Conried recreated their roles as Charlie Halper and Uncle Tonoose.

105. **Mama's Family** NBC, 1983–1984; Syn., 1986

Thelma "Mama" Harper (Vicki Lawrence) is a cantankerous widow who lives at 1542 Ray Lane in Raytown, U.S.A. Also living with her are her son, Vinton (Ken Berry), his wife, Naomi (Dorothy Lyman), and Sonia and Vinton, Jr. (Karin Argoud, Eric Brown), Vint's children from a failed first marriage (to a woman named Mitzi, who ran out on him). Their address is also given as 1542 Ray Way. James Ray founded the town; the Tomb of the Unknown Raytonian is the major tourist attraction and Ray Point is the make-out spot.

Mama's late husband, who called her "Snooky Ookems," was named Carl. Thelma is a member of the Raytown Community Church League and the founder of M.O.P. (Mothers Opposing Pornography). She inherited Captain Petey, the parrot of her "crazy" Uncle Cyrus (who thought he was a pirate), and wears a perfume called Obsession. She uses Easy-Off to clean the stove and can force people to tell the truth with a stare she calls the "Look." Mama attempted to market Mother Harper's Miracle Tonic (a cold remedy that contained her secret ingredient—pure vanilla extract. With its 35 percent alcohol content, the tonic intoxicated users). She has a treasured recipe (Million Dollar Fudge) and held a job as a receptionist at the Raytown Travel Agency. Mama's house was originally a brothel called Ma Beaudine's and was located at 10 Decatur Road. As a kid she was jump rope champion of the second grade; she won first runner-up in the Lovely Be Lady Grandma U.S.A. Pageant.

Vinton was born on April 23 and weighed 8 pounds, 2 ounces (he was 22 inches long). He works as a locksmith for Kwick Keys (owned by the Bernice Corporation) and has a *TV Guide* collection dating back to 1958. He is a member of the Mystic Order of the Cobra Club and hangs out at the Bigger Jigger Bar (where he won a talent contest by imitating Fred Astaire; the success went to his head and he tried to break into show business as Vinnie Vegas). Vinton has an insurance policy with Mutual of Raytown and eats Dino Puffs cereal for breakfast (not for its high fiber count but for the free dinosaur that comes in every box). As a kid, Vinton had a pet rabbit named Fluffy.

Naomi Oates, "the sexiest woman in Raytown," married Vinton in 1983. She had four previous marriages, to Bill, George, Leonard and Tom. Naomi, called "Skeeter" by Vinton, works as a cashier at the Food Circus supermarket. Thelma dislikes Naomi and believes "she is the kind of girl mothers fear their sons will marry." Naomi wrestled (as the "Queen Bee") in the women's wrestling championships (she battled the Masked Mabels and Vinton was her ringside attendant, the "Bee Keeper"). Red licorice is Naomi's favorite candy, and as a kid she had a dog named Marlon.

Sonia and Vinton, Jr., nicknamed Buzz, attended Raytown High School. Sonia, who has a midnight curfew, was named after her cousin, "a school teacher for 35 years who went berserk and set the gym on fire." Buzz has a 1 A.M. curfew. He and Sonia were dropped from the syndicated version. Replacing them was Bubba Higgins (Allan Kayser), the son of Mama's neurotic daughter, Eunice Higgins (Carol Burnett). Thelma is also the mother of Ellen Jackson (Betty White), a widowed society woman. Bubba attended Raytown Junior College.

Fran Crawley (Rue McClanahan), Thelma's sister, writes an advice column "for the local paper that is thrown on the porch." Iola Boylen (Beverly Archer) is Thelma's longtime friend and neighbor, a spinster who lives with her never-seen, domineering mother. Iola sews, enjoys arts and crafts and is a member of the Peppermint Playhouse Theater Company. Peter Matz composed the theme, "Bless My Happy Home."

Origins

The program is based on a series of skits that were originally performed on ***The Carol Burnett Show*** from 1974 to 1978. Carol Burnett played Eunice Higgins; Harvey Korman was her husband, Ed; Vicki Lawrence, her mother Thelma Harper; Ken Berry, her brother Philip Harper; and Betty White, Eunice's sister Ellen.

On 3/15/82, CBS aired ***Eunice***, a 90-minute special that reunited the original cast. Act 1, set in 1955, details the bumbling courtship of Eunice and Ed. Act 2, set in 1963, finds Eunice dreaming of becoming an actress when Philip, a successful writer, returns home for a visit. Act 3, set in 1973, finds Eunice's life falling apart and her drifting into alcoholism. The final act is set in 1978 and finds Eunice attempting to get her life back together again (dealing with her sharp-tongued mother, Thelma, and social-climbing sister, Ellen).

106. Margie ABC, 1961–1962

Margie Clayton (Cynthia Pepper) is a pretty teenage girl who lives at 36 Chestnut Lane in the small town of Madison during the 1920s with her parents, Harvey and Nora (Dave Willock, Wesley Marie Tackitt), and brother, Cornell (Johnny Bangert); Central 4734 is their phone number. Margie and her friends Maybelle Jackson (Penny Parker) and Heywood Botts (Tommy Ivo) attend Madison High School (Crawford's Ice Cream Parlor is the after-school hangout). Maybelle lives at 63 Oak Tree Lane; Margie is editor of the school newspaper, the *Bugle*; Harvey is a loan officer of the Great Eastern Savings Bank. Lionel Newman composed the theme adaptation of the song "Margie."

107. The Marriage NBC, 1954

Ben Marriott (Hume Cronyn), an attorney with the firm of Burns and Marriott, and his wife, Liz (Jessica Tandy), a former buyer for Hunt's Department Store, live at 31 West 43rd Street in Manhattan. They are the parents of Emily and Peter (Susan Strasberg, Malcolm Broderick). Ben and Liz bank at the Center Trust Company and Ben's biggest challenge is to balance the checkbook. Emily, whose hair curls in 18.3 and 7/10 seconds when she gets a permanent, is not permitted to eat chocolate ice cream (Liz says "It's bad for your skin"). Emily attends Grant High School and her at-home dates consist of "listening to the phonograph and popping corn." Peter likes building antique model cars and reading comic books while taking a bath. The family heirloom is a bible that has been handed down from their grandfather. Based on the radio series (NBC, 1953–54).

108. The Mary Tyler Moore Show CBS, 1970–1977

WJM-TV, Channel 12, is a local, independent station in Minneapolis, Minnesota. Mary Richards (Mary Tyler Moore) is an attractive, single woman in her thirties who works as the assistant producer of *The Six O'Clock News* program. Lou Grant (Edward Asner) produces the show, Murray Slaughter (Gavin McLeod) writes it, and Ted Baxter (Ted Knight) is the newscaster.

Mary, a Presbyterian, lives in Apartment D at 119 North Weatherly (her rent is $125 a month). She was born in Roseburg, Minnesota, and was head cheerleader and most popular girl in high school (her parents gave her a brown Hudson as a graduation gift). Mary keeps complete records on everything she does or buys and makes chocolate chip cookies to impress guests. She enjoys a chef's salad for lunch, does charity work for the YWCA and helps support her grandmother (she sends her $45 a month). Vodka and tonic is her favorite drink and if somebody's stomach growls, Mary believes people will think it is hers. She washes her hair before she goes to the hairdresser and cares about what other people think of her. Her favorite movie is *Gone with the Wind* and her IQ is 118.

Mary has a large *M* on her living room wall, a picture of herself with a poodle on her home desk (near the front door) and can type 65 words a minute. She earned $18,000 in 1969 and is known for throwing terrible parties. Mary was later promoted to producer when Lou decided to make himself the executive producer.

Mary originally sought a secretarial job at the station (which was filled when she applied. Lou offered her the producer's job which paid $10 a week less). Mary has spunk (which Lou hates) and "a nice caboose" (which he likes). It was at Mary's parties that Lou "had some of the worst times of my life"; he also broke up with his wife, Edie (Priscilla Morrill), at one of them. Lou likes to drink and his favorite watering hole is the Happy Hour Bar; his bar bill comes to the station on the 15th of each month. Lou keeps a bottle of liquor in the bottom right drawer of his desk and a picture of himself as a college football player is on his office wall. Lou's favorite actor is John Wayne. He realizes that no matter how hard he tries, his show will never become a ratings winner. Lou enjoys his solitude but finds his life plagued by Sue Ann Nivens (Betty White), the host of the station's *Happy Homemaker Show*, who has advice for everybody and has made it her goal to snag Lou. Though technically not a spinoff, *Lou Grant* (CBS, 1977–1982) allowed Ed Asner to continue as that character in a dramatic series as the city editor of the *Tribune*, the second-largest newspaper in Los Angeles.

Ted Baxter, the incompetent newsman, is a Republican. He has trouble pronouncing words and relies on Murray's talent as a writer to make him look intelligent. Ted also uses Murray's opinions and hopes Murray's will agree with what the president has to say (as he and the president like to think alike). Murray earns much less than Ted ($31,000 a year) and calls Ted's cue cards "Idiot cards." He has an IQ of 125 and has been married to Marie (Joyce Bulifant) since 1955 (Marie's maiden name is McGuire and 555-3727 is their home phone number).

Ted likes to read other people's mail and has made it a goal to be a part of everyone's business. He married the sweet and trusting Georgette Franklin (Georgia Engel), a window dresser at Hempell's Department Store. Ted has a fake newspaper headline on his office wall that reads "Ted Baxter Wins Three Emmys." His hero is Walter Cronkite and he longs for an anchor job in New York. He started his own business, the Ted Baxter Famous Broadcasting School, and calls the station's control room "the technical place." Ted hates to part with money and pays a high school senior $5 a year to prepare his taxes. *Snow White* is Ted's favorite Disney movie and he signs off with "Good Night and Good News." Ted takes six sugars in his coffee, eats at Antonio's Restaurant and was Farmer Ted, the commercial spokesman for Ma and Pa's Country Sausage. In the last episode, Ted mentions he has a dog named WJM.

Rhoda Jo Beth Morganstern (Valerie Harper) is Mary's upstairs neighbor. She is a window dresser at Hempell's Department Store and joins Mary for lunch each afternoon at the station's cafeteria. Rhoda is Jewish. She was born in the Bronx, New York, in December 1941. She won her third grade science fair with a model of the human brain; as a teenager she worked as an usher at Loew's State Theater; and in high school she was a member of a gang called the Sharkettes. She has a goldfish (Goldfish) and was issued a $40 summons for feeding yogurt to a buffalo at the Minneapolis Zoo. Rhoda has a weight problem and tries to eat healthy but is often tempted to eat sweets (and complains that "I should just apply it to my hips"). She calls Mary "Mare."

When Rhoda returns to New York for a two-week vacation, the spinoff series *Rhoda* begins (CBS, 1974–1978). It is here that she meets and marries Joe Gerard (David Groh), the owner of the New York Wrecking Company. They set up housekeeping in Apartment 9B at 332 West 46th Street in Manhattan and Rhoda begins her own decorating business, Windows by Rhoda. Two years later, Rhoda and Joe divorce. She moves to a new apartment (6G, but also seen as 4G) and works for the Doyle Costume Company. Her sister, Brenda Morganstern (Julie Kavner), lives in Apartment 2D and works as a teller at the midtown branch of the First Security Bank in Manhattan. Rhoda's parents, Ida and Martin Morganstern (Nancy Walker, Harold Gould), live in the Bronx near Fordham Road at 3517 Grand Concourse.

On February 7, 2000, ABC aired the TV movie *Mary and Rhoda* that updated the lives of Mary and Rhoda. Mary now lives at 415 84th Street in New York City and is a segment producer for WNYT, Channel 6, a TV news station. She is a recent widow and the mother of Rose (Joie Lenz), an English major at N.Y.U. Mary's late husband, Steve Crowin, was a congressman who died in a rock climbing accident. Mary had previously worked as an in-studio producer for ABC News. She quit to spend time with Rose but had to return to work when she found her husband has squandered all their money on his campaign.

Rhoda, a professional photographer, is divorced from Jean Paul Russo and is the mother of Meredith (Marisa Ryan), a medical school student at Barnard College. Rhoda left Jean Paul for cheating on her and spent several years in Paris. She returned to New York to begin her career (using her maiden name of Morganstern) and to be near her daughter.

Phyllis Lindstrom (Cloris Leachman) owns the building in which Mary lives (although in the pilot Phyllis was a tenant). She is a Democrat, is married to the never-seen Lars (a dermatologist), and is the mother of Bess (Lisa Gerritsen). Bess is very close to Mary and calls her "Aunt Mary." According to Phyllis, "wearing makeup and putting on her mother's wigs" is what Bess does best. In 1975, following the death of Lars, Phyllis and Bess move to San Francisco and the spinoff series, *Phyllis* (CBS, 1975–1977), begins. Phyllis and Bess live at 4482 Bayview Drive and Phyllis first finds work as an assistant to Julie Erskine (Barbara Colby, Liz Torres) at Erskine's Commercial Photography Studio. A year later, she quits to become the administrative assistant to Dan Valenti (Carmine Caridi) of the San Francisco board of administration.

The clocks seen in the station's newsroom are static models (the hands do not move). The station's beloved Chuckles the Clown (Mark Gordon, Richard Schaal) suffered a horrible fate: while dressed as Peter Peanut, the grand marshal of a parade, a rogue elephant crushed him to death in an attempt to shell him. The last episode finds Mary, Lou and Murray being fired while a new team is brought on to work with Ted. Sonny Curtis sings the theme, "Love Is All Around."

109.   M*A*S*H CBS, 1972–1983

During wartime the medical corps fights for every life. Helicopters go right to the battlefields to return wounded soldiers to nearby MASH units. One such Mobile Army Surgical Hospital is the 4077, a unit built on barren ground five miles from the Korean War front in one of the most brutal climates on earth—unbearably hot in the summer, subzero temperatures in the winter. The 4077 is anything but classy. Its doctors and nurses often operate under battle conditions risking their lives to save others. In order to remain sane amid the insanities of war, the personnel act somewhat abnormally.

Captain Benjamin Franklin Pierce (Alan Alda), the doctor most opposed to the war, constantly defies authority. He was born in Crabtree Cove, Maine, and was nicknamed "Hawkeye" by his father (after the main character in *The Last of the Mohicans*. "My father was crazy about that book. He was crazy about Indians"). The nurse-chasing Hawkeye was drafted (he was working in a hospital at the time). He has the dog tag number 19095607 and will not carry a gun. He calls the unit a cesspool and his tent the "Swamp" (where he has a still for making martinis—"the wellspring of life" as he calls them. He has also made it his goal "to find the driest martini that can be found in these parts").

Hawkeye "is the best cutter in the outfit; he is certified in chest and general surgery" and holds the position of chief surgeon (for which he earns $413.50 a month). He complains about the food ("We eat fish and liver day after day. It's against the Geneva Convention. I've eaten a river of liver and an ocean of fish"). What he misses most is "a mattress thicker than a matzoh, my own bathroom and any woman out of uniform and the entire state of Maine." He thinks of himself as the "social director of the heart" for all the temporary relationships he has with nurses.

Hawkeye turns his mind off and hopes it will all go away—"But it doesn't work ... you go back to your job and try to forget there is a war going on." Hawkeye reads *The Joys of Nudity* magazine and starred in the Army documentary *Yankee Doodle Doctor* (as a wacky, Groucho Marx–like surgeon). When the Army shipped a half million tongue depressors to the unit, Hawkeye used them to build a "Monument to Stupidity" but also to represent all the wounded who have passed through the 4077. To relax, Hawkeye collapses after a day of surgery and drinks. He says also "that at night I dream I'm awake."

Hawkeye calls his tentmate Captain "Trapper" John McIntire (Wayne Rogers) "Champion of the oppressed and molester of registered nurses." Trapper was a boxing champion in college and fought in the Army's Inner Camp Boxing Tournament as "Kid Doctor" (he weighed in at 175 pounds). Trapper enjoys smoking cigars and playing poker with Hawkeye, but would like to go AWOL to see his wife and kids. He shares Hawkeye's love of playing practical jokes. When the locals need medical help, Trapper is the one they turn to. He reads *Field and Stream* and *Popular Mechanics* magazines; he played a Harpo Marx–like surgeon in the *Yankee Doodle Doctor* Army film. As a kid Hawkeye had a imaginary friend named Tuttle that he blamed for doing things that got him in trouble. To cover up their smuggling efforts—

to get camp supplies to Sister Theresa's orphanage—Hawkeye and Trapper say they are delivering supplies on orders from a Captain Jonathan Tuttle.

Trapper and Hawkeye never had a chance to say goodbye (Hawkeye returns from R&R in Tokyo with "The Mount Rushmore of hangovers" to learn that Trapper was transferred stateside two hours earlier).

Captain B.J. Hunnicutt (Mike Farrell) replaces Trapper John. B.J. (name never revealed) was born in Mill Valley, California. He is a surgeon fresh from civilian residency and is married to Peggy (May 23 is their wedding anniversary). B.J. attended Stanford Medical School (top 10 in his class) and received the bronze Star (saved a soldier under fire). He is a clean-cut, even-tempered family man who is tempted by nurses but avoids their advances ("I'm hopelessly and passionately in love with my wife"). "Horseplay—taking your frustrations out on other people"—relaxes B.J. B.J., called "Beej" by Hawkeye, misses his wife's cooking.

Major Frank Burns (Larry Linville) also shares a tent with Hawkeye. Frank, nicknamed "Ferret Face," had a lucrative practice before being called up. Hawkeye claims that Frank became a doctor for the money ("He married money and is crazy about money"). Frank says he toyed with the idea of becoming a doctor in high school then decided to do so when his mother asked him ("She's the guiding light of my life"; he keeps a picture of her in a silver frame by his bed). Frank keeps in touch with his patients with his "What's Up Front Doc" letters so they won't forget him. Frank brags about his "$35,000 house and two cars" and misses his country club and 30-foot yacht. Frank played the lead in his college production of *Romeo and Juliet* and likes his pork chops with extra fat. He uses the brokerage house of Sanders, Landers and Flynn in New York City and has set his goal to expose Hawkeye for constantly defying military rules (Hawkeye would like to see Frank transferred to another base—"preferably an enemy base"). Frank is married and fears his wife will discover he is having an affair with Major Margaret Houlihan (Loretta Swit).

Margaret, nicknamed "Hot Lips," is the head nurse and earns $400 a month. She has a spotless record, has been a chief nurse for ten years and "is a woman of passion but a stickler for rules" (which sometimes alienates her from her nurses, "who never make me a part of their activities"). Margaret is regular Army; she would like all the doctors and nurses to behave in a military manner but realizes they won't ("They're terribly unruly and undisciplined and I thank God for each and every one of them when those casualties roll in"). Despite the deplorable conditions, Margaret tries to be beautiful and alluring. She uses her sex appeal to wrap superiors around her finger, and acts tough. But when the shellings start, she becomes frightened

("I don't like being afraid, it scares me"). "I miss the beauty parlor in Tokyo and a sense of order and discipline," Margaret says. She treasures the brushes her father gave to her (which she uses to brush her hair 100 times a night). When Margaret hugs Frank he loses control and falls to pieces; he likes Margaret to call him "Tiger."

While Margaret becomes turned on when Frank flares his nostrils ("I get so excited") she knows he "thinks of me as a bag of desirable bones." She would like Frank to know "I have a mind and a brain." When she found someone who did, she left Frank and married Major Donald Penobscott (Beeson Carroll, Mike Henry). This caused Frank to have a breakdown and he was transferred to a stateside hospital in Indiana; he also received a promotion to lieutenant colonel.

When Margaret yells at Hawkeye, he tells her "Your voice sounds like a songbird drowning in hot tar." If Margaret sees a nurse warming up to Hawkeye (or Trapper), she tells the men "You stay away from my nurses— they're off limits to you." If she finds a nurse is too attractive, she transfers her in an attempt to keep her away from Hawkeye.

Charles Emerson Winchester III (David Ogden Stiers) replaces Frank as Hawkeye and B.J.'s new tentmate. Charles is a pompous Bostonian. He was educated at Harvard and had been working at Tokyo General Hospital before his transfer. He loves classical music (Gustav Mahler is his favorite composer) and fine wine. He reads the *Boston Globe* (sent to him by his sister, Hanoria) and is called "Major Windbag" by Margaret when he talks about himself. Charles, a gourmet, feels that "breakfast at the 4077 makes you look forward to lunch." He sends a tape-recorded message home to his parents and says "classical music reminds me that there is still some grace and culture in the world." He also says he's a good doctor "because I do one thing at a time. I do it very well, then I move on." Winchester says that "the meatball surgery that is performed in the OR is causing my skills to deteriorate; they're wasting away."

Colonel Henry Blake (McLean Stevenson) first commanded the 4077. He was born in Bloomington, Illinois, and loves fishing (and is often seen wearing his green fishing cap). He was more like "one of the boys" as opposed to being a leader (he found Hawkeye's antics amusing). Though in charge, he was actually lost without the help of the company clerk (Radar). Henry ordered adult films from the Tabasco Film Company in Havana, Cuba, and sent notices to the various tents to announce things (as nobody listened to him when he spoke). Although married to Mildred, Henry tries to impress the nurses with fishing stories and fishing equipment. In one episode he mentions "I left a growing practice and a wife with a fistful of credit cards at home."

Henry believes Frank "is the biggest horse's patootie on this post" and "the only thing G.I. about him is athlete's foot." Henry's joyous transfer turns to sadness when the 4077 learns that his transport plane is shot down over the Sea of Japan and there are no survivors. Before leaving, Henry kissed Margaret on the lips and told Radar "to behave yourself or I'm gonna come back and kick your butt." Henry is often seen wearing a black sweater with a red *I* (for Illinois State College) and drinks from a mug with the same colors.

Frank becomes the temporary commanding officer and tries to introduce order and discipline "to make this a more enjoyable war for all of us." After Frank's short reign as the C.O., Colonel Sherman Potter (Harry Morgan) becomes the new leader of the 4077. Potter, a career army man, was born in Riverbend, Missouri, although he later mentions he is from Hannibal, Missouri. He is married to Mildred (no relation to Henry's wife) who calls him "Puddin' Head." He began practicing medicine in 1932. Sherman loves horses (Radar found him one named Sophie). Unlike Henry, Sherman finds Hawkeye's antics a violation of army rules but realizes why he is doing it and never punishes him. Potter finds relief from the insanity by painting (he paints sitting on a saddle and wears a cowboy hat; pictures of horses are on the wall behind his desk). He shares drinks with Hawkeye and B.J., wears a Hawaiian shirt when he relaxes, and considers his troops at the 4077 "the best group of people I ever worked with." He was stationed in England during World War II. Harry Morgan originally played General Bartford Hamilton Steele, a spit-and-polish military man in the episode "The General Flipped at Dawn" (9/10/74).

Corporal Walter Eugene O'Reilly (Gary Burghoff) is the company clerk. He was born in Iowa and has the nickname "Radar" (for his ability to perceive what others think). He writes the announcements heard over the P.A. system and drinks only Grape Nehi. His serial number is 3911880 and he has mailed a jeep home piece by piece. Radar has a pet mouse (Daisy), rabbits (Fluffy and Bingo), and guinea pigs (Bongo, Babette, Mannie, Moe and Jack). Radar manages to do the impossible: acquire needed items without the hassle of red tape (usually through bartering). When Henry is out of his office, Radar smokes his cigars and drinks his brandy. As a kid, Radar had an imaginary friend named Shirley, and mentioned that his hobby is peeking through the hole in the nurses shower tent.

Radar received a hardship discharge when his Uncle Ed died and he became his family's sole support. Radar left behind his most cherished possession, his teddy bear (which he placed on Hawkeye's bed). In a follow-up letter we learn that Walter O'Reilly, gentleman farmer, has taken an evening job in the local general store to pay the bills.

Maxwell Klinger (Jamie Farr) is the company's "resident loon." He is a corpsman and pretends to be insane to get a Section 8 psychiatric discharge. He is first a corporal then a sergeant and dresses in women's clothes hoping to convince his superiors "that I'm nuts." He patrols in a skirt, wore a special Carmen Miranda dress for Henry's farewell and purchases his gowns from Mr. Syd of Toledo. Klinger became the clerk after Radar and "hates the damned army but I love these people." He calls the trucks that bring in the wounded "the bad humor trucks." He "goes for a dollar like a puppy goes for slippers" says Potter about Klinger's love of money. Klinger printed the camp newsletter, *M*A*S*H Notes* ($2 monthly subscription fee; 10 cents newsstand price per issue), and writes the advice column "Dear Aunt Sadie" (Margaret writes "About Faces," a beauty column). Klinger doesn't relax ("If I do someone will think I like it here"). In the last episode, he married Soon-Lee (Rosalind Chao), a migrant farm worker.

Father Francis Mulcahy (George Morgan, William Christopher) is a first lieutenant and the unit's chaplain. He raises money for the Sister Theresa Orphanage and finds his faith in God challenged every day by the horrors he sees. He relaxes by playing poker ("Shearing the flock" as he says); all his winnings go to help Korean children. He mentioned that the only thing he will miss "is the Korean children and all their smiles."

Visiting generals call the 4077 "a nut house, a mad house"; it is closest to the Kimpo Airfield in Seoul. Rosie's Bar is the local unit's watering hole (where Klinger sometimes works as the bartender). There is a signpost on the grounds with arrows pointing to Coney Island, San Francisco, Tokyo and Burbank. When Margaret decided to make a time capsule so "future generations will know who we were here," Hawkeye contributed Radar's teddy bear; Charles, a bottle of cognac; Klinger, his Scarlett O'Hara dress; and B.J. a broken helicopter fan belt. Fox Movietone News did a documentary on the 4077 on 10/9/52. Johnny Mandel composed the theme, "Suicide Is Painless."

Updates

1. *After-M*A*S*H*, CBS, 1983–1984. Following his retirement from the Army in 1953, Colonel Potter (Harry Morgan) returns to his home in Riverbend, Missouri, where he becomes chief of staff at the General Pershing V.A. Hospital. Potter contacts two former Army buddies, Maxwell Klinger (Jamie Farr) and Father Francis Mulcahy (William Christopher), who accept his invitation to work with him at the hospital. Rosalind Chao recreates her role as Max's wife, Soon-Lee, and Potter's wife, Mildred, is played by Barbara Townsend (and then by Anne Pitoniak).

2. *W*A*L*T*E*R*, CBS, 7/17/84. An unsold pilot that was set to focus on the after–M*A*S*H life of Walter O'Reilly (Gary Burghoff) as he gives up the family farm and moves to St. Louis to become a police officer.

110.   Mayor of the Town Syn., 1954

Springdale is a small American town with a kindly old Mayor (Thomas Mitchell) who resides in an old-fashioned house on Elm Street with his nephew Roscoe Gardner (David Saber) and his housekeeper, Marilly (Kathleen Freeman). The Mayor enjoys sitting in his easy chair and reading the *Morning Chronicle* by the fireplace. He has an office on Main Street and each night before going to bed, he winds the clock, places the fire screen on the fireplace, puts the damper down and locks the front door. Each year he suffers from "post–Christmas mental hangover" (everything is dull, flat and uninteresting) that takes him the whole month of January to get over. Roscoe, nicknamed Butch, attends Springdale Elementary School. Marilly says the mischievous Butch "can do more damage doing nothing than 20 people doing something." When Butch is naughty, he is sent to bed early. Marilly prepares stewed chicken when guests arrive and talks endlessly about everything. The family has a pet cat (Sweet Alice) and a goldfish (Mr. Weismuller, named after Johnny Weismuller). Capitol City is the nearest metropolis (60 miles away). Based on the radio series (1941–49) with Lionel Barrymore as the mayor.

111.   **Meet Corliss Archer** CBS, 1951–1952; Syn., 1954–1955

The house at 32 Oak Street is owned by Harry Archer (Fred Shields, John Eldredge), a private-practice attorney, and his wife, Janet (Frieda Inescourt, Irene Tedrow, Mary Brian). They are the parents of Corliss (Lugene Sanders, Ann Baker), a pretty 16-year-old high school sophomore with a knack for getting into trouble. Corliss has a weekly allowance of $1; she has two eggs, toast and orange juice for breakfast and enjoys lasagna the most for dinner. She has a tendency to drop the toothpaste tube cap down the drain, loves Gregory Peck movies and believed she could sing—until she tried to join the school's glee club and was told "If I sang with the glee club, there would be no glee in the glee club." Dexter Franklin (Bobby Ellis) is Corliss's boyfriend and "the man I plan to marry one day." Dexter, a steak and potatoes man, loves Marilyn Monroe movies and also has an allowance of $1 a week. Harry and Janet have been married for 18 years. Based on the radio series (1943–56) with Janet Waldo, Priscilla Lyon and Lugene Sanders as Corliss Archer. On 8/5/56 NBC broadcast a rare color special called *Meet*

Corliss Archer that found Corliss (Robin Morgan) playing matchmaker for her Uncle George (Steve Chase). Jerome Cowan and Polly Rowles were Harry and Janet; Warren Berlinger was Dexter.

112.   **Meet Millie** CBS, 1952–1956

Millie Bronson (Elena Verdugo) is a secretary for investment counselor Johnny Boone, Jr. (Ross Ford). She lives at 137 West 41st Street, Apartment 3B in Manhattan with her mother, Bertha (Florence Halop), and longs to marry her boss. Millie attended Central High School and finds herself the victim of her mother's endless matchmaking attempts. Mama, as Bertha is called, is 48 years old but tells everyone she is 37. She and Millie vacation each year at the Live Right Lodge. Alfred E. Prinzmetal (Marvin Kaplan) is their friend, a seemingly permanently unemployed young man who lives with his parents and his pet parrot, Irving. Alfred doesn't understand women; "they're too complicated. I'll wait until there is something else to marry." Last-season episodes find Millie, Mama and Alfred as ranchhands on the Weems cattle ranch in Texas. Irving Miller composed the *Meet Millie* theme. Based on the radio series (CBS, 1951–53) with Audrey Totter then Elena Verdugo as Millie.

113.   **Mister Ed** Syn., 1960–1961; CBS, 1961–1966

The house at 17230 Valley Spring Lane in Los Angeles was purchased from Golden Acres Real Estate by Wilbur and Carol Post (Alan Young, Connie Hines), a young married couple. Wilbur, an architect, sets up his office in the barn and finds that the horse left by the previous owner can speak. The horse is named Mister Ed (voice of Allan "Rocky" Lane) and will only speak to Wilbur because he is the only human he likes well enough to talk to. Mister Ed, who weighed 96 pounds at birth, calls himself the "play-boy horse of Los Angeles" (he is always chasing fillies). He loves carrots, has a fear of heights and believes *filly* is the prettiest word in the English language. Wilbur's (and Ed's) birth sign is Taurus and he drives a car with the plate FIM 921. Wilbur is a member of the Lawndale Men's Club and his address was also given as 17340 Valley Boulevard, 17290 Valley Spring Lane, and 1720 Valley Road; Poplar 9-1769 is his phone number. Carol, who measures 36-22-36, is a former professional dancer who now teaches dancing at Miss Irene's in Hollywood. Her maiden name was given as both Carlisle and Higgins. Jay Livingston and Ray Evans composed the theme. The original unaired pilot, *The Wonderful World of Wilbur Pope*, starred Scott McKay as Wilbur Pope, Mister Ed's owner, and Sandra White as his wife, Carlotta.

114. The Monkees NBC, 1966–1968

The apartment at 1334 Beachwood Street in a town called Centerville is occupied by Micky Dolenz, Davy Jones, Mike Nesmith and Peter Tork, a rock group known as the Monkees (their address is also given as 1438 Beachwood Street, Los Angeles). A life-size dummy named Mr. Snyder also lives with the band. Davy plays tambourine; Micky, the drums; Peter, keyboard and bass guitar; and Mike, guitar. They have recorded such songs as "I'm a Believer," "Last Train to Clarksville" and "Daydream Believer" but are constantly out of work and seeking gigs.

They drive the Monkeemobile, a 1966 GTO with room for six, a parachute and an eight-track stereo system; its license plate is NPH 623. The band's first job was for a Sweet 16 party at the Riviera Country Club (they sang "I Wanna Be Free" and were paid $150). They were chosen "Typical Young Americans" by *Sheik* magazine and were extras (for $30 a day) in the beach movie *I Married a Teenager from Out of Town*. When the boys go out to a restaurant, Peter takes a doggie bag for himself—not for the dog he doesn't have. The group uses the incompetent Urgent Answering Service and the following signs can be seen in their apartment: "Money Is the Root of All Evil," "Denver Chamber of Commerce," "Bus Stop" and "No Smoking in Street Clothes."

Davy, born in England, is the most sensible member of the group. Micky was born in Burbank and was called "Goo Goo Eyes" by his mother. In one episode, Micky mentions that "I haven't been to the circus since I was a kid" and proceeds to sing the theme to the TV series *Circus Boy* (in which he starred as a kid under the name Mickey Braddock). Micky also played his vicious double, a killer named Baby Face Morales, "the most wanted man in America."

Peter was born in Connecticut and is shy around girls. He first attended a private school but he didn't like it so his mother put him in public school. Peter cries at card tricks, gets the hiccups when he auditions for producers, has hay fever and is prone to seasickness. Mike was born in Texas and was an Eagle Scout as a kid. He collects fortune cookies to feed to that dog that Peter doesn't have.

In the opening theme, over the song "Hey, Hey, We're the Monkees," Peter's name is seen four times—once for his own credit and once for each of the other three Monkees.

Update

The New Monkees, Syn., 1987. Jared Chandler, Dino Kovacs, Marty Ross and Larry Saltis are the new Monkees in a failed attempt to revive the charm of the original series. The boys live in a very large and bizarre old mansion and are cared for by Manfred the butler (Gordon Cas-Heim). They have a computer named Helen (voice of Liz Godfrey) and each episode features "two oldies and a new adventure."

115.   Mork and Mindy ABC, 1978–1982

The apartment at 1619 Pine Street in Boulder, Colorado, is home to Mindy McConnell (Pam Dawber), the host of *Wake Up, Boulder*, an early morning talk show on KTNS, Channel 31. Her roommate is Mork (Robin Williams), an alien from the planet Ork, who has been assigned to study life on Earth. Mindy, the first girl in Boulder to play Little League baseball, drives a jeep with the plate ML 29HJ. She attended Boulder High School and then the University of Colorado (majoring in journalism). She first worked for her father, Fred (Conrad Janis), at the McConnell Music Store, then as a newscaster for KTNS. Fred, a widower, is later conductor of the Boulder City Orchestra. On Ork, a planet 200 million miles from Earth with three moons, Mork worked as a dinner diver in a lobster tank before he was chosen by their leader, Orson (voice of Ralph James), to become an Earth observer (Mork relates his observations to Orson via mind-transference "Scorpio reports"). On Earth, Mork works as a counselor at the Pine Tree Day Care Center. Orkans evolved from the chicken (their space ships resemble eggs). Mork was born in a test tube, attended Ork prep school and travels through time via his size eight red sequined time traveling shoes. He has a pet Orkan nauger chump (a furry creature he calls Beebo) and an Earth caterpillar he calls Bob. Shortly after Mork and Mindy marry in 1981, Mork becomes pregnant and lays an egg. It hatches and they become the parents of an "elderly" baby named Mearth (Jonathan Winters). Orkan children are born old and become young with time. Mearth has a teddy bear (Teddy) and attends Ork prep school via the 828 transport beam. Mork's greeting is "Na-nu, Na-nu." Perry Botkin composed the theme.

116.   The Mothers-in-Law NBC, 1967–1969

Suzy and Jerry Buell (Deborah Walley, Jerry Fogel) are newlyweds whose lives are constantly interrupted by their meddling mothers, Eve Hubbard and Kaye Buell (Eve Arden, Kaye Ballard). Eve, Suzy's mother, is married to Herb (Herbert Rudley), an attorney; Kaye, Jerry's mother, is married to Roger (Roger C. Carmel, Richard Deacon), a TV scriptwriter. Eve and Herb live at 1805 Ridgeway Drive in Los Angeles (where Suzy and Jerry, students at UCLA, live in their converted garage). Kaye and Roger live next door at 1803 Ridgeway. Roger wrote previously for radio; Kaye was a singer (Angelina DiVina, "The Little Girl with the Big Voice") in the Ozzie Snick Orchestra and with Charlie Banks and His Ten Tellers. Kay Cole played Suzie in the unaired pilot. Wilbur Hatch composed the theme.

117. The Munsters CBS, 1964–1966

The spooky, run-down house at 1313 Mockingbird Lane in the town of Mockingbird Heights is home to Herman and Lily Munster (Fred Gwynne, Yvonne DeCarlo), their son, Edward Wolfgang (Butch Patrick), their niece, Marilyn (Beverley Owen, Pat Priest), and Lily's father, Count Vladimir "Grandpa" Dracula (Al Lewis). With the exception of Marilyn, who is normal-looking, the family members resemble film monsters of the 1930s and believe they are normal and everyone else is strange.

Herman, the father, resembles Frankenstein. He is 150 years old and stands seven feet three inches tall. He weighs "three spins on the bathroom scale" and has a body temperature of 62.8 degrees. His blood pressure is minus three, his pulse, 15, and heartbeat, none. Herman was assembled at the Heidelberg School of Medicine ("I was in several jars for six years") and works as a gravedigger for the Gateman, Goodbury and Graves Funeral Parlor. He writes poems for *Mortician's Monthly* magazine ("Going Out to Pasture" was his first poem) and has a hot rod with the license plate HAJ 302. "Goldilocks and the Three Bears" is his favorite fairy tale and he has a ham radio with the call letters W6XRL4. Herman also held jobs as a rodeo bronco buster, Chinese laundry presser, welder and private detective (agent 702 for the Kempner Detective Agency). When Herman gets mad he stomps his feet (and shakes the house) and says "Darn, darn, darn" when something goes wrong.

Lily, the daughter of the infamous Count Dracula, is Herman's hauntingly beautiful wife. She wears a dress made from coffin lining and claims to be 304 years old (she and Herman were married in Transylvania in 1865. They had to leave shortly after when angry villagers drove them out of town with torches and threatened to burn them at the stake). Lily and Herman enjoy Bat Milk yogurt and Bundles for Transylvania is Lily's favorite charity. While Lily, who cooks and untidies the house (applying dirt and cobwebs), doesn't need to work, she held a job as a welder to buy Herman an anniversary gift.

Grandpa, a vampire by birth, is also "a 378-year-old mad scientist" (he has a lab in the dungeon and the only copy of the plans Dr. Frankenstein used to give life not only to Herman, but to his twin brother, a con artist named Charlie, and to Johan, their primitive, afraid of his own shadow prototype; both played by Fred Gwynne).

Grandpa, born in Transylvania, has been married 167 times and has a pet bat named Igor ("A mouse with wings who joined the Translvanian Air Force"). His favorite TV show is *My Three Sons* and he has a transistorized divining rod that picks up reruns of *My Little Margie*.

Marilyn is the black sheep of the family. She appears lovely to the viewer, but grotesque in her family's eyes (in some episodes she is Lily's niece; in others she is Herman's niece). Marilyn attends State University (studying art) and has a bedroom that is bright and cheery. She accepts her family but feels she is so ugly that she will never attract a man (she fails to realize that once a new boyfriend sees Herman, it is he who scares them off, not she).

Edward, called Eddie, attends Mockingbird Heights Elementary School. He resembles a werewolf and has a wolfman doll he calls Woof Woof. Eddie has a pet snake named Elmer (who lives under the garbage pail in the backyard). In one episode, Eddie had a mechanical twin brother, made by Grandpa, named Boris the Robot (Rory Stevens).

Spot is the family's pet fire-breathing dragon (he was found by Grandpa while digging in the backyard. He lives under the living room staircase and eats Doggie's Din Din pet food). There's also Kitty Kat (a cat who roars like a lion) and Grandpa's unnamed raven who says "Never More." John Carradine plays Herman's employer, Mr. Gateman. Jack Marshall composed the theme, "At the Munsters."

Origins

The Munsters, 1964. The original, unaired color pilot (the series is in black and white) starred Fred Gwynne (Herman Munster), Joan Marshall (his wife, Phoebe), Al Lewis (Grandpa), Beverley Owen (Marilyn) and Happy Derman (Eddie). The episode, titled "My Fair Munster," found Marilyn "frightening off" a boyfriend after he sees Herman.

Updates

1. *The Munsters' Revenge*, NBC, 2/27/81. A TV movie that finds Herman and Grandpa (Fred Gwynne, Al Lewis) attempting to clear the family name when they are arrested as the Monster Muggers. Yvonne DeCarlo

recreated her role as Lily while Jo McDonnell became Marilyn and K.C. Martel, Eddie.

2. The Munsters Today, Syn., 1988–1991. In 1966 Grandpa (Howard Morton) conducted an experiment that placed himself, Herman (John Schuck), Lily (Lee Meriwether), Marilyn (Hilary Van Dyke), and Eddie (Jason Marsden) in a state of suspended animation for 22 years. They awake to a new world and still reside at 1313 Mockingbird Lane (555-1313 is their phone number) but changes occurred in their characters.

Herman, now six feet eight inches tall, was created in Dr. Frankenstein's lab in Transylvania over 300 years ago. His teeth squeak when he gets thirsty; his eyes are brown, blue and indeterminate; and his neck bolts (for the electricity that supplied life) itch when he gets an idea. He works as a gravedigger for the Gateman, Goodbury and Graves Funeral Parlor (phone 1-800-FOREVER) and received the Golden Shovel award for being the best at his job. His hero is TV's Judge Wopner (*The People's Court*) and he is a member of the Christina Applegate (*Married with Children*) Fan Club. For a bedtime snack Herman enjoys weasel burgers and refried armadillo bladders (which give him nightmares); rack of lamb is his favorite dinner. He owns stock in Amalgamated Crematorium and attempted but failed to start his own funeral business, The House of Herman.

Lily is 324 years old and married Herman 299 years ago. Before she married, Lily worked as a singer at Club Dead in Transylvania. She won the beauty pageant title "Miss Transylvania of 1655" and the Silver Shroud Award for fashion design. Her normal body temperature is 25.8 degrees and "Transylvania the Beautiful" is her favorite song. Lily, whom Herman calls "Lillikins," gives birth within 24 hours of becoming pregnant (a tradition with vampires in her family).

Grandpa, the original Count Dracula and mad scientist, attended the University of Transylvania and majored in philosophy. He was a member of the Sigma Alpha Aorta fraternity and, with Genghis Khan, opened the first blood bank in Transylvania. Grandpa is a member of the A.V.A. (American Vampire Association) and once had a business sharpening fangs. He was married to Katja (Jo de Winter), Lily's mother, for many decades (she left him when she got tired of ironing capes and mopping dungeons). Dracu-Cola is Grandpa's favorite drink; leeches and cream, his favorite food; and for dinner he enjoys stuffed piranha (poison oak pancakes are his favorite breakfast). He has a pet bat (Igor), a lab rat (Stanley), a computer (Sam), and Leonard, the skeleton he befriended in college and who now lives in the dungeon.

Marilyn is the blonde and beautiful black sheep of the family. She is now 17 years old and a student at Mockingbird Heights High School. She reads *Teen Scene* magazine and desperately wants a larger bosom ("a 36D") to attract boys. She mentioned she was studying art but also wanted to be an actress and then a magazine writer-editor. She has a porcelain bunny collection and the cheerleading team award Bronx Pom Poms. Marilyn appeared in her school's production of *To Kill a Mockingbird* and her relationship to the family is not known (she is a niece, but Herman and Lily are not sure to which side of the family she belongs).

Eddie now attends Mockingbird Heights High School and wants to become a rock video producer. He is a member of the Dukes Little-League baseball team and has a pet Tasmanian devil named Irving. He buys his clothes at Kiddie Casuals and rocky road is his favorite flavor of ice cream.

The Munsters also own Munster Moor, a swamp at 1313th Avenue; Grave Diggers Mutual, "The Good Hands People," insure the house. Spot, the fire-breathing dragon, still lives under the staircase; Maxine is the sea serpent that lives in the moat surrounding the house; and Boris is the name of the boar's head mounted on the living room wall.

3. Here Come the Munsters, Fox, 10/31/95. A TV movie that relates how the Munster family was forced to leave their home in Transylvania (by angry villagers) and how they came to America to live with their niece, Marilyn, at 1313 Mockingbird Lane in Los Angeles (Marilyn's last name is now Hyde, not Munster as in all the previous versions). **Cast:** Edward Herrmann (Herman Munster), Veronica Hamel (Lily Munster), Robert Morse (Grandpa), Christine Taylor (Marilyn Hyde), Mathew Botuchis (Eddie Munster).

Note: There is also *Munster, Go Home*, a 1966 color pilot that was to continue from where the CBS series left off. It was apparently refused by the networks and released theatrically instead. The story finds the family traveling to England to claim an inheritance. **Cast:** Fred Gwynne (Herman Munster), Yvonne DeCarlo (Lily Munster), Al Lewis (Grandpa), Debbie Watson (Marilyn Munster), Butch Patrick (Eddie Munster).

118. My Favorite Martian CBS, 1963–1966

Exagitious 12½ (Ray Walston) is a Martian anthropologist exploring the Earth when his "flying saucer" suddenly locks onto the flight path of the X-15, a plane being tested by the U.S. Air Force. In an attempt to avoid a collision, the Martian's ship becomes damaged and crashlands. He is found by Tim O'Hara (Bill Bixby), a reporter for the Los Angeles *Sun*, who witnessed the incident. Tim takes the stranded alien to his apartment at 21 Elm Street. To protect him, Tim names him Uncle Martin, a relative who has come to stay with him. They later retrieve the space ship and hide it in the garage (Martin is unable to repair it because the materials he needs are still unknown on Earth). Martin has a superior intellect and is the greatest living authority on Earth history (he advised people from William Shakespeare to Thomas Jefferson). Martin can levitate objects with his right index finger, disappear by raising the antenna in the back of his head, speak to and understand animals, read minds and project his dreams. He is most fearful of thunderstorms because if he is struck by lightning, he gets "Popsy" (uncontrollably appearing and disappearing). Martin is puzzled by human emotion and believes humans lack intelligence. Tim gets up for work at 8:00 A.M. (he has three alarm clocks set to ring within seconds of each other) and drives a car with the plate JFI 561. Tim's landlady, Lorelei Brown (Pamela Britton), is a pretty but slightly dizzy widow. She is famous for her fudge brownies, gives bridge lessons, sells Christmas cards and beauty creams, plays the stock market with a Ouija board and is studying real estate. Bill Brennan (Alan Hewitt) is Lorelei's romantic interest, a detective with the 12th Precinct of the L.A.P.D. He is called the "Human Bulldog" and is suspicious of Tim and Martin (whose antennae quiver when Bill is near). George Greeley composed the theme.

119.   **My Friend Irma** CBS, 1952–1954

"If she thinks it could be dangerous," says Jane Stacy (Cathy Lewis), the level-headed roommate of Irma Peterson (Marie Wilson), a beautiful and shapely "dumb blonde" whose well-meaning intentions always backfire. Irma and Jane share Apartment 3B (later 2C) at Mrs. O'Reilly's Boarding House at 185 West 73rd Street in Manhattan.

Irma was born in New York City and loves the excitement of big-city life. She works as a secretary for Milton J. Clyde (Donald MacBride), owner of the Clyde Real Estate Company at 631 East 41st Street. Irma attended the Grace Street Elementary School and Madison High School. She is sweet and sensitive and realizes that she is not as smart as other people. She talks to walls "to clear the cobwebs out of my mind," reads "Flash Gordon" comic books and "when I don't want people to know I know something, I pretend I'm dumb." When Irma eats a banana, she peels it, tosses the fruit aside and munches on the inside of the skin; she believes that when the French kiss on the cheek, it is their version of shaking hands to say goodbye. Irma is always fashionably dressed; she is a picture of beauty, a good housekeeper and an ample cook, but is head over heels in love with the wrong man—Al (Sid Tomack), "The best customer at the state unemployment office." The averse-to-work Al is a con artist who calls Irma "Chicken." Jane believes he "is a live wire and it is only a matter of time before they hook him up and put a chair under him."

Jane was born in Connecticut and lived with her parents at 1362 Post Valley Road before coming to New York to fulfill a dream: marrying a rich man. Jane believes only money can buy happiness and begins her quest by becoming the personal secretary to Richard Rhinelander (Brooks West), the wealthy owner of the Richard Rhinelander Investment Company at 113 Park Avenue. Jane secretly loves Richard and desperately tries to impress him, but feels her chances will be ruined by Irma, who is well below his social scale. Richard is a graduate of Harvard Business School and, despite his encounters with Irma, finds her delightful. Jane attended Willow High School and talks directly to the audience to relate her feelings as the story progresses. She met Irma quite by accident while looking for an apartment. Irma, who never looks where she is going, bumped into Jane and knocked her to the ground. In the process of helping her to her feet, Irma ripped Jane's dress. When Irma learned that Jane was looking for a place to live, she offered to let her live with her—in "a one-room furnished basement Irma calls home."

Before leaving the series in 1953 (she was transferred to Panama), Jane summed up Irma with "Mother Nature gave some girls brains, intelligence and cleverness. But with Irma, Mother Nature slipped her a mickey." Kay Foster (Mary Shipp) is Irma's new roommate. Irma appeared onstage and explained in an opening curtain speech that Kay responded to her newspaper ad and became her new roommate. Kay is bright and beautiful and works as a reporter for the *New York Globe*. She, too, speaks directly to the audience and comments on the situations that develop as a result of Irma's antics. Kay was born in Ohio and attended Ohio State College (majoring in journalism).

There were plans for Irma to marry and continue the series as *My Wife Irma*. While this never happened, Al was dropped to give Irma a more respectable boyfriend—Joe Vance (Hal March), a neatly dressed, intelligent, hard-working man (for the Spic and Span Cleaners). Joe called Irma "Beautiful" and gave her a "used" engagement ring when he proposed (he purchased the microscopic diamond in the ring from a friend when he broke up with his girl). Irma didn't mind; she loved Joe and accepted it. Kay's boyfriend is Brad Jackson (Gerald Mohr), a reporter for the *Globe*.

Gloria Gordon appears as Kathleen O'Reilly, the owner of the boarding house; Sig Arno is Professor Kropotkin, Irma's neighbor, who plays violin at the Paradise Burlesque Theater (later the Gypsy Tea Room). To avoid the hassle of always having to do her nails, Marie Wilson wears white gloves in virtually every episode.

Origins

The series is based on the radio program *My Friend Irma* (CBS, 1947–1954) with Marie Wilson (as Irma Peterson), Cathy Lewis and Joan Banks (as Jane Stacy), Leif Erickson (as Richard Rhinelander), John Brown (as Al), Hans Conried (as Professor Kropotkin), Alan Reed (as Milton J. Clyde) and Gloria Gordon (as Kathleen O'Reilly).

120.   **My Little Margie** CBS, 1952–1953; NBC, 1953–1955

Marjorie "Margie" Albright (Gale Storm) and her father, Vernon "Vern" Albright (Charles Farrell), live in Apartment 10A of the Carlton Arms Hotel in New York City; Carlton 3-8966 is their phone number.

Margie is 21 and beautiful. She is a talented dancer and dreams of attending the International Dance Ball ("I've wanted to attend ever since I learned to dance."). Margie does not have a regular job and appears to live off an allowance given to her by her father. She mentioned that she first worked as "a beauty consultant" (handing out samples of cosmetics) at Stacey's Department Store and held various part-time jobs as a waitress, dancer instructor and salesclerk. She attended Gorman Elementary School, Lexington High School and Manhattan College. Margie possesses Irish blood from her mother (who died shortly after her birth) and is easily angered when something bothers her. Margie also has a bad habit—smoking (various episodes show her reaching for, lighting up and smoking a cigarette).

While Margie can have any man she chooses, she has chosen Freddy Wilson (Don Hayden) as her boyfriend. Vern considers Freddy "a goofball" and calls him "a droop." He wishes Margie would show a little more taste in boyfriends, but Margie insists "There is nothing wrong with Freddy."

Freddy seems permanently suited for unemployment. He works at various jobs, but, as Vern says, "Freddy is the only person who got fired from five different jobs in one week." He also thinks "that Freddy is too lazy to work. One night he only dreamed he was working and he was pooped for the next two days." Margie believes Freddy is smart ("He's won several contests working crossword puzzles") and did hold two jobs for longer than a day: night watchman ("Not one night was stolen when I was watching them") and as a window mattress demonstrator (sleeping) at Farley's Furniture Store. Despite this, Vern still feels "Freddy is only qualified to be a mental case ... even his draft board rejected him and sent him home with a note pinned to his chest: 'If this is dead we don't want it; if this is alive, we don't believe it.'"

Margie claims she first learned about men from Freddy—"When we were three years old and he pointed one out to me." When Freddy does get a job, Margie misses him (as they would spend the afternoon together) and there is food in the refrigerator ("Freddy would eat all the leftovers" says Vern). Freddy's favorite TV show is *Captain Stratosphere* and he wrote a play called *Girl Against the World* ("The heartwarming story of Gwendolyn Lovequist, a typical American girl with the odds stacked up against her").

Vern is 50 years old and works as a counselor for Honeywell and Todd Investment Counselors in Manhattan. He attended Boston University (where he starred in several school plays) and was a captain during the war. He enjoys playing golf, watching "old Charlie Farrell movies on TV" ("I wouldn't miss them for anything," he says, referring to the films he made in his real-life career as an actor) and has a bad habit of "staying out late, dancing and exhausting himself." Vern does it "because it's fun" and believes age has nothing to do with it—"I have the constitution of a 17-year-old boy" (which Margie wishes he'd give back). Vern has his shoes polished at Joe's Shoe Stand and eats Boomies, the atomic energy cereal, for breakfast (so Margie can use the boxtops for the Junior League Toy Drive). In the episode "Margie's Millionth Member," Margie and Vern are seen hosting an unnamed science-fiction show for adults on WBCA-TV. They play "The first father-daughter space team." The show is never mentioned or seen again.

Vern often says "I've got to teach that girl a lesson" when Margie meddles in his business affairs. He tries to do so but when Margie finds out, she turns the tables on him and tries to teach *him* a lesson—which is the basic plot of virtually every episode.

Vern's romantic interest, Roberta Townsend (Hillary Brooke), works as a secretary and lives across the hall from him in Apartment 10B. Living in Apartment 10C is Clarissa Odetts (Gertrude Hoffman), Margie's 82-year-old neighbor. Mrs. Odetts, as she is called, has British ancestors who date back to Valley Forge and had dreamed of becoming an actress; she enjoys helping Margie turn the tables on Vern and likes to look in on the Albrights (which Vern says she does all the time—"through the keyhole"). Margie sometimes babysits for Clarissa's ten-year-old granddaughter, Norma Jean Odetts (Sheila James), "a little monster" (as she calls herself) who thinks Margie is unfair to children (for being strict). George Honeywell (Clarence Kolb) is Vern's boss; Charlie (Willie Best) is the building's elevator operator. Lud Gluskin composed the *My Little Margie* theme.

121.   My Living Doll CBS, 1964–1965

U.S. Air Force project AF 709 is a beautiful female robot built by Dr. Carl Miller (Henry Beckman) and assigned to psychologist Dr. Bob McDonald (Bob Cummings) to mold her character (for a program to send robots into outer space). The robot poses as Rhoda Miller (Julie Newmar), Carl's niece, and lives with Bob and his widowed sister, Irene Adams (Doris Dowling), at 5600 Wilshire Boulevard (Rhoda is said to be a patient who requires special attention).

Rhoda is made of low modulus polyethylene plastics, miniature computers "and assorted components." She stands five feet ten inches tall, has blonde hair and measures 37-26-36. On her back are four small birthmarks that are actually emergency control buttons (her main "off" switch is located in her right elbow). Rhoda's eyes provide a source of power obtained from light and she has microscopic sensors that keep her body temperature at 98.6 degrees. Her memory bank contains 50 million items of information. Bob works at the Cory Psychiatric Clinic and is chairman of its fund-raising committee. He is also a ladies' man and dines at the Galaxy Club in Los Angeles. When Bob Cummings left the series after 21 episodes (he and Julie could not get along), Bob's neighbor Peter Robinson (Jack Mullavey) became Rhoda's guardian; Bob was said to have been sent to Pakistan. George Greeley composed the theme, "Living Doll."

122.   My Mother the Car NBC, 1965–1966

The theme tells us that everyone "comes back" via reincarnation, though in a different form. For the late Agatha Crabtree, a car, a run-down 1928 Porter, is her choice for reincarnation. It was on August 23, 1949, that Agatha passed away but it was not until September 14, 1965, that her son Dave Crabtree (Jerry Van Dyke) found her. While looking for a used car, Dave spots the Porter with a sign on it that reads "Fixer Upper." Intrigued by the car, Dave gets in, touches the radio and hears a female voice say "Hello Davey." Dave responds "Mother?" and is startled to learn that his mother (voice of Ann Sothern) is now a car (Agatha was fond of automobiles and chose this vehicle by which to return and help guide Dave's life).

Dave pays $200 for the car, returns home and finds his wife and children object to the eyesore and want a station wagon. In an attempt to make Mother more presentable, Dave has her overhauled at Doc Benson's Auto Clinic and painted red at A. Schreib's Auto Painting. The family still objects, but Mother is still wanted—not only by Dave but by Captain Bernard Mancini

(Avery Schreiber), an easily exasperated, eccentric antique car collector, who missed buying the car by minutes at the lot. Despite Dave's continual refusal to sell Mother, Mancini has set his goal to have "our vehicle" (as he calls it). He calls Dave everything but Crabtree when speaking to him (for example, Crabmeat, Kravitz, Crabmaster, Kragle); he always responds with "whatever" when Dave corrects him.

Dave and Barbara Natwick (Maggie Pierce) were sweethearts at Irvington High School. They married four years later (1957) when Dave graduated from law school. They purchased a home at 213 Hampton Street, and when the series begins, they are the parents of two children, Cindy and Randy (Cynthia Eilbacher, Randy Whipple). The family dog is Moon and their phone number is Madison 6-4699.

Mother will speak only to Dave and has her original Stops on a Dime Brakes (for which she did a TV commercial produced by the Video Advertising Agency). Mother sees through her headlights and her license plate reads PZR 317. She has a Stromley-Gaxton carburetor that contains 16 nuts, 14 screws and three bolts.

Dave places Mother in the garage each night after the 11 o'clock news (to protect her from the dew) and places a blanket on her radiator (so she won't catch cold). He stays with her five minutes before returning to the house. Mother watches her favorite TV show, *Jalopy Derby*, on the $10 used set Dave purchased for her. Paul Hampton sings the theme, "My Mother the Car."

123. My Three Sons ABC, 1960–1965; CBS, 1965–1972

Steve Douglas (Fred MacMurray) is a widower and the father of Mike, Robbie and Chip (Tim Considine, Don Grady, Stanley Livingston). Steve is an aeronautical engineer for Universal Research and Development and lives at 837 Mill Street in the town of Bryant Park (later episodes are set in North Hollywood, California, and Steve works for Walters Industries). Tramp is the family dog. Larson 0-6719 is their phone number and JXN 127 is Steve's license plate.

Steve married schoolteacher Barbara Harper (Beverly Garland) in 1969, a widow with a young daughter named Dodie (Dawn Lyn). Mike, studying to become a teacher at State College, is a member of the Sigma Gamma Chi fraternity. He marries Sally Ann Morrison (Meredith MacRae) in 1965 and moves east to teach psychology. Robbie attended Webster Elementary School and then Bryant Park High. He married Katie Miller (Tina Cole) in 1967 and became the father of triplets. Chip attended Webster Elementary and was a member of the Moose Patrol scouting troop. He married Polly Williams (Ronne Troup) in 1970. In 1965 Steve adopts Ernie Thompson (Barry Livingston) when his parents are killed; how they died is not explained. He attends the Susie B. Dorsey School and Buchanan Elementary. William Michael Francis Aloysious O'Casey (William Frawley), nicknamed "Bub," first cares for the family; he is replaced by his brother Charles O'Casey (William Demarest), a former merchant marine who is fondly called "Uncle Charlie." Bub was a member of the Brotherhood of the Cavaliers; Charlie was born in Sandusky, Ohio. Frank DeVol composed the theme, "My Three Sons."

124.   Nancy NBC, 1970–1971

The theme paints *Nancy* as a love story, and the lovers are Nancy Smith (Renne Jarrett), the daughter of the President of the United States, and Adam Hudson (John Fink), a small-town (Center City, Iowa) veterinarian. Nancy is at her family residence in Center City when her horse, Lady, becomes ill. Adam is the vet she calls for help. They meet, fall in love and marry and set up housekeeping on the former Swenson farm in Center City. Nancy can speak English, French, Italian, German and Spanish and received a $700 half-carat round diamond in a gold setting wedding ring from Adam. Although Nancy was born in Center City, she spent much of her time in Washington, D.C., and attended Georgetown University. Adam, also born in Center City, attended Center City High and Iowa State College. Unlike Nancy, who is somewhat authoritative, Adam is laid back and easy-going; so much so that he often performs services for people who are unable to pay their bills. Abby Townsend (Celeste Holm) is Nancy's guardian; Willie Wilson (Eddie Applegate) is Adam's friend, a reporter for the *Daily Clarion*. Sid Ramin composed the theme.

125.   Nanny and the Professor ABC, 1970–1971

Phoebe Figalilly (Juliet Mills) is a pretty British nanny who cares for Hal, Jr., Prudence and Bentley (David Doremus, Kim Richards, Trent Lehman), the children of Professor Harold Everett (Richard Long), a widower who teaches math at Clinton College in Los Angeles. Nanny lives with the Everetts at 10327 Oak Street, and although the theme song speaks of her "magic," she is neither a witch nor a magician but has the ability to spread love and joy (nice things happen around her). Phoebe prefers to be called "Nanny" (she calls Harold "Professor" and Bentley by his nickname, "Butch"). Nanny has an antique car she calls Arabella and the family pets are Waldo (dog), Sebastian (rooster), Mike and Mertyl (guinea pigs) and Jerome and Geraldine (goats). Harry Nilsson performs the theme, "Nanny."

The New Addams Family *see* The Addams Family

The New Gidget *see* Gidget

The New Leave It to Beaver *see* Leave It to Beaver

126.   The New Loretta Young Show CBS, 1962–1963

Christine Massey (Loretta Young) is a widow and the mother of seven children: Vickie (Beverly Washburn), Maria (Tracy Statford), Marnie (Celia Kaye), Judy (Sandy Drescher) twins Dack and Dirk (Dack and Dirk Rambo) and Binkie (Carol Sydes). She is a children's book author and lives in a conservative neighborhood (at 7816 Willow Road) in the small town of Ellendale, Connecticut. She has lived in the town for 14 years and is engaged to Paul Belzer (James Philbrook), the editor of *Manhattan Magazine*, (whom the kids call "Mr. B"). The show is called "New" because it is a departure from Loretta's prior anthology series, *A Letter to Loretta* and *The Loretta Young Show*.

The New WKRP in Cincinnati *see* WKRP in Cincinnati

127.   Newhart CBS, 1982–1990

The Stratford Inn at 28 Westbrook Road (off Route 22) in River City, Vermont, is a 200-year-old establishment that is now owned by Dick Loudon (Bob Newhart), a history buff and how-to book author, and his wife, Joanna (Mary Frann). Dick has written such books as *How to Make Your Dream Bathroom*, *Pillow Talk* (making pillows) and *Installation and Care of Your Low Maintenance Lawn Sprinkler*. He also hosts *Vermont Today* on WPIV-TV, Channel 8. Dick attended Cunningham Elementary School, had a pet goldfish (Ethel Merman) and spent a summer at Camp Cowapoka.

In college he played drums with the Jazz Tones band and was called "Slats" Loudon. Dick wears a size 8½DDD shoe and loves fishing. His first novel was *Murder at the Stratley* (a takeoff of the Stratford Inn). Joanna was born in Gainsville, Ohio. She and Dick met in New York when they both worked for the same ad agency. Joanna, maiden name McKenna, is a real estate broker and hosts *Your House Is My House* (later called *Hot Houses*) on WPIV. She loves to wear sweaters but on her birthday, Dick always gives her a yellow scarf.

George Utley (Tom Poston) is the handyman. He is a member of the Beaver Lodge and has a favorite hammer he calls "Old Blue." He invented the board game "Handyman: The Feel Good Game" and bird-watches at Johnny Kaye Lake. He keeps a lucky penny in his shoe or sock, and *Barnaby Jones* and the mythical *It's Always Moisha* are his favorite TV shows. As a kid he was a fan of *The Goldbergs* radio series.

Leslie Vander Kellen (Jennifer Holms) was the original maid (who left to attend Oxford). Her cousin (also termed sister), Stephanie Vander Kellen (Julia Duffy) replaced her. Stephanie is rich and spoiled and took the job to experience real life. She starred in the WPIV series *Seein' Double* (wherein she played teenage twins Jody and Judy Bumpter). The show was produced by her boyfriend, Michael Harris (Peter Scolari). When Michael is fired for insulting the boss's daughter, he first works for Circus of Shoes (as a salesman), then Menke's Market (as a produce clerk) and finally as a mime. He calls Stephanie "Cupcake," "Gumdrop" and "Muffin" and has a section of his apartment (9B) dedicated to her ("Cupcake Corner"). He also invented the holiday "Cupcake Day" in order to give her presents. As a kid Michael appeared as the singing assistant on the TV show *Captain Cook's Playhouse*.

Larry, Darryl and Darryl (William Sanderson, Tony Papenfuss, John Volstedt) are three strange brothers who operate the Minuteman Cafe. Larry, the only brother who speaks, is a graduate of Mount Pilard Technical School; Darryl One attended Oxford University; Darryl Two majored in royalty under a rowing scholarship at Cambridge University.

The final episode shows that the 5,000-room Takadechi Hotel and Golf Course has been built around the inn that Dick refused to sell. When Dick is hit in the head with a golf ball the screen goes black. When Dick awakens in bed he is not Dick Loudon but Bob Hartley (from *The Bob Newhart Show*) and his wife is Emily (Suzanne Pleshette) not Joanna. When Emily asks Bob what is wrong he relates his dream about the Stratford Inn. Apparently, *Newhart* was Dr. Bob Hartley's dream. Henry Mancini composed "The Newhart Theme."

128. Night Court NBC, 1984–1992

Harry T. Stone (Harry Anderson) is a night court arraignment judge who is famous for his "$55 and time served sentences." He presides in room 808 of New York's Manhattan Criminal Courts Building and processes 12 percent fewer cases than any other judge in his position (due to his lecturing defendants). The building is also called the Municipal Court House and Harry's sessions can also be seen in room 1808 on the 18th floor.

Harry attended East Chesapeake State College. As a kid he had a teddy bear (Jamboree) and a dog named Oliver (in another episode he says he had a dog named Otto that he took for rides in his red wagon). He now has a rabbit (Cecil) and a stuffed armadillo (Clarence). As a teen he stole a 1964 Cadillac for a joy ride. He received two nights in jail and two weeks in a reformatory for crashing the car into a liquor store. Harry's true love is magic. Harry Houdini is his hero and *Magic Time* was his favorite TV show.

A picture of actress Jean Harlow hangs on the wall in Harry's office and he has a photo of his idol, singer Mel Tormé, on his desk. He owns every record Mel has made and has vowed to marry the first girl who is impressed by that. Harry bowls at Bowl-a-Lane Alleys and likes cherry Kool-Aid and Fresca soda; he eats Zipp Bitts cereal for breakfast.

A Mercury-head dime is Harry's good luck charm. He appeared in a TV pilot about a kid attorney called *The Littlest Lawyer* and teaches law classes at the Ed Koch Community College (named after the former N.Y. mayor. A pigeon that got caught in the air-conditioning vent is the school's mascot). Harry is also faculty advisor for the school's newspaper, the *Harpoon*, and was voted "Man of the Month" (by the Society of Goodfellows) and "Most Fascinating Judge in New York" (by the Empire Magicians' Society).

Christine Sullivan (Markie Post), the beautiful legal-aid attorney, lost her first case, defending a man who tried to dismantle a record store with his bare hands (she cried, hyperventilated and had to be dragged out of the courtroom). She was born in the town of North Tonawanda near Buffalo, N.Y. She had a dog (Puddles) and dreamed of competing as an ice skater in the Olympics but the ice stopped her ("It's slippery on that stuff"). Christine attended Buffalo State College and majored in psychology ("I'm an expert on depression"). She measures 37-23-35 and lost the "Miss Greater Buffalo Beauty Pageant of 1978" when she took a stand for women's rights.

Christine has a collection of Princess Diana porcelain thimbles and likes her job "because I serve justice and help the downtrodden" (she also says "the most artistic people I get as clients are hookers with makeup skills").

She has an unseen car with Happy Face hubcaps and lived in apartments 1611E, 616 and 7C (addresses not given). Christine is a member of "Ha Ha" (Happy Alone, Happy Adults; "Happy to Be Happy" is their slogan) and became the inspiration for street artist Ian McKee (Bill Calvert) who painted a large, nude mural of her on a warehouse door called "The Naked Body of Justice." Christine, called "Peaches" by her father, wrote the book *Mommy's World* under the pen name Mother Sullivan.

In 1990 Christine became pregnant after an affair with undercover police officer Tony Juliano (Ray Abruzzo). They married but divorced in 1992. Their son, Charles Otis, was born on 5/2/90 and Christine handed out videos of the event called "Charles Otis Juliano—The Movie." Christine later ran for and was elected congresswoman for the 13th District. She moves to Washington, D.C., in the last episode (5/13/92) to pursue that goal.

Dan Fielding (John Larroquette) is the prosecuting attorney. He was born in Paris, Louisiana, as Reinhold Fielding Elmore (he changed his name when he started school). Dan grew up on a farm and lived with pigs in his room (he was six before he realized he wasn't related to them). As an infant he had a potato painted to look like a pet turtle called Scruffy and in 1967 worked as a lifeguard at the Lone Star Beach Club in Galveston, Texas.

Dan lives in an apartment on Hauser Street off Third Avenue. He is a ladies' man and calls his car, a Mercedes with the plate HOT TO TROT, the "Dan Mobile." He is an army reservist and owns stock in the Fletko Corporation (a company that tears down landmarks). He is also the overseer of the Phil Foundation, a charity that helps the needy, and the host of a put-down TV show called *In Your Face* (when Christine became pregnant he referred to her breasts as "Puppies" and started an on-the-air contest called "Guess the Size of Her Boobs"). In one episode, Dan dreams of becoming a judge ("To wear black satin and send people to jail"); in another, it is becoming a lawyer with the firm of Taylor, Woods and Johnson. Dan picks up girls, who call him the "Prince of Passion," at the Sticky Wickey Club, and in the last episode, he quit his job to pursue his dream girl, Christine, in Washington.

Nostradamus "Bull" Shannon (Richard Moll) is the tall, bald bailiff whose friends think he "is dumber than dirt." He previously worked as an usher at the Majestic Theater and lives in Apartment 7 with a giant *B* on the door and a large concrete sofa in his living room that he made himself ("durable, practical and easy to patch"). His favorite TV show is *The Smurfs* and he has pet pythons called Bertha and Harvey.

Bull weighs 250 pounds and makes $320 a week. He attempted to write a children's book called *Bully the Dragon* (but it scared kids). He then wrote

The Azzari Sisters: An Adventure in Fun, The Snake Pit of Chuckie's Mind and *Bull on Bull* (which, after 426 rejections, he had published by the vanity press Random Author). Bull eats Frosted Neon Nuggets cereal for breakfast. He entered its "Little Tikes Golly-Gee-O-Rama" contest and won the mystery prize—the Shatner Turbo 2000 Whimberly Wig. Because Christine is so nice to him, Bull calls her "a lily pad in a pond full of sludge." Bull still believes in Santa Claus, had a short career as a wrestler (Bull, the Battling Bailiff) and is devoted to Harry ("I'd swallow molten lava for that man. Fortunately, he never asked me").

Bull, a member of the Volunteer Father Organization, enjoys Snickers bars as a treat. On 11/20/91 Bull married Wanda (Cathy Appleby) on the roof of the courthouse. He wore his mother's wedding dress (which she made into a jacket) and Harry performed the ceremony. The last episode finds Bull being taken to Jupiter by aliens to become somebody—"The man who can reach the items on our top shelves."

Mac Robinson (Charles Robinson) is the court clerk. He was a singer with a group called the Starlights ("Before they became famous") and did a tour of duty in Vietnam during the war. At this time he helped a Vietnamese family overcome the ravages of a recent bombing and a 12-year-old girl named Quon Le Dac fell in love with him. Years later (1985), Quon Le (Denice Kumagai) leaves Vietnam to find her hero. She and Mac marry and Quon Le finds work as a checker at the Vegetable Mart. She and Mac attempted to market a cookie she makes as "Mac Snakes."

Mac originally took night classes in law at City College. When he taped 60 hours of Bull's wedding and turned it into a 90-minute movie called *Connubial Fusion*, he switched majors to film.

Rosalind "Roz" Russell (Marsha Warfield) is Bull's female counterpart and earns $410 a week. Before becoming a bailiff, Roz worked as a stewardess for Paramus Airlines. It was an annoying group of passengers that made Roz realize that her goal in life "was to kick butt." She is a volunteer for Toys for Toddlers (a youth center on Canal Street) and hates to have her picture taken (people say she resembles comedian Slappy White). She was married for six weeks to musician Eugene Westfall (Roger E. Mosley) of the Expectations, whom she met at her senior prom.

In the pilot, Gail Strickland played Sheila Gardner, the public defender. Sheila was replaced by Liz Williams (Paula Kelly). Wilhelmina "Billie" Young (Ellen Foley) replaced Liz. Mary (Deborah Harmon) replaced Billie and Christine (Markie Post) replaced Mary as the legal aid attorney.

Lana Wagner (Karen Austin) was the original court clerk. She was replaced by Charli Tracy (D.D. Howard) and Mac (Charles Robinson) replaced her.

Selma Hacker (Selma Diamond) was the original female bailiff. She was replaced by Florence Kleiner (Florence Halop) and Roz (Marsha Warfield) replaced Florence.

Lisette Hocheiser (Joleen Lutz) is the court stenographer. She is a pretty, curly-haired blonde who knits sweaters for birds and enjoys folding socks. She whines to get what she wants and has a goldfish (Orca), a plush giraffe (Too Tall) and a favorite lamp (Sparky). She sells Cantel Cosmetics on the side and attends mosaic classes. Jack Elliott composed the *Night Court* theme.

129.   The Odd Couple ABC, 1970–1975

"Can two divorced men share an apartment without driving each other crazy?" These words, heard during the opening theme, refer to Oscar Madison (Jack Klugman) and Felix Unger (Tony Randall), a slob and a perfectionist, who share Apartment 1102 at 1049 Park Avenue (at 74th Street and Central Park West) in New York City.

Oscar, a sportswriter for the *New York Herald*, also hosts a radio program called *The Oscar Madison Sports Talk Show* (later titled *Oscar Madison's Greatest Moments in Sports*). He first worked as a copywriter for *Playboy* magazine then as a sports reporter for the *New York Times*. "Reckless" is his favorite song; lasagna and French fries his favorite dinner; and Boston cream pie his favorite dessert. Catsup is his favorite food topping and he drinks beer for breakfast. Oscar wears a size 11D shoe and is addicted to gambling. In one episode, Oscar mentions he was born at the Lady of Angels Hospital in Philadelphia; in another, he claims to have been born in Chicago. As a kid he attended the Langly Tippy-Toe Dancing School and was enrolled in James Polk High School. Oscar was married to Blanche (Brett Somers) for eight years (they divorced due to excessive arguing). Oscar acquired the apartment by looking through the obituaries to see who had died in the better neighborhoods (a postman named Irving Cohen was the previous tenant).

Felix is excessively neat. He is a self-employed photographer ("Portraits a Specialty") and is a member of a band (The Sophisticates) and the Lexington Avenue Opera Club (he subscribes to *Opera News* magazine). Felix is also a member of the Radio Actors' Guild (as a kid he appeared on *Let's Pretend*) and in college had his own radio show (*Felix*). During World War II, when Felix was stationed in England, he was a member of the 22nd Training Film Platoon, Educational Division of the Special Services, and starred in the Army training film *How to Take a Shower* (he claims to have originated the line "Men, don't let this happen to you"). He also won the Silver Canteen Award for his song about Adolph Hitler called "To a Sour Kraut." Felix, a lieutenant at the time, was later transferred to Greenland and retired as a captain.

Felix first mentions he was born in Toledo, Ohio, then in Chicago (his family moved to Oklahoma and finally to Glenview, New York, where he was raised on a farm). Felix suffers from sinus attacks, has a pet parrot (Albert) and won the Dink Advertising Award for his Fataway Diet Pills TV commercial. Felix is the father of Edna (Pamelyn Fedin, Doney Oatman) and Leonard (Leif Garrett, Willie Aames) and was married to Gloria (Janis Hansen) who divorced him after seven years of marriage (due to his excessive neatness). Felix's first girlfriend was "Big Bertha"; Orville Kruger ("the boy with the odd-shaped head") was his best friend. Felix and his brother, Floyd, were called "Spic and Span"; Floyd now makes Unger Bubble Gum. Floyd calls Felix "Big F"; Felix calls Floyd "Little F."

Felix lived in New Rochelle, New York, before moving in with his friend Oscar. It is first mentioned that Oscar and Felix met when they were jurors for the trial of Leo Garvey (who was accused of driving his roommate crazy); next, they met as kids in Chicago; finally, when they were young men working for *Playboy* magazine (Oscar, writing copy; Felix as a photographer named Spencer Benedict— "You don't think I'm going to use my real name to shoot nudies").

Oscar and Felix wrote the song "Happy and Peppy and Bursting with Love" for singer Jaye P. Morgan and appeared on TV's *Let's Make a Deal* in a horse costume (Felix was the head; Oscar the rear). Nino's Italian Restaurant is their favorite eatery.

Myrna Turner (Penny Marshall) is Oscar's secretary. She was born in the Bronx, is disorganized, sloppy and lazy (Oscar's ideal work mate). She calls Oscar "Mr. M" and is a Scorpio (born in November). She is forever having boyfriend trouble, especially with "Sheldn" (Rob Reiner); "They forgot the *o* on my birth certificate." While Myrna is attractive, she says she'll never be a lady ("I talk nasal, I have an unproud bust and I sit like a frog"). Murray Greschner (Al Molinaro) is Oscar and Felix's friend, a police officer with the N.Y.P.D.; Miriam Welby (Elinor Donahue) is Felix's romantic interest; and Dr. Nancy Cunningham (Joan Hotchkis) is Oscar's lady love. Neil Hefti composed *The Odd Couple* theme.

Update

The New Odd Couple, ABC, 1982–1983. A black version of *The Odd Couple* with Ron Glass as Felix Unger and Demond Wilson as Oscar Madison. The series used scripts from the original programs and featured Liz Torres as Oscar's secretary, Mira, and John Schuck as Officer Murray Greschner.

130.   One Day at a Time CBS, 1975–1984

Ann Romano (Bonnie Franklin) is a 34-year-old divorcee and the mother of Barbara and Julie Cooper (Valerie Bertinelli, Mackenzie Phillips). Ann retains her maiden name ("because I want to be a liberated woman and master of my own fate"), while her daughters carry their father's last name (Ed Cooper, played by Joseph Campanella). Ann, Julie and Barbara live at 1344 Hartford Drive, Apartment 402, in Indianapolis, Indiana; 555-4142 is their phone number.

Ann first worked as an account executive for the Connors and Davenport Ad Agency. Rutledge Toys was her biggest account and her boss, Al Connors (John Hillerman), called her M.S. Romano (not Ms. He pronounced the *M* and *S* as separate letters). Ann next became the co-owner of the Romano and Handris Ad Agency when she and Nick Handris (Ron Rifkin) began their own company (later called Handris and Associates). When the business failed, Ann and her former rival at Connors and Davenport, Francine Webster (Shelley Fabares), pooled their resources and began the Romano and Webster Ad Agency (Star Time Ice Cream was their first big account).

Ann was born in Logansport, Indiana, and attended Logansport High School. Mocha almond is her favorite flavor of ice cream. She first dated David Kane (Richard Masur), her divorce lawyer (with the firm of McInerney, Wollman, Kollman and Schwartz), then Sam Royer (Howard Hesseman), an architect she married on 5/16/83. She and Sam moved to 322 Bedford Street, Apartment 422.

Julie, the older, more troublesome daughter, has a plush bear (Tu Tu Bear) and wears a size 32B bra. Her favorite snacks are pickles and bananas and celery and ice cream. Julie, a graduate of Jefferson High school, first worked as a receptionist for a veterinarian at the Curran Animal Center. She then held jobs as a freelance fashion designer and as a counselor at the Free Clinic. She married Max Horvath (Michael Lembeck), a flight attendant for PMA Airlines, on 10/10/79. When Max is laid off, he turns to writing. When he is unable to sell his stories, he becomes a waiter at Barney's Tavern. To improve herself, Julie attended classes at the Berkum Management Institute in Ohio; she later became the manager of an unnamed doughnut shop. She and Max are later the parents of a daughter they name Annie (J.D. and R.C. Dilley; Paige and Lauren Maloney). Max calls his mother-in-law, Ann, "Shortie" and she and Julie have accounts at the First Security Bank (1-222-1220-877-02453 is Julie's account number).

Barbara was a tomboy who evolved into a beautiful young woman. She attended Jefferson High school (where she wore jersey 4 on the girls basketball team) and then City College (but dropped out when she couldn't handle the work load). She first worked as a countergirl at Quickie Burger, then as a salesclerk at Olympia Sporting Goods (owned by Erickson Enterprises) and finally as a travel agent at Gonagin Travel. Rocky road is her favorite flavor of ice cream and her favorite snack is a huge banana split. As a kid Barbara ate a caterpillar when Julie told her it was a fuzzy Tootsie Roll. At Jefferson High, Julie and Barbara were envious of Trish the Dish, a well-endowed (but not-seen) girl who attracted all the boys. To become attractive to boys, Julie padded her bra with tissues, while Barbara pretended to be on the pill—and paid dearly when she attracted a boy who thought he could have his way with her.

Barbara married Mark Royer (Boyd Gaines), a dentist, on 10/3/82. It was at this time that she learned that her dream of raising a family could never happen as an incurable medical condition made her incapable of conceiving.

Former Navy man Dwayne F. Schneider (Pat Harrington, Jr.) is the building's superintendent (he lives in Apartment 1 in the basement) and is a member of I.B.M. (Indianapolis Building Maintenance). Dwayne was born in Secaucus, New Jersey, and at the age of two months was a diaper ad model. He attended Irvington High School and married in 1957. (The marriage lasted only one week. His wife got up one morning, hot-wired his truck and just took off. In the pilot episode, Dwayne is married although his wife is not seen; in a later episode, he says he was married for five days and got a divorce.)

Dwayne uses the C.B. handle "Super Stud." He is a member of the Secret Order of the Beavers Lodge, North Central Chapter (he is activities chairman and entertainment producer for the lodge). He invested $10,000 in one of Ann and Francine's accounts—Georgette Jeans; he frequents the Boom Boom Room of the Purple Pig Club and the Alibi Room Bar.

Nanette Fabray played Ann's mother, Kathryn Romano (who calls Ann "Muffin"), and Mary Louise Weller was Ginny Wroblinki, Ann's sexy neighbor, a waitress at the Alibi Room Bar. Jeff and Nancy Barry composed the theme, "One Day at a Time."

Spinoff

Another Man's Shoes, CBS, 5/28/84. An unsold series for Pat Harrington, Jr. The story finds Dwayne Schneider in Daytona Beach, Florida, where he is planning to take his niece and nephew Lori and Keith Schneider (Natalie Klinger, Corey Feldman) back to Indianapolis with him after the death of their father (his brother). He is sidetracked by Jackie Cahill

(Candace Azzara), the owner of Jackie's Arcade (at 17 Boardwalk at Morgan Beach) who offers him a job as her maintenance man. With his "adopted family" gone (Ann, Julie and Barbara are married), Dwayne elects to stay in Florida and raise his brother's children.

131.   Our Miss Brooks CBS, 1952–1956

Connie Brooks (Eve Arden), an English teacher at Madison High School in the town of Madison, lives at Mrs. Davis's Boarding House on Carroll Avenue. Last-season episodes find her teaching at Mrs. Nestor's Elementary School in the San Fernando Valley when Madison High is demolished for a freeway. Connie enjoys "Schoolteacher's B&B" (bath and bed) after a trying day. She shops at Sherry's Department Store and enjoys pancakes and tomato juice for breakfast. Connie is in love with Philip Boynton (Robert Rockwell), the shy biology teacher (also the track team coach and a member of the Elk's Club). Philip was born in Seattle and attended Cavendish High School. He has a pet lab frog (McDougall) and carries jelly beans with him at all times (for quick energy). He plays the ukulele and realizes that when it comes to women "I'm not the most aggressive chap in the world."

Osgood Conklin (Gale Gordon) is the easily upset, stern principal (a major during World War II; four years in charge of Camp Fabrick in Ohio; a member of the Elk's Club). Walter Denton (Richard Crenna) is the featured student, a member of the track team who drives a $30 hot rod. He is in love with Osgood's daughter Harriet (Gloria McMillan) who feels "Walter is my life, my future, my all" (until she fancies someone else, then its "Who needs Walter"). Osgood feels Connie is his "faculty comrade" and Gloria feels her father acts like a principal even at home. Mrs. Davis (Jane Morgan) has a cat named Minerva. Wilbur Hatch composed the theme. Based on the radio series (CBS, 1948–57) with Eve Arden.

132.   Ozzie's Girls Syn., 1973–1974

Ozzie and Harriet Nelson (Themselves) are a retired couple who live at 1822 Sycamore Street in the town of Hilldale. Their sons, David and Ricky, have moved out, and to fill a void in their lives, they advertise in the *Campus News* for someone to rent their sons' former room. College co-eds Susan Hamilton (Susan Sennett) and Jennifer MacKenzie (Brenda Sykes; her character later became Brenda MacKenzie) answer the ad. The girls pay the difference between what it now costs the Nelsons to run the house with them living there then before. The school Brenda and Susan attend is called the "Campus" or the "College." Brenda is an Aquarius, sophisticated and neat. Susan is a hippie type and disorganized. She is a Pisces and plays the guitar. Her father calls her "Charlie" (her mother calls her father, whose name is George, "Jackson"). Ozzie is a Pisces and Harriet a Moonchild. Frank McKelvey composed the theme.

133.   **Paper Moon** ABC, 1974–1975

Moses "Moze" Prey (Christopher Connelly), a salesman for the Dixie Bible Company, drives a 1931 Roadster with the plate 68132. He is accompanied by Adelaide "Addie" Loggins (Jodie Foster), an 11-year-old girl who believes, "because I look like you," that Moze is her father. (Addie was born on November 19, 1922, in Oak View, Kansas, and weighed 6 pounds 2 ounces. She later moved to 47 Bridge Corner in Ophelia, Kansas, where her mother, Essie Mae Loggins, was killed in a car accident. Addie only knows that her father deserted her, but when Moze came to the funeral, Addie formed the connection and made herself part of his life.) Addie keeps her treasures in an old cigar box; Moze uses a fake gold tooth to sell a gold-embossed deluxe Bible edition. Based on the feature film.

134.   **The Partridge Family** ABC, 1970–1974

A 1957 Chevrolet school bus, psychedelically painted and bearing the license plate NLX 590, is the on-the-road home to a group of singers known as the Partridge Family, as they tour the country. There is also a warning sign on the back of the bus—"Careful. Nervous Mother Driving." Shirley Partridge (Shirley Jones) is the mother, and with her children, Keith, Laurie, Danny, Chris and Tracy, they form the Partridge Family, "America's newest singing sensation."

When not traveling, the family lives at 698 Sycamore Road in San Pueblo, California (address also given as the 700 block on Vassario Road). Shirley, maiden name Renfrew, is a widow. She worked at the Bank of San Pueblo before joining the family as a singer. It was ten-year-old Danny who borrowed recording equipment from his school, made a tape of them singing and convinced agent Reuben Kincaid (Dave Madden) to take a chance on them. They first performed the song "Together" at Caesar's Palace in Las Vegas (in a show headlined by Johnny Cash). This led to a recording contract and success (their first album, "The Partridge Family," had a picture of a partridge on it). The family also has a dog named Simone.

"Most mothers have to worry about drugs and violence with their sons, but all your ding-a-ling son does is think about girls" says Laurie about her brother Keith. Keith (David Cassidy) is the eldest child and writes the songs for his family (he also plays guitar). He was also the first family member to experience the problems of popularity when the girls ("who never liked me before") started chasing after him. Keith first attended San Pueblo High School and then San Pueblo Junior College. Keith is a member of the school basketball team (jersey 15) and his favorite foods are meatloaf and steak and potatoes. Laurie believes Keith only dates dumb girls because "they believe all the corny pickup lines he uses." Keith reads *Playpen* magazine ("for the short stories") and attempted to become a film producer after he saw an experimental movie. With Danny as his backer, they made a film called *16½* (originally titled *A History of the World* "but we ran out of film during the 16th century" says Danny). The film was shown to the public at the Royal Theater (for which Danny and Keith were paid $100). Muldoon's Point is Keith's favorite makeout spot.

Laurie (Susan Dey) attends San Pueblo High School and reads *Liberal Outlook* magazine. While very pretty, Laurie never faced the problems of popularity with boys. She is a teenage women's libber, plays the keyboard, and sometimes objects to Keith's lyrics (which she feels are degrading to women; Keith writes love songs). Laurie was born on December 10 and blue is her favorite color.

Danny (Danny Bonaduce) is the schemer of the family and always out to make a dollar ("He usually comes up with six to eight schemes a week," says Reuben, who believes "he is a 40-year-old midget in a kid outfit"). Danny plays bass guitar and keeps his money in a piggy bank that he hides in an old Wild West–style safe in his room. Danny has one share of stock in A.T.&T. preferred (his most cherished possession) and a stamp collection. He reads *U.S. Finance and Monetary Report* magazine and won a race horse (F. Scott) in a raffle. When he thought school was a waste of time, he dropped out to become a songwriter (but found out it takes an education to be one). He also tried becoming a business tycoon and a standup comedian with old vaudeville jokes. Danny, a bit awkward around girls, became the object of 11-year-old Julie Lawrence (Jodie Foster) as she tried to get a date with him. His hangouts are the Sweet Shoppe and the Taco Stand.

Tracy (Suzanne Crough), who plays tambourine, and Chris (Jeremy Gelbwaks, Brian Forster), who plays drums, are the youngest members of the family. As part of the family's Christmas tradition, Tracy places a piece of mistletoe over her head and is kissed by each member of the family. Reuben always manages to drop by when Shirley bakes an apple pie (he gives Tracy a dime to call him). In third-season episodes, Shirley (a widow) used her maiden name to enroll in college to complete her courses in psychology. When someone calls on the family at home, Shirley worries about how the house looks while Keith worries about how his hair looks.

In real life, the Partridge Family had a number of songs, but only one, "I Think I Love You," ever made it to the top ten (in 1970; 16 weeks on the Billboard charts). "When We're Singing" by Wes Farrell and Diane Hilderbrand was the first-season theme; "Come on Get Happy" by Wes Farrell and Danny Janssen was used as the theme for the remainder of the series.

Spinoffs

1. *Getting Together*, ABC, 1971–1972. Bobby Conway (Bobby Sherman) and Lionel Poindexter (Wes Stern) are unknown songwriters who were united in the "Knight in Shining Armour" episode of *The Partridge Family* (3/19/71). Bobby writes music, plays a number of instruments, but can't write lyrics. Lionel is tone deaf, can't play instruments, but can write lyrics (Bobby says "He's weird but okay"). They team, move to Los Angeles and with no money "try for the brass ring in the roughest business in the world." Bobby cares for his sister Jennifer (Susan Neher) and works as a technician in a recording studio. Lionel was raised at St. Michael's Orphanage and works at various part-time jobs. "Stephanie" was the first song they wrote together.

2. *Partridge Family: 2200 A.D.*, CBS, 1974–1975. An animated series in which a futuristic Partridge Family find misadventure as they tour the various planets. *Voices:* Sherry Alberoni (Shirley), Susan Dey (Laurie), Danny Bonaduce (Danny), Chuck McLennan (Keith), Suzanne Crough (Tracy), Brian Forster (Chris), David Madden (Reuben Kincaid).

135. The Patty Duke Show ABC, 1963–1966

Martin Lane (William Schallert), his wife, Natalie (Jean Byron), and their children, Patty (Patty Duke) and Ross (Paul O'Keefe), live at 8 Remsen Drive in Brooklyn Heights, New York. Also living with them is Catherine "Cathy" Margaret Rollin Lane (Patty Duke), Patty's sophisticated look-alike cousin.

Cathy is the daughter of Martin's brother Kenneth (William Schallert), a foreign correspondent for the *New York Chronicle*. Because his assignments constantly uproot Cathy, Kenneth arranged for Cathy to live with Martin until she completes her high school education.

Patty and Cathy attend Brooklyn Heights High School (they are sophomores when the series begins). Their after-school hangout is the Shake Shop (later called Leslie's Ice Cream Parlor). Together they attempted several moneymaking ventures: the Worldwide Dress Company (selling Catnip dresses designed by Cathy for $9.95); Mother Patty's Preserves (a jam, bottled in jars from the Fleming Bottle Company, based on a recipe Cathy found in a book by Charles III. Patty used the slogan "The Jam of Kings—King of the Jams"); and the Doctors Baby Sitting Service (which folded when Patty had no sitters and too many kids).

Patty is the typical teenage girl. She was born in December and wears a size five dress. She was editor of her high school newspaper, the *Bugle*, and worked as a hospital candy striper and a waitress and singer at the Pink Percolator, a coffeehouse that served 75 flavors of coffee (when she sang, Patty used the name "Pittsburgh Patty"). When she read an article about a teenage prodigy, Patty felt she too could become one and wrote a book called *I Was a Teenage Teenager* (a story about "love, war, poverty, death and cooking recipes"). The vanity press Frye Publishing produced 100 copies. Patty and her boyfriend, Richard Harrison (Eddie Applegate), have been dating for five years. He attends the same school as Patty and worked as her manager at the Pink Percolator. He is bedazzled by Patty's antics and remains true to her ("no matter how much trouble I get into"). Richard's father, Jonathan (David Doyle), is first mentioned as being a banker then a highway construction worker. Sue Ellen Turner (Kitty Sullivan) is Patty's nemesis and rival for Richard. She is rich and spoiled and enjoys making Patty's life miserable. Patty calls her father "Poppo."

Cathy previously lived in Glasgow, Scotland, and attended a private school called Mrs. Tuttle's of Mountain Briar (where she was the debating champion). Cathy wears a size five dress and has a built-in lie detector: she gets the hiccups if she tells a fib. Cathy is sedate, enjoys reading poetry and is a member of the literary club at school. She is a straight A student while Patty is the average C student. Cathy is not as popular with boys as Patty and feels her European upbringing has hindered her in this respect. Her father calls her "Kit Kat."

Although her father, Gaylord Lane (George Gaynes), does not resemble Martin, his daughter Betsy (Patty Duke) bears a remarkable resemblance to Patty and Cathy. Betsy is a blonde bombshell who hails from Atlanta, Georgia. Her visit to the Lanes caused a rift in the family when she devised a plan to discredit Cathy so she would leave and Betsy could move in. (Betsy felt unwanted. She was sent to boarding schools so her parents could devote time to their business.) Patty called her a "Confederate Cleopatra" (for trying to steal Richard). Betsy's security blanket was her doll, Sara Jane.

Martin works as the managing editor of the *New York Chronicle* (the *Record* is the paper's competition). Martin was captain of his college football team and married Natalie in 1943 when she was 17 years old (they honey-mooned at Lake George in New York State). Natalie is a Pisces; Martin is a Virgo (William Schallert also played a third role, that of his uncle Jed Lane). Ross attends P.S. 8 grammar school and has an allowance of 50 cents a week. He enjoys building model airplanes and often makes extra money by help-ing either Patty or Cathy when they are at odds and each needs to know what the other is doing. He has a dog named Tiger and Taurus is his birth sign.

The Lane family ancestors include Lieutenant Noah Lane, the first Union officer captured at Bull Run, and Joshua Lane, who established the first general store in Vermont. The Lanes' home is also historic. It was built in 1720 by Adam Prescott, whose son Jonathan served under General George Washington. Adam's daughter Jane offered the house to General Howe and charmed him in order to give Washington and his troops time to rest and regroup. The Lanes' phone number is 624-1098. Rita McLaughlin plays Patty when Patty Duke is Cathy and Cathy when Patty Duke is Patty.

TV Movie Update

The Patty Duke Show—Still Rockin' in Brooklyn Heights, CBS, 4/27/99. The original cast reunites in a story that finds Patty, now the prin-cipal of Brooklyn Heights High School, struggling to save the school from Sue Ellen (now played by Cindy Williams) who wants to demolish it and build a shopping mall. Patty and Richard had married, but divorced after 27 years. Cathy was a widow and living in Scotland. Ross worked as a musi-cian in a Broadway play, and Martin and Natalie had retired and moved to Florida.

136.   The Paul Lynde Show ABC, 1972–1973

Paul Simms (Paul Lynde) is an attorney with the firm of McNish and Simms in Ocean Grove, California. He lives with his wife, Martha (Elizabeth Allen), at 3 Prescott Drive and has a double martini when he comes home from work. He is easily exasperated and believes he is in a rat race "and the rats are winning." His eldest daughter, Barbara (Jane Actman), is married to Howie Dickerson (John Calvin), a genius she met at college (he was going through the dictionary looking for mistakes). Paul dislikes the annoying Howie, who works as a caddy, and feels he may be the reason why he is headed for a nervous breakdown. Howie has been around the world three times, charts the stock market for fun, is a walking encyclopedia and a connoisseur of fine wine. Paul's younger daughter, Sally (Pamelyn Ferdin), is fascinated by Howie and believes he is the smartest person she knows. Sally attends Ocean Grove Junior High School. Shorty Rogers composed the theme.

137. The People's Choice NBC, 1955–1958

Socrates "Sock" Miller (Jackie Cooper), a graduate of Cornell University, works for the Bureau of Fish and Wildlife. He lives with his aunt Augusta "Gus" Bennett (Margaret Irving) at the Paradise Park Trailer Camp in New City, California (which is famous for its lettuce crops). Sock is engaged to and later marries Amanda "Mandy" Peoples (Patricia Breslin), daughter of Mayor John Peoples (Paul Maxey). Also living with Sock is his basset hound, Cleo, whom Sock won in a poker game when he was a corporal during the Korean War. Cleo expresses her thoughts (voice of Mary Jane Croft) as situations unfold. As a puppy Cleo would hang out in the dynamite shed; Sock was the platoon's bayonet champion. Sock later becomes the fifth district councilman (with an office on the first floor of the municipal building), then sales manager of Barkerville, a housing development with 294 homes (houses sell for $15,999; Sock and Mandy live rent-free in model house 119). Sock calls Mandy, who attended Valley Junior High School, his "Ruby Throated Hummingbird"; the mayor calls Sock "Nature Boy" and Gus, whom he later marries, "Mousey." Lou Kosloff composed the theme.

138. Pete and Gladys CBS, 1960–1962

Elm Street is a quiet little block in Westwood, California, that is lined with Palm trees. The house at 726 is owned by Pete Porter (Harry Morgan), a salesman for the Springer, Slocum and Klever Insurance Company in Los Angeles, and his scatterbrained wife, Gladys (Cara Williams). Granite 5-5055 is their phone number. *Life Can Be a Problem* is their favorite TV show; and Petroni's is their favorite Italian restaurant (the song "Santa Lucia" is heard in the background when they attend).

Although Pete would like "a normal, conventional, everyday housewife, I have Gladys instead." He loves Gladys and "I've gotten used to her. I'm addicted to her." On *December Bride* (see that entry), the program of which *Pete and Gladys* is a spinoff, Gladys was never seen. She was only a reference and "a tyrant and total boss over Pete … . I'm not henpecked, I'm buzzard-pecked," said Pete. "I wear the pants in the family. Even though Gladys makes them, I still wear them." He summed up the symbols of his marriage as "a padlock, chains and a straitjacket." Pete mentioned he was interested in magic and that he and Gladys had a daughter named Linda (both aspects dropped from the series).

Pete spent his military career as a clerk in the PX during World War II (although he told Gladys he was a war hero for singlehandedly capturing a Japanese patrol). While Pete says he has a hobby ("saving money"), Gladys felt he should have a more realistic one so he won't be so irritable—restoring old cars. The hobby became hers when she bought a 1924 Hupmobile Roadster (plate JFH 647) for $20 and went about restoring it herself. "Gladys's real hobby," says Pete, "is taking things back to the store."

Gladys appeared on the TV show *Lucky Lady*, performed with Mickey Rooney in a benefit for the children's hospital, bowls (with Sindler bowling balls) with the Westwood Women's League, and is the entertainment chairman of the Junior Matron's League. When Gladys does something wrong she tells Pete "I'll pack my bags and be out of your life in a hour."

Paul Porter (Gale Gordon) is Pete's favorite uncle. He gave Pete his first pair of roller-skates and believes "Gladys is an idiot." Uncle Paul, as he is called, is an antique dealer and so overbearing that Gladys falls apart trying to impress him. When they first met, Gladys offered to light Uncle Paul's cigar by using a candle. The wax dripped onto his tie and ignited it; in an attempt to douse the fire, Gladys threw a pot of cream of tomato soup on him. In some episodes, Uncle Paul mentions "that I do not smoke." In other episodes, he is seen lighting up and smoking a cigarette. Wilbur Hatch and Fred Steiner composed the *Pete and Gladys* theme.

139. Peter Loves Mary NBC, 1960–1961

Peter Lindsey and his wife, Mary (Peter Lind Hayes, Mary Healy), are a show business couple who decide to settle down after 20 years on the road. Peter, a comedian, and Mary, a singer/dancer, are the parents of Leslie and Steve (Merry Martin, Gil Smith). They take up residence at 130 Maple Street in Oakdale, a small town in Connecticut. Mary is a member of the PTA, garden and book clubs; Peter, who still performs locally at the Imperial Room in Manhattan, is president of the Keep Oakdale Beautiful Committee. Leslie and Steve attend the Oakdale School. The Lou Porter Theatrical Agency handled Peter and Mary's bookings.

140. Petticoat Junction CBS, 1963–1970

The theme song invites viewers to relax at "the junction," i.e., Petticoat Junction, where Kate Bradley (Bea Benaderet) owns the Shady Rest, a rural hotel in the town of Hooterville (a community of 72 farms). Kate is a widow and the mother of Billie Jo (Jeannine Riley, Gunilla Hutton, Meredith MacRae), Bobbie Jo (Pat Woodell, Lori Saunders) and Betty Jo (Linda Kaye Henning), three beautiful girls who enjoy swimming in the water tower of the Cannonball Express, the 1890s steam engine, coal car and combination mail/baggage/coach car that services the area. (It is owned by the C.F.& W. Railroad and the girls' petticoats can be seen hanging over the rim of the tower when they swim.

Early episodes find Homer Bedlowe, the railroad vice president played by Charles Lane, attempting to scrap the Cannonball in hopes of becoming a company big shot.) Joe Carson (Edgar Buchanan), called "Uncle Joe," assists Kate in running the hotel (he enjoys sitting in his rocking chair on the front porch and is a member of the Hooterville Volunteer Fire Department). Billie Jo attends classes at the Pixley Secretarial School; Bobbie Jo and Betty Jo attend Hooterville High School. Uncle Joe organized the girls into the singing group, the Lady Bugs, and teamed with pilot Steve Elliott (Mike Minor) to form the Carson-Elliott Cropdusting Company. Steve later marries Betty Jo. The family dog is named Boy.

When Kate, known for her "Bachelor's Butter," died in 1968, she was replaced by Dr. Janet Craig (June Lockhart) as the show's mother figure; Uncle Joe became manager of the hotel. Curt Massy composed the theme.

141.   The Phil Silvers Show CBS, 1955–1959

Ernest Bilko (Phil Silvers), serial number 10542699, is a master sergeant (and master con artist) stationed at the Camp Freemont Army Base at Fort Baxter, Kansas. He is in charge of the 3rd Platoon, 24th Division, Company B Motor Pool and manipulates the Army for his personal benefit. His company includes privates Duane B. Doberman (Maurice Gosfield), Dino Paparelli (Billy Sands), Sam Fender (Herbie Faye) and Corporal Henshaw (Allan Melvin). Rupert Ritzik (Joe E. Ross) is the base cook and Bilko's main patsy. He is married to the always nagging Emma (Beatrice Pons) and eats Crispy Crunchies breakfast cereal; *Captain Dan, Space Man* is his favorite TV show. WAC Master Sergeant Joan Hogan (Elisabeth Fraser) is Bilko's girlfriend and John T. Hall (Paul Ford) is the C.O. Also known as *Sergeant Bilko* and *You'll Never Get Rich*.

142.   Private Secretary CBS, 1953–1957

Susan "Susie" Camille McNamara (Ann Sothern) is the private secretary to Peter Sands (Don Porter), owner of International Artists, a theatrical agency at 10 East 56th Street (Suite 2201; Plaza 5-1955 is its phone number). Susie, a graduate of Mumford High School in Indiana, types 65 words a minute and takes 125 words a minute by shorthand. She is a Libra and lives at the Brockhurst Apartments (Apartment H) on East 92nd Street in Manhattan. Susie was a WAVE for three years and began working for Peter in 1945. Peter, birth sign Aries, established the agency after serving four years with the Air Force. He calls Susie "the most faithful and loyal secretary I ever had" and enjoys looking at women's legs ("I enjoy exercising that privilege"). Violet "Vi" Praskins (Ann Tyrrell), the agency's receptionist, is a Scorpio and interested in horoscopes. She reads *Advanced Astrology* magazine and began working for Peter in 1949. The series is also known as *Susie.*

143.   Professional Father CBS, 1955

Dr. Thomas Wilson (Steve Dunne) is a child psychologist who says that "Patience is the key to all problems." But he has little patience himself when it comes to his family and their problems. Steve lives at 11 Van Nest Lane with his wife, Helen (Barbara Billingsley), and children Kathryn (Beverly Washburn) and Thomas, Jr. (Ted Marc). Kathryn, called Kit by Helen and Kitten by Thomas, has a tendency to trip over things (Thomas says "She's just clumsy"); Kit responds with "no damage" after such incidents. Thomas, Jr., called Twig, is a member of the Beavers baseball team; both children attend Sweeter Elementary School. Thomas enjoys fly fishing at the "Lake" and when he is faced with a troubled boy at work, he gives him a broken clock to fix (he has a closet full of clocks and uses them as a form of therapy). Twig says "holy haystack" when something excites him; Helen feels that her motherly instincts are all that are needed to solve her family's problems.

144.   Punky Brewster NBC, 1984–1986; Syn., 1986–1988

Penelope "Punky" Brewster (Soleil Moon Frye) is a seven-year-old girl who was abandoned by her mother (Susan) in a Chicago shopping mall. Punky believes "that maybe my mother just forgot about me, but one day she'll come back and we'll live happily ever after." But until that time, she lives with her adoptive father, Henry Warnimont (George Gaynes), a 60-year-old widower who found her in an empty apartment (2D) of a building he manages (Henry won a petition to care for Punky when it was found she had no one else).

Punky, Henry and Punky's dog, Brandon, now live in Apartment 2A at 2520 Michigan Avenue in Chicago. Punky originally slept on the couch in the living room. When Henry allowed Punky to change his study into her bedroom (and paint it in a number of funky colors) she found her place— "I'm not nobody anymore, I'm Punky Brewster." Her bed is an old flower cart with a mattress attached. The window has the sun painted on it; her window shade has the moon and stars decaled on it. Punky has a Felix the Cat alarm clock and loves to wear miniskirts. She eats Sugar Beasties cereal for breakfast and has a treehouse in the backyard. She listens to radio station WATD and says "Rock and roll is the answer to everything." Orange is Punky's favorite color. When she was younger she pretended to be Rapunzel and ran down the street with bathroom tissue hanging from her head. She was called "Gunky Brewster" when she first started school (not named; she later attends Fenster Hall). Punky's most cherished Christmas memory is the warm feeling she would get when her mother made cranberry pudding. Punky believes that everything will get better no matter how bad things look— "That's Punky Power" she says.

Henry hopes that Punky will remain a tomboy "for another 30 or 40 years." He says she has a marvelous imagination ("When I ask her to do chores, she comes up with brilliant excuses") and says that her bedroom is so colorful "that it could blind a Smurf." Henry is a photographer (owner of Warnimont Studios) and collects old *National Geographic* magazines. He drives a never-seen 1955 DeSoto; has an alarm in his wallet; and received the Department of Motor Vehicles Highway Award, the Order of the Crosswalk. Henry was a merchant seaman during World War II and his idol as a kid was Jack Benny (whom he listened to on the radio). Henry was married many years ago to a woman named Claudia (she died a year after they were married; his dream of having a child came true when Punky came into his life). Henry's fondest memory of Christmas is when he would visit his grandfather in Massachusetts and they would go into the woods to chop down a tree. The tradition changed when he was 12 years old: it was the year his grandfather was attacked by a moose and the tradition of buying store-bought trees began. Punky and Henry's first Christmas together was somewhat mystical. While Punky's wish that she be reunited with her mother didn't come true, Santa did leave her something: her mother's musical jewelry box; the gift Punky made for her mother, earrings, was gone. Was it a miracle? Punky thinks so "because all you have to do is believe."

Cherie Johnson (Herself) and Margaux Kramer (Ami Foster) are Punky's best friends. Cherie lives in Apartment 3A with her grandmother Betty Johnson (Susie Garrett), a nurse at Cook County Hospital (Betty has been caring for Cherie since her parents' death). Margaux is very pretty, very rich and very spoiled. She lives in a mansion on Oak Lane and 555-RICH is her phone number. She takes lessons from her mother on how to fire servants and "when it comes time for marriage, I'll look through *Who's Who* to see who has what." Margaux's house "has so many rooms that you need a map to find your way around" (her bedroom is in the east wing). There are metal detectors at the front door and Margaux has her own masseuse, beautician and manicurist. She also has a collection of dolls; her most cherished one is the ballerina that dances to the song "Beautiful Dreamer" ("She comforts me when I'm sad" says Margaux).

Punky, Margaux and Cherie shared cabin 12 at Camp Kookalookie (across the lake was the boys' camp, Camp Scratchanichee); they share homeroom 103 at school and acted together in the school's Christmas play *The Saddest Raindrop* (Punky was a sad raindrop turned by the winter wind into a beautiful snowflake). The girls won a trip to Disneyland when they wrote *Gruesome Ghost Stories: The Mystery of Horror House* for the WHXY old-time radio contest. Punky and Cherie tried to make money by selling Lady Contempo Cosmetics door to door.

Brandon, Punky's dog, is made almost human (he buys his own Calvin Klein Flea Powder at $75, and sends flowers, at $55, to his friend Lady). When Brandon is good he gets an Oreo cookie.

There is a real Punky Brewster—Peyton B. Rutledge (who appears in the episode of 11/10/85, "The Search"). Peyton, known in her childhood as "Punky Brewster," was the daughter of the headmaster of the prep school that then NBC head Brandon Tartikoff had attended (he remembered the name and suggested it for the show). Gary Portnoy sings the theme, "Everytime You Turn Around."

145. **The Real McCoys** ABC, 1957–1962; CBS, 1962–1963

The McCoys are a proud but poor farming family living in Smokey Corners, West Virginia. Amos McCoy (Walter Brennan) is the head of the family. He lives with his grandson Luke McCoy (Richard Crenna), Luke's wife, Kate (Kathleen Nolan), and Luke's sister and brother Hassie (Lydia Reed) and Little Luke (Michael Winkelman). One day Amos receives notice that his brother Ben has died and that he has inherited Ben's ranch in the San Fernando Valley. With their worldly belongings packed on their 1920s car, the McCoys head west to take possession of the 20-acre McCoy farm (4½ miles outside of town). There they acquire Pepino Garcia (Tony Martinez), the hired hand who had worked for Ben.

The Sun Mortgage and Loan Company holds the mortgage on the farm (located on the Back Road; Valley 4276 is their phone number). Amos and

Luke grow a variety of crops—tomatoes, lettuce, potatoes, apples, peaches and alfalfa (apples are sold to Mother Norman's Frozen Apple Pie Company; alfalfa to the Tilford Stables). They also have 56 egg-laying hens (Marie, Loretta, Ethel, Harriet, Henrietta and Lazy Susan are their favorites) and are members of the Valley Co-op Poultry Association. The family also has a milk cow (Bessie; later Agnes, then Rosemary), a bull (Old Abe) and a horse (Rick). Their car, a Model A Ford Touring Car (license plate LBV 179), was first called Gertrude and then Emily.

Amos, fondly called Grandpa, was born in 1894 in Smokey Corners; his late wife was named Julie. He is an expert at bird calls and uses the "McCoy Tonic" to cure his ailments (an alcoholic beverage recipe that has been in the family for over 100 years). When it comes to planting crops, Grandpa knows what goes where by tasting the dirt—"I got a taste for dirt." Amos claims the McCoy family history includes two moonshiners, a horse thief, and a riverboat gambler. He also says "No McCoy ever backs out of a problem" and enjoys pitching horseshoes, fishing, playing checkers and relaxing in his rocking chair on the front porch. Amos is also a member of the Royal Order of the Mystic Nile Lodge (where he is Grand Imperial Mummy) and president of the West Valley Grange Association. Grandpa is musically inclined (he plays the jug that usually holds moonshine) and in his youth, he was the only spooner with a gramophone in his canoe. Amos calls his tractor Iron Mule (it is stubborn and rarely starts). He is most embarrassed by the fact that he can't read or write.

Luke, real name Lucius, married Kate Purvis shortly before leaving West Virginia. They honeymooned at the Colonial Palms Motel and stayed in room 204. "Margie" was the song they danced to when they first met at the June Social (another episode claims they first met in Sunday School). Luke calls Kate "Sugar Babe" ("Honey Babe" in the pilot). In his youth, Luke wrote a song called "In the Name of Rotten Love." He entered an amateur radio contest and sang the song "In the Hills of West Virginny." He took a job as dog catcher (badge 7014; car code AR 3) when the farm was between crops. Luke is also a member of the Grange Association and the Mystic Nile Lodge (which raises money for charity, promotes brotherhood in the community, and helps people in need). Luke was the state arm-wrestling champion of West Virginia and a member of its state militia marching band.

Kate, famous for her cooking, won the Prize Foods of California Home Baking Preserves Contest with her piccalilli (she received a blue ribbon) and a $50 gift certificate for winning the Mrs. Homemaker Contest at the Carter Brothers General Store. Kate is a member of the Charity Clothing Drive and the Ladies' Auxiliary, and earns money by sewing.

Luke's parents are deceased. He and Kate care for Luke's sister Hassie and his younger brother Little Luke (Luke's parents were so excited when the baby was born they named him Luke—forgetting they already had a son named Luke). Tallahassee, nicknamed Hassie, is 13 years old when the series begins. She earns spending money by babysitting and pledged the Alpha Beta Sigma sorority at Valley High School (the Malt Shop is the original after-school hangout; later it's the Soda Fountain). In her senior year at Valley High, Hassie joined the "in crowd" of teenage girls called the "Bunch." Hassie's favorite colors are red and silver and she has her hair done at Armand's Beauty Parlor (she was the first in her school to wear the latest craze from France—the bouffant beehive, which cost her $3.50).

Little Luke was the only McCoy to be born in a hospital. He attends Valley Elementary School and is a member of the Valley Town Tigers little-league team (jersey 4). Little Luke's school is also referred to as "that school Little Luke attends" (Grandpa believes "it is a prison with all those rooms"). Little Luke enjoys fishing (sometimes cutting school to do so) and had his first job delivering papers (he made $10.24 in his first week). When Little Luke has nothing to say it means something is bothering him. In one episode he has a dog named Mack (that appeared to be part of the family, but it never turned up again).

Grandpa considers Pepino to be a McCoy until he does something wrong and "is fired from the family." Pepino lives in "the room in the barn" and calls Amos "Señor Grandpa." He makes $15 a week and believes in superstitions and potions (which he gets from Gladys Hunnicutt, the Owl Lady; played by Jeanette Nolan). Pepino also cares for Pepinita, Rosemary's calf.

George MacMichael (Andy Clyde) is Amos's best friend (they play checkers every Wednesday night). He runs "the farm up the hill" from the McCoys with his sister Flora (Madge Blake). Amos says "George is a cranky old bachelor who ought to be put out to pasture." George, a World War I veteran, was voted commander of the local VFW (Veterans of Foreign Wars), Post 192.

"The McCoys have a weakness for flattery," says Grandpa. The family keeps their money in the sugar bowl in the dish cabinet (sometimes it's the cookie jar) and Luke says "Grandpa has a mind like a steel cash register when it comes to money." When the family needs something special, they serve Grandpa ice cream and apple pie for dessert. When their strawberry crop failed (a drought), the McCoys took part-time jobs to get them through the weeks ahead: Amos, salesman at McGinnis's Hardware Store; Luke, salesman at the feed store; Kate, salesgirl at the Knit Shop; Hassie, countergirl at the Malt Shop; and Little Luke, stock boy at Clark's Department Store.

At the start of the 1962–63 season, viewers see Hassie leaving home for college. Little Luke is said "to be at camp" and Luke has been a widower for a year and a half (no mention is made as to how Kate "died"). George and Pepino are given featured roles and Luke becomes involved with various women as he seeks a wife. He is often featured dating his new neighbor, Louise Howard (Janet DeGore), a widow from Cleveland with a young son named Gregg (Butch Patrick). Joan Blondell played Louise's aunt Winnie Jordan, a former stage star, who tried to spark a romance between Luke and Louise. In the first non–Kate episode, the McCoys' cousin Tilda (Tina Louise) appears to help Amos, Luke and Pepino care for the house (the backwoods Tilda is amazed by electric lights, running water, a gas oven, and having her own room).

Harry Ruby composed *The Real McCoys* theme with Jimmie Rodgers performing the vocal in last-season episodes. CBS daytime reruns of the series were broadcast as *The McCoys*.

Rhoda *see* The Mary Tyler Moore Show

The Ropers *see* Three's Company

146.   The Sandy Duncan Show CBS, 1971–1972

Starring as the "Yummy Peanut Butter Girl" and being the spokesperson for John E. Appleseed Used Cars are two of the television commercial jobs done by Sandy Stockton (Sandy Duncan), a student teacher at UCLA who also works for Maggie Prescott (Nita Talbot), owner of the Prescott Advertising Agency. Sandy lives in Apartment 2A of the Royal Weatherly Hotel at 130 North Weatherly Boulevard. This version of the series aired as *Funny Face*.

Under the title of *The Sandy Duncan Show*, Sandy is still a student teacher but she now works as a part-time secretary for Bert Quinn (Tom Bosley), senior member of the Quinn and Cohen Advertising Agency at 5099 Linden Boulevard in Los Angeles. Sandy resides at the same address and her phone number is 555-3444. Jack Jones sings the theme, "The Kind of Girl She Is."

147.   Sanford and Son NBC, 1972–1977

Fred G. Sanford (Redd Foxx) is a cantankerous 65-year-old widower who refuses to retire. He was married to a woman named Elizabeth and is the father of Lamont (Demond Wilson), a 34-year-old who is anxious not to follow in his father's footsteps.

Fred and Lamont run Sanford and Son Salvage, a junkyard at 9114 South Central in Los Angeles. In 1972, Fred has been a widower for 23 years. He was born in Georgia and grew up in poverty (he slept in the same room with four of his siblings). He now has his own business, his own home (although it is furnished with other people's "trash") and feels he is living a life of luxury. Fred was unable to receive a full education. He attended the Dickinson Elementary School but had to drop out in eighth grade to work and help support his family. He held a number of jobs but turned his talent as a dancer into his livelihood when he teamed with a girl named Juanita and performed on the vaudeville stage. Fred saved what money he could and retired from show business to begin his dream: the Sanford junk empire.

Fred is set in his ways and is distrustful of people. When he doesn't get his way, he feigns a heart attack (he puts his hand on his heart, looks up to Heaven and says "I'm coming Elizabeth, this is it, the big one"); it was mentioned that he had 15 major heart attacks in the first episode. If there is work to be done, Fred's "arth-i-ritis" suddenly kicks in and Lamont finds himself doing what has to be done. Fred needs to wear glasses but refuses to see an eye doctor. He has a desk drawer filled with pairs of discarded eye glasses that he rummages through when he needs to read something. He loves fried foods and drinks an alcoholic beverage called "Ripple." When someone makes a smart remark, Fred makes a fist and says "How would you like one across the lip?"

Lamont, affectionately called "Dummy" by Fred, can't stand being poor. He refuses to call himself a junk dealer ("I'm a collector") and "one of these days I'm gonna split this joint because I'm sick of doing all the work." Lamont attended South Central High but not college as Fred couldn't afford the tuition. Lamont and his best friend, the always in trouble with the law Rollo Larson (Nathaniel Taylor), managed an all-girl rock group called the Three Degrees. Grady Wilson (Whitman Mayo) is Fred's best friend and Julio Fuentes (Gregory Sierra) is the next-door neighbor that Fred dislikes (Julio has a goat named Chico that often wanders onto Fred's property).

Esther Anderson (LaWanda Page) is Fred's sister-in-law. She is usually called Aunt Esther and she and Fred simply do not like each other (much of the comedy stems from the insults the two throw at each other). Aunt Esther is deeply religious and is trying to reform Fred (whom she calls a heathen). Donna Harris (Lynn Hamilton) is Fred's romantic interest. She is much younger than Fred, but Fred couldn't care less about what other people think. Quincy Jones composed the *Sanford and Son* theme.

Origins

The series is based on the British comedy *Steptoe and Son* (BBC, 1963–1973). It is about Albert Ladysmith Steptoe (Wilford Brambell) and his son Harold Kitchener Steptoe (Harry H. Corbett), a team of "rag and bone men" (junk dealers). While Fred and Lamont had a beat-up old pickup truck, Albert and Harold had two cart horses named Hercules and Delilah.

NBC first attempted to adapt the series to American TV in 1965 with an unaired pilot called *Steptoe and Son* with Lee Tracy as Albert and Aldo Ray as Harold. Before achieving success with a black version of a white show, Norman Lear produced an unaired pilot called *Steptoe and Son* with Barnard Hughes and Paul Sorvino as Albert and Harold.

Spinoffs

1. *Grady*, NBC, 1975–1976. Fred's best friend, Grady Wilson (Whitman Mayo), leaves Los Angeles to move in with his married daughter Ellie Marshall (Carol Cole) and her family: her husband, Hal (Joe Morton), and their children, Laurie (Rosanne Katon) and Haywood (Haywood Nelson), at 636 Carlisle Street in Santa Monica. When the series failed, Grady returned to *Sanford and Son*.

2. *Sanford Arms*, NBC, 1977. Here, Phil Wheeler (Theodore Wilson), a retired army man, buys the Sanford and Son junkyard from Fred (who has decided to retire) and turns it into the Sanford Arms Rooming House. He is assisted by his children Angie and Nat (Tina Andrews, John Earl). The series ran for four episodes.

3. *Sanford*, NBC, 1980–1981. Fred has his junkyard back but Lamont is no longer his partner (he left the business in 1977 to work on the Alaska pipeline). Fred is now teamed with Cal Pettie (Dennis Burkley), a not-too-bright friend of Lamont's who paid Fred $2,000 for a share of the business. Cal, an overweight southerner, calls Fred "Mr. Sanford." Fred's address was given as 4707 South Central in Watts and he is seen dating Evelyn Lewis (Marguerite Ray), a wealthy woman who lived at 77 Kantwell Drive in Beverly Hills (she didn't mind dating beneath her social scale as she loved Fred and accepted him for what he was).

148.   So This Is Hollywood NBC, 1955

Kim Tracy (Virginia Gibson) is an aspiring actress with Imperial Artists Studios in Hollywood. She made her film debut in *Dark Rapture* and has been described as "fresh with natural charm; freckles across the nose, tomboyish grin, the perfect girl next door." Kim lives at the La Paloma Courts on Sweeter Street and shares a small apartment with Queenie Dugan (Mitzi Green), a stuntwoman at Imperial Artists. Kim and Queenie share a room and are seen sleeping in the same bed (an extreme TV rarity at this time). They are awakened each morning at 8:00 A.M. when the daily paper is delivered and hits the window. Queenie and her boyfriend, Hubie Dodd (Gordon Jones), earn $70 a stunt. Kim and Queenie have drinks at Casey's Bar; Hollywood 2211 is the phone number for Imperial Artists. William Lava composed the theme.

149.   Star of the Family ABC, 1982

Jennie Lee Krebbs (Kathy Maisnik) is a 16-year-old girl who aspires to be a singer. She lives at 7136 La Salle Drive in Southern California with her father, Buddy (Brian Dennehy), and brother Douggie (Michael Dudikoff). Buddy, a widower, has the real name of Leslie and is captain of fire company 64. The not-too-bright Douggie, real name Douglas, and Jennie attend Monroe High School. Kathy Maisnik sings the theme, "Movin' Along."

150.   Stockard Channing in Just Friends CBS, 1979

Stockard Channing plays Susan Hughes, a girl on the rebound from a broken marriage, who works as the assistant manager of the Fountain of Youth Health Spa in Beverly Hills. Coral (Sydney Goldsmith), Susan's girlfriend, works at the spa's juice bar. In 1980, after the title became *The Stockard Channing Show*, Stockard is Susan Goodenow, an undercover investigator for the *Big Ripoff*, a consumer advocate program on KXLA-TV in Los Angeles. The station is owned by Gus Clyde (Max Showalter), a former actor who calls KXLA the "House That Gus Built." Earline Cunningham (Sydney Goldsmith) is the station's sexy but dim-witted receptionist. Earline lives at 123 Morning Glory Circle; Susan resides at 196 North Langley Drive (555-3004 is her phone number). Delaney Bramlett composed "Stockard's Theme."

151.   The Stu Erwin Show ABC, 1950–1955

Stu Erwin (Himself), the principal of Alexander Hamilton High School, lives at 143 Melville Avenue in the town of Hamilton, with his wife, June (June Collyer Erwin), and his daughters Joyce (Ann Todd, Merry Anders) and Jackie (Sheila James). Stu, a member of the University Club, teaches night classes in civics for adults. He reads a paper called the *Daily Star* and

IT2N 514 is his license plate. June, a member of the Women's Club, reads *Women's Home Companion* magazine. Joyce first attends Hamilton High and then State College. Divine Scent is her favorite perfume; fried chicken is her favorite dinner; and her allowance is one dollar a week. Jackie, a student at Hamilton High in 1954, receives an allowance of 50 cents a week. She is a tomboy ("collects bugs, bottles, beetles and butterflies") and has a pet frog named Elmer. Jackie likes freshly made strawberry jam and eating dinner in the kitchen ("It's closer to second helpings"). Biff's Ice Cream Parlor is the after-school hangout. Willie (Willie Best), a Baptist from North Carolina, works as the school's custodian, basketball team equipment team manager and handyman for Stu around the house.

Also known as *Life with the Erwins*, *The New Stu Erwin Show* and *Trouble with Father*.

152.   **Sugar Time** ABC, 1977–1978

"Girls, girls, girls, don't you wanna love 'em," says the theme. The girls referred to are Maxx Douglas, Maggie Barton and Diane Zuckerman (Barbi Benton, Marianne Black, Didi Carr), singers who comprise the group Sugar Time. The girls live together in an apartment at 363 Lindhaven Street and perform at the Tryout Room, a Los Angeles nightclub. Maxx, an instructor at the Health Spa, worked previously as a go-go dancer. She is a bit dense and mentioned she was born in Cleveland (later, Texas). Diane, born in the Bronx, works as a dental assistant; and Maggie, who teaches children to dance at the Willow School, formed the group (she met Maxx at the spa; Diane at the dental office). "Goodbye, Eddie" is the first song they performed together. When onstage, Diane stands in the middle, Maggie to the left and Maxx to the right. Barbi, Didi and Marianne sing the theme, "Girls, Girls, Girls."

153.   **The Tab Hunter Show** NBC, 1960–1961

Beautiful girls posing as swimsuit models are one of the perks for Paul Morgan (Tab Hunter), a cartoonist who draws the comic strip "Bachelor at Large" for John Larsen (Jerome Cowan), the owner of Comics, Incorporated, a publication that produces "mostly comics for kids." Paul's bachelor pad is his swank beach house at 3600 Malibu Road in Malibu Beach, California. Paul's friend, the wealthy Peter Fairfield III (Richard Erdman) squanders money ("I'm terribly rich") and enjoys the pleasure of Paul's company for the girls he gets to meet. Peter calls John "a grouchy old bear" and attending cocktail parties is the hardest work John does (he says "I need to do so for business"). Swimsuit photos of some of the girls Paul uses as models can be seen on his living room wall. Pete Rugolo composed the theme.

154.   Tammy ABC, 1965–1966

Tammy Tarleton (Debbie Watson) is a pretty 18-year-old bayou girl who lives with her grandfather Mordecai Tarleton (Denver Pyle) on the *Ellen B*, a riverboat that is moored on the Louisiana Shore in Ducheau Parish. They have a dog (Delilah), a cow (Beulah) and a goat (Nan). Tammy is an excellent cook (famous for her "river vittles," such as hog liver soup, poke weed salad, stuffed catfish and mustard greens). Tammy, a graduate of nearby Seminole College, works as a secretary to John Brent (Donald Woods), a wealthy widower who runs Brent Enterprises from his home at Brentwood Hall. Lavinia Tate (Dorothy Green) is the woman seeking to marry John. She despises Tammy, her sweetness and her river talk, and schemes to get her fired so her daughter Gloria (Linda Marshall) can assume the secretarial position. Lavinia has a dog named King Alfonse of Normandy. Tammy can type 200 words a minute and add faster than an adding machine ("It sort of comes naturally to me, like smelling to a skunk"). Based on the novels *Tammy Out of Time* and *Tammy Tell Me True*.

155.   The Tammy Grimes Show ABC, 1966

Tammy Ward (Tammy Grimes) is a spendthrift young heiress who cannot collect her multimillion dollar inheritance until she reaches the age of 30. She lives at 365 Central Park West (467-7671 is her phone number) and works as the customer relations officer at the Perpetual Savings Bank of New York (the "Bank with a Heart"). Her uncle Simon Grimsley (Hiram Sherman) is the bank president and her twin brother, Terence Ward (Dick Sargent), is the bank's vice president (he lives at 51 Gramercy Place). Johnny Williams composed "The Theme from the Tammy Grimes Show."

156.   That Girl ABC, 1966–1971

In a small apartment at 344 West 78th Street near the FDR Drive in New York City lives Ann Marie (Marlo Thomas), a young woman who has come to Manhattan to fulfill her dream of becoming an actress. Ann was born in the mythical small town of Fenwick, New York. She is five feet, 5½ inches tall, weighs 100 pounds (later 108 pounds), and wears a size six dress and a 6A shoe (by the episode "Secret Ballot" she appears to be 21 years of age). Ann was called "Punky Puss" as a child, organized her dolls by name, and was voted "best snowball thrower" in Putnam County (when she and her family moved to Brewster, New York, her current home town). Ann attended Camp Winnepoo (where she won a medal for best actress in the camp play), worked as a meter maid (in Fenwick), and attended Brewster College (where she was a member of the Brewster Community Playhouse acting group). She was also nicknamed "Twinkle Fingers Marie, the Speedy Steno" for her rapid shorthand. When Ann was five years old she managed to get her elbow stuck in a peanut butter jar; in adult life, she tried toe bowling and got her big toe stuck in a bowling ball (which released itself when her toe relaxed). Before leaving Brewster, Ann taught elementary school.

Ann's rent is $88.43 a month and her phone number is Plaza 3-0598 (207 is her phone answering service code number). In the pilot episodes (both aired and unaired) Ann lived at the East End Hotel on East 70th Street. Her address was later given as 344 West 70th Street, Apartment 4D (although it is seen as only "D" on her door); she later resides at 627 East 54th Street, Apartment 2C.

Ann's first job (unaired pilot) was as a waitress. In the series, the second filmed episode aired first and showed Ann performing in a TV commercial for Jungle Madness perfume. In the second aired episode (actually the reworked pilot), Ann is seen leaving Brewster for New York and working as a mop on the children's TV show *The Merry Mop-a-Teers*.

Ann appeared as a contestant on the game shows *The Mating Game* (to help her reporter boyfriend get a story) and *Get Rich Quick*. She played Doris the Ding-a-ling, a woman with multiple personalities, on an unnamed soap opera. Her most embarrassing moment occurred on a live broadcast of the TV series *The Ladykiller* (wherein Ann played a dead bank teller who opened her eyes on-camera; her end credit read "The Girl ... Ann Marie"). Ann appeared in television commercials for No Freeze Anti Freeze, Action Soda, POP Soft Drinks and Creamy Soap.

Ann also performed on stage. She costarred with Ethel Merman in a two-week Lincoln Center revival of *Gypsy*, and performed on the Broadway stage in *The Revolutionary Heart* and *The Knights of Queen Mary*.

Ann's off–Broadway productions are *And Everything Nice* (tried and closed in Philadelphia), *The Queen of Diamonds* (in St. Louis), *A Preponderance of Artichokes* and *Honor's Stain* (both in Manhattan). Ann was also the understudy to Sandy Stafford (Sally Kellerman), a famous Broadway star.

Ann's modeling credits include: pajama model at Unifit; Miss Everything (for the New York Has Everything convention at the Coliseum); Girl

Friday Productions Model; Miss Chicken Big (spokesgirl for the Chicken Big, Inc. fast food chain—"We Fry Harder"); model to British photographer Noel Prince (Gary Marshall); roving clothes model at Sardi's Restaurant (where she performed scenes from movies while modeling). Ann also appeared nude in *Playpen* magazine (her face on another girl's body).

Ann's nonacting jobs included: cosmetics salesgirl at Best & Company; perfume salesgirl at Macy's; door-to-door salesgirl for Smart and Stunning Shoes; waitress at the Cave (a nightclub); department store Christmas elf and sales announcer; and spokesperson for the U.S. Air Force (to promote women in the space program).

To help further her career, Ann joined the Benedict Workshop of the Dramatic Arts (run by the stern Jules Benedict, played by Billy De Wolfe). He has a sign on his office door that reads "Never Enter Here." She was also accepted by the Gilliam and Norris Theatrical Agency (represented most often by her agent, Seymour Schwimmer, played by Don Penny). Ann's dream is to purchase the rights to the book *A Woman's Story* by Joseph Nelson and star in a movie version of it.

Donald "Don" Hollinger (Ted Bessell), a reporter for *Newsview* magazine, is Ann's boyfriend. He was born in Toledo, Ohio (but later says Shelton, Ohio, then St. Louis, Missouri). He is a rather sloppy housekeeper and lives in Apartment 1 on West 54th Street in Manhattan. He drinks milk with corned beef sandwiches and wrote an unpublished novel called *City of Strangers.* He is a bit older than Ann (34 by the episode "Secret Ballot") and has a red Mustang with the license plate 4G82 H 9. He won the Humanitarian Award for his writing and BRyant 9-9978 is his phone number. In the unaired pilot, Ted Bessell plays Don Blue Sky, Ann's Native American boyfriend and agent. Don and Ann became engaged at the start of the last season but no wedding occurred before the series left the air. His and Ann's favorite eatery is Nino's Restaurant. *Newsview* magazine is located at 1330 Sixth Avenue in Manhattan.

Lou and Helen Marie (Lew Parker, Rosemary DeCamp) are Ann's parents. Lou owns the La Parisienne Restaurant in Brewster. He is a member of the Shriner's Club, the Brewster Boosters, and the Brewster Country Club (where each year, during its annual show, he performs the song "Minnie the Moocher"). Lou dislikes Ann in long earrings and short skirts and doesn't really approve of her becoming an actress (he finally accepted her when she directed his club's annual show). Lou won the 1969 Golden Knife and Fork Award as Restaurateur of the Year and the 1947 Safest Driver Award. Lou, who is not too fond of Don, calls him "Hollinger." Lou's competition is Tony's Restaurant. When Ann was told she had "a rotten name for an actress" (most producers asked "Ann Marie who?"), she toyed with the idea of changing her name to Marie Brewster (combining her last name and her home town) but never did it.

Frank Faylen played Don's father, Bert (also called Ed and Harold), and Mabel Albertson was his wife, Mildred (also called Lillian). In the unaired pilot, Harold Gould and Penny Santon played Ann's parents, Lew and Helen. Earle Hagen and Sam Denoff composed the *That Girl* theme.

157.   That's My Boy CBS, 1954–1955

John Jackson (Eddie Mayehoff) was a star football player at Rossmore College. He is the school's most famous alumnus. He played quarterback and earned the nickname "Jarrin' Jack" for "hitting them hard, fast and low." He wore jersey 66. Jack now lives at 734 Appletree Lane in Rossmore, Ohio, and is head of the Jackson and Patterson engineering firm. He is married to Alice (Rochelle Hudson), a former tennis star, and is the father of Jack Jackson, Jr. (Gil Stratton, Jr.), an 18-year-old who wears glasses, is clumsy, allergic to strawberries, and prone to hay fever and sinus attacks. Junior, as he is called, is also a weakling and has no interest in sports. He is a freshman at Rossmore. Jack's efforts to change Junior and relive his college days are the focal point of the series. Based on the feature film.

158.   This Is Alice Syn., 1958–1959

Alice Holliday (Patty Ann Gerrity) is a nine-year-old girl who lives with her parents, Chet and Clarissa Mae (Tommy Farrell, Phyllis Coates), and grandfather Colonel Dixon (Lucien Littlefield) at 857 Elm Street in River Glen, a small town in New Jersey (population 24,695; elevation 322 feet). Alice and her friends Stingy Jones (Jimmy Baird) and Clarence "Soapy" Weaver (Stephen Wooton) attend the River Glen Elementary School (their classes are held in room 4B). Alice is president of the All for One Club and has several pets: Pegasus (pony), Rudolph (frog) and Henry and Matilda (flies). Chet is a reporter for the *Star Herald*; Clarissa Mae was born in Georgia where her family owns a peanut plantation. The colonel is Clarissa Mae's father.

159.   Three's Company ABC, 1977–1984

Apartment 201 of the Ropers Apartment House in Santa Monica, California, is home to Janet Wood (Joyce DeWitt), Christmas "Chrissy" Snow (Suzanne Somers) and Jack Tripper (John Ritter), three singles attempting to live a strictly platonic relationship.

Janet and Chrissy originally share the apartment with Eleanor Garvey (Marianne Black). When Eleanor leaves to get married (to a man named Teddy, whom she later divorces), Janet and Chrissy throw a farewell party that gets Janet and a party crasher (Jack) so drunk that Janet attempts a striptease and Jack falls asleep in the bathtub. Janet and Chrissy need a new roommate to help pay the $300 a month rent. When they find Jack and learn he is living at the YMCA and can do something neither of them can—cook— they rent him Eleanor's old room (to the right of the living room) for $100 a month. To convince their landlords, Stanley and Helen Roper (Norman Fell, Audra Lindley), that "there will be no funny business," Janet tells Stanley that Jack is gay—a charade he must continue throughout the entire series run.

Janet was born in Massachusetts and works as a salesgirl (later manager) of the Arcade Florist Shop. She talks and nags and usually gets her way by doing so ("People just give in to shut me up"). She is the practical one of the group and is looking to marry and settle down. Janet exercises to keep her figure but feels she has one shortcoming: her small breasts (she contemplated implants in the hope of attracting men but decided against it). Janet did change her looks, however, to see if blondes have more fun—she wore a blonde wig over her black hair. Her original reasoning was that "if I get a last-minute date I don't have to wash my hair ... I'll just run in and put it on" (she did have more fun but discarded the wig when she found it was changing her personality). Janet panics when she gets upset and in the last episode, she accepted the marriage proposal of her boyfriend, art dealer Philip Dawson (David Ruprecht).

Jack is a cooking student at the L.A. Technical School (specializing in French cuisine; poached salmon aspic is his specialty). Eggs Madeira was the first meal he prepared for Janet and Chrissy. Jack represented the school in the Tenth Annual California Bake-Off with a chocolate mousse pie (his instructors considered him a top pastry student). He lost when Chrissy accidentally ate the pie and replaced it with a store bought one from Hoffmeyer's Bakery.

Jack's father called him "Junior" and as a kid, Jack was a Davy Crockett fan. He attended San Diego High School and served a hitch in the Navy; he has a tattoo on his behind that says "The Love Butt." After graduating ("You're looking at the Galloping Gourmet of 1980") Jack acquired a fulltime job as chef at Angelino's Italian Restaurant. He later opens his own French eatery called Jack's Bistro (at 834 Ocean Vista, Los Angeles). The last episode finds Jack returning home from a chefs' convention in San Francisco and falling in love with Victoria "Vicky" Bradford (Mary Cadorette), the stewardess who came to Jack's assistance when the plane encountered turbulence and Jack, who is afraid to fly, panicked. The spinoff series, *Three's a Crowd* (ABC, 1984–1985), begins when Jack and Vicky move into Apartment 203 (over the bistro, now at 834 Ocean Vista in Ocean Vista, California). Vicky is a flight attendant for Trans-Allied Airlines and her father, James Bradford (Robert Mandan), is Jack's landlord and the "three" of the title (he disapproves of Vicky living with Jack and constantly intrudes in their lives). James owns the Allied Waste Disposal Company and is married to Claudia (Jessica Walter). The series is also known as *Three's Company, Too.*

Chrissy is the beautiful, blonde daughter of a minister. She was born in Fresno on Christmas Day (hence her name) and works as a secretary for an unnamed company (possibly J.C. Braddock & Company as her employer is a woman named J.C. Braddock, played by Emmaline Henry). Chrissy also sold cosmetics for the Easy Time Cosmetics Company. Jack and Janet worry about Chrissy. She is sweet and trusting and they feel her naivete may attract the wrong kind of man (she has a habit of turning men on without realizing she is doing it). Chrissy does dumb things, cries when she gets upset and feels she is disturbing Jack by asking him to do something ("The day you stop disturbing me," says Jack, "is the day I go see my doctor"). Chrissy has a habit of sleepwalking (in a shortie nightgown) when she goes to bed worrying (a situation that started as a kid. Being the daughter of a minister, she had to be the best in bible class, the best in school, the best at everything). A contract dispute forced Suzanne Somers to leave the series. She was first seen in cameos (a quick phone call to Jack and Janet telling them she is in Fresno caring for her sick mother) then written out when her cousin Cynthia "Cindy" Snow (Jenilee Harrison) arrives to become their new roommate ("Chrissy said I could stay here while she's gone"). Cindy is tall, and like Chrissy, blonde and beautiful. She is also clumsy and accident-prone (Jack is most often on the receiving end of her mishaps). She has a basset hound named Wilbur, is a student at UCLA and earns extra money as a secretary or by hiring herself out as a maid.

When Cindy moves into a dormitory near school, Terri Alden (Priscilla Barnes) becomes Janet and Jack's new roommate. Terri, a nurse at Wilshire Memorial Hospital in Los Angeles, was born in Indiana. She and Jack first met when Jack cut his finger and went to the hospital for a tetanus shot. Although Terri is the new roommate, Cindy still appears (she is seen in the opening theme and stops by to visit). Terri is also a blonde beauty who agrees to keep Jack's secret. She is warm and caring but easily exasperated; she shares the room to the left of the living room with Janet (as did Cindy). In the last episode, Terri leaves for a job opportunity in Hawaii.

Larry Dallas (Richard Kline) is Jack's friend, a playboy who lives in Apartment 304 at the Ropers. He is a rather dishonest used car salesman (for an unnamed company; he calls himself "Honest Larry, the used car salesman"). He is always in need of money and always borrowing it from Jack. He and Jack have drinks (usually beer) at the Regal Beagle, a bar styled after a British pub, and lust for Greedy Gretchen (Teresa Ganzel), a girl who is apparently the ideal dream date.

Stanley and Helen Roper own the apartment house. They are an older couple who live on the ground floor. Stanley has a hard time parting with money and believes Jack is gay while Helen knows he is straight. Helen, a USO entertainer during World War II, craves love and affection but just doesn't get it (Stanley always finds an excuse to avoid romantic situations). Helen says she wakes up with a headache every morning—"Stanley." Stanley always manages to intrude on a conversation that leads him to believe that Jack may not be a committed gay, but later realizes that Jack won't change "because you can't tinker with a tinkerbell." Helen has a dog (Muffin) and a parakeet (Stanley) and her mother calls Stanley "Herbert." When Stanley and Helen decide to retire they sell the apartment house to Bart Furley (Hamilton Camp) and move to the Royal Condominium at 46 Peacock Drive in Chevia Hills, California. The spinoff series, *The Ropers* (ABC, 1979–1980), then aired. Here Helen and Stanley try to fit into a plush neighborhood where their living style is frowned upon by Jeffrey Brookes III (Jeffrey Tambor), a snobbish real estate agent who feels the Ropers will bring down property values (he is also president of the Royal Dale Homeowners Association). He is married to Anne (Patricia McCormack), who approves of her neighbors, and is the father of David (Evan Cohen), who finds a friend in Stanley.

When the Ropers moved, Bart needed someone to manage the building he just bought. He appoints his brother Ralph Furley (Don Knotts) to oversee things ("I'm the new manager, landlord in residence so to speak. I'll be in total charge"). Ralph dresses in outlandish outfits and believes he is a ladies' man. He is not comfortable with Jack, Janet and Terri's living arrangement and hopes to change all that "by making a man out of Jack" (teaching him the secrets to liking and dating women). While Ralph does maintain the building, he finds that placing a picture of himself over a crack in the wall to be the easiest solution. Julia Rinker and (the other) Ray Charles perform the theme, "Three's Company."

Origins

Three's Company is based on the British series *Man About the House*. It is about Robin Tripp (Richard O'Sullivan), a male cookery student who shares a flat with Jo (Sally Thomsett) and Chrissy (Paula Wilcox). This series was spunoff into *Robin's Nest* (which became the basis for *Three's a Crowd*). In *Robin's Nest*, Robin (Richard O'Sullivan) becomes a qualified chef and he and his girlfriend, Victoria Nicholls (Tessa Wyatt), move above a defunct restaurant they turn into a bistro called Robin's Nest. *Man About the House* featured Brian Murphy and Yootha Joyce as George and Mildred Roper, Robin, Jo and Chrissy's landlords. These characters were also spunoff into their own series, *George and Mildred* (which became *The Ropers* in the U.S.). In *George and Mildred*, the Ropers sell their apartment house and move into an exclusive and classy British neighborhood at 46 Peacock Crescent, Hampton Wick, Middlesex. Their neighbors are Jeffrey Fourmile (Norman Eshley), his wife, Anne (Sheila Fern), and their son, Tristan (Nicholas Bond-Owen).

160.   The Tom Ewell Show CBS, 1960–1961

Tom Potter (Tom Ewell) is the lone male in a house full of women: his wife, Fran (Marilyn Erskine), their children, Carol, Debbie and Cissy (Cindy Robbins, Sherry Alberoni, Eileen Chesis), and Fran's mother, Irene Brady (Mabel Albertson). Tom owns the Potter Real Estate Company on Main Street and lives at 611 Elm Street in Las Palmas, California. Tom believes "the Potter family has three wonderful girls, each a queen in her own right" until they ask for money "and become the three gold diggers." Carol, 17, is smart, fashion-conscious and attends Las Palmas High School. *Teenage House Hop* is her favorite TV show. Debbie, 11, and Cissy (real name Catherine) attend the Richmond Street Elementary School. Debbie had a job delivering newspapers for the *Gazette* and started her own gossip sheet, *The Debbie Daily*. Six-year-old Cissy "is sweet, adorable and huggable" says Tom. She had a job walking Bismark, the neighbor's dog. Debbie prefers entering the house through the living room window. She then does a cartwheel and heads for her room (Tom says she is the only one of the girls who can do cartwheels). Cissy has blonde hair like her sisters in some episodes; in others it is black or dark brown (the series is in black and white). Tom calls Irene "Mother Brady." Jerry Fielding composed "The Theme from the Tom Ewell Show."

161.   Too Close for Comfort ABC, 1980–1983; Syn., 1984–1986

Henry and Muriel Rush (Ted Knight, Nancy Dussault) are the owners of a former brothel turned Victorian two-story house on Buena Vista Street in San Francisco. They are also the overprotective parents of Jackie and Sarah (Deborah Van Valkenburg, Lydia Cornell), two beautiful young women who rent the downstairs apartment for $300 a month.

Henry is an artist whose first job was painting turtles. He now draws and writes his creation "Cosmic Cow," a comic strip about a space crime fighter. "Cosmic Cow" is published by Random Comics (a division of Wainwright Publishing) and Henry's biggest challenge "is to draw an udder so it is not offensive." Muriel, who receives $150 a week from Henry to run the house, is a freelance photographer. In her youth she was a singer known as Muriel Martin and performed with Al Crowler and His Orchestra. Henry and Muriel honeymooned at the Golden Pines Hotel and in each episode, Henry is seen wearing a different college sweatshirt. In April 1986, Henry and Muriel relocate to Marin County, California (at which time Jackie and Sarah have moved away). Henry becomes co-owner (49 percent) of a weekly newspaper (the *Marin Bugler*) with Hope Stinson (Pat Carroll), the editor (who owns 51 percent). Hope's late husband, Norris, founded the paper in 1951; Brutus is the name of the dog on the paper's masthead. This version was initially titled *The Ted Knight Show* but retitled *Too Close for Comfort* when syndicated with the earlier version of the series.

Jackie, the older sister (22), is excessively neat and jealous of women with fuller figures (she is thin, wears a size 32A bra and often feels men reject her because "of my lack of cleavage"). She first worked as a teller at the Bay City Bank, then as a salesgirl at Balaban's Department Store and finally as a freelance fashion designer.

Sarah considers herself a "ten." She wears a size 36C bra, is somewhat lazy and an untidy housekeeper. The constant attention men give Sarah makes Jackie extremely jealous. Sarah attended San Francisco State College and first worked as a "wench waitress" at the Fox and Hound Bar. She was next a teller at the Bay City Bank, and then the weather girl for KTSF-TV's *Dawn in San Francisco* program. She tried to make money by marketing Cosmic Cow Cookies (but had to quit when she was slapped with a copyright infringement suit).

Monroe Ficus (Jim Bullock) was a college friend of Sarah's who befriended Henry and eventually moved into Henry's converted attic apartment (at $300 a month). Monroe was a communications major (with a minor in journalism) and worked as a security guard at the Riverwood Shopping Mall (at $200 a week). He was named security guard of the month (Officer April) for catching a lady stealing pantyhose and he has a pet hamster named Spunky. In Marin County episodes, Monroe assists Henry at the paper. He also hopes to become a standup comedian and performs as Buddy Ficus at the Comedy Shack.

Origins

The series is based on the British comedy *Keep It in the Family*. It is about Dudley Rush (Robert Gillespie), a comic-strip cartoonist (of "Barney, the Bionic Bulldog"), and his wife Muriel (Pauline Yates), as they struggle to keep tabs on their beautiful daughters, Jacqui (Jenny Quayle) and Susan (Stacy Dorning), when they move into the basement of the Rush home.

162. Topper CBS, 1953–1955

The house at 101 Yardley Avenue in New York is home to Cosmo Topper (Leo G. Carroll), his wife, Henrietta (Lee Patrick), and its former owners, the ghosts of George and Marian Kerby (Robert Sterling, Anne Jeffreys), and their dog Neil (Buck).

Topper, a henpecked bank vice president, inherited the ghosts three months after the Kerbys' death in Switzerland. (As part of their fifth wedding anniversary celebration, George and Marian decided to go skiing. Fifty miles from nowhere Marian's ski broke. While arguing about what to do, a drunken Saint Bernard came to their rescue. Before anything could be done, the three perished in an avalanche.)

George and Marian have come back, apparently, to bring some fun into Topper's dull life (an exact reason is not given). While measuring the floor for a carpet, Topper first realizes he has ghosts when he sees Marian's shapely legs, then the rest of her materialize. George then appears and Cosmo finds that his life is about to change forever as the ghosts will appear and speak only to him (coping with their antics and explaining unusual occurrences to other people becomes his biggest concern).

George and Marian consider Topper's home to be theirs. Marian, an excellent cook, calls Cosmo "Topper Darling" while George, a former playboy who still has an eye for the ladies, calls Topper "Old Man." George and Marian's idea of eating out is to invite themselves to someone's home and pilfer food. If they materialize and dematerialize too often they become exhausted ("It uses up our ectoplasm," says Marian).

Because of his resemblance to George's cousin, Marian named the dog Neil. "Neil is crazy about bones and beer" says Marian and by ten A.M. has had four martinis, two old fashioneds and a can of beer.

Every morning when Topper checks the mail Marian asks "Anything for us?" "Not unless it's from the dead letter office" replies Cosmo. George and Marian hate mediums ("They're pushy," says Marian, "trying to get us to appear whenever they want"). Cosmo has a bank account of $3,500.27

and entertains clients at Manhattan's Club 22. He is associated with the following banks: National Security Bank, City Bank, Gotham Trust Company and City Trust and Savings. Humphrey Schuyler (Thurston Hall), the bank president (all listed), enjoys raising chickens on his upstate farm (Hildergarde is his prize-winning chicken). To battle inflation, Topper invented the "Seven Cent Dime" (If an increase in the price of sugar causes a nickel candy bar to cost a dime, "the maker can use my new dime and only raise the price to seven cents").

Henrietta sees many unusual things and accepts her husband's explanations, but believes Cosmo amuses himself by pretending to be haunted by three ghosts. She is most baffled by the front door—"It opens and closes by itself" (actually by George and Marian who prefer to enter and exit the house by opening the door as opposed to passing through it). It was Henrietta who talked Cosmo into moving (thinking their apartment was too small). Her parents never liked Cosmo; they believed he was not good enough for her. Henrietta is a member of the Ladies' Drama Committee.

Over the course of the series, the Toppers had three maids: a girl named Vilma who appeared in the pilot but without a credit; Katie (Kathleen Freeman), a maid from the Abba Agency; and Maggie (Edna Skinner). The Toppers' mailbox (near the front gate) is a scale model of their home; their address is also given as 635 Yardley (in the pilot) and later 101 Maple Street. Cosmo's license plate reads 2K 6308. Cosmo paid $16,000 for the house. (Its market value was $27,000, but when the agent tried to cheat Topper, saying it was worth $28,000, George and Marian stepped in and made the house appear to be falling apart. The agent was glad to unload it at $16,000.)

Origins

1. *The Adventures of Topper*, NBC Radio, 1945. Roland Young is Cosmo Topper, Hope Emerson, his wife, Malvena, and Paul Mason and Frances Chaney, George and Marian Kerby. Here George and Marian became ghosts after a car accident.

2. *Topper*, unaired pilot, produced for CBS TV in 1950. Jack Sheehan is Cosmo Topper, Carol Goodner, his wife (Mrs. Topper), and Joseph Boland and Susan Shaw, George and Marian Kerby.

Updates

1. *Topper Returns*, NBC, 4/19/73. An unsold pilot with Roddy McDowall as Cosmo's nephew Cosmo Topper, Jr., who inherits his late uncle's possessions, including the ghosts of George and Marian Kerby (John Fink, Stefanie Powers).

2. Topper, ABC, 11/9/79. An unsold TV movie/pilot with Jack Warden (Cosmo Topper), Rue McClanahan (his wife, Clara) and Andrew Stevens and Kate Jackson (George and Marian Kerby). Here Topper is a lawyer and the Kerbys have a dog named Sam. All versions are based on characters created by Thorne Smith.

163.   Two Girls Named Smith ABC, 1951

"And now new liquid Glim presents 'Two Girls Named Smith' starring Marcia Henderson as Babs and Peggy French as Frances." Announcer Vince Williams spoke these opening theme words to introduce viewers to Babs and Fran Smith, cousins who have come to New York City to further their dreams: Babs as a singer; Fran as a fashion designer. Babs and Fran are originally from Omaha, Nebraska, and now share a small apartment at 514 East 51st Street (Plaza 3-0707 is their phone number; a painting titled "Aristide Braunt" can be seen on their living room wall near the telephone). Babs works as a stenographer while taking singing lessons and hoping for her big break. She is timid and shy and has been described as "a nice, sweet, pretty kid"; her dream became a reality when she was chosen to replace the lead in the Broadway play *Stairway to Venus* ("I never dreamed anything so wonderful could happen to a little girl from Omaha" said Babs when she got the part). Fran, the older of the cousins, works for East Side Fashions and is dating Attorney Jeffrey Carter (Kermit Kegley). Peggy Ann Garner originally played Babs. The show ends with Babs and Fran facing the camera and saying "And now it's time to be saying goodbye from 'Two Girls Named Smith.' Bye bye." The sponsor, Glim, was a liquid dishwashing detergent. Jacques Press composed the theme.

164.   Valentine's Day ABC, 1964–1965

Valentine Farrow (Anthony Franciosa) is a handsome playboy bachelor who lives in a brownstone on 23rd Street in Manhattan with his cook, housekeeper and best friend, Rocky Sin (Jack Soo). Val works as the nonfiction editor for Brackett and Dunstall, a publishing house at 50 Park Avenue. Val collects books and paintings and when he is asked "Why don't you get married?" he responds "You sound like my mother" (whom Val corresponds with once a week; he concludes his letters with "Your year-round Valentine"). Val has his laundry done at Mama Zimmerman's Hungarian Hand Laundry and is called "Boss" by Rocky. Rocky and Val met during the Korean War. Rocky has a gambling problem; he worked for his father's import business before the war. Libby Freeman (Janet Waldo) is Val's gorgeous, ever-efficient secretary (she earns $125 a week). Jeff Alexander composed the theme.

165.   Welcome Back, Kotter ABC, 1975–1979

In 1965 Gabe Kotter (Gabe Kaplan) lived in a Brooklyn, New York, neighborhood so tough that "the gangs didn't carry guns. They inserted the bullets manually." He was a radical student at James Buchanan High School in Bensonhurst and coined the phrase "Sweathogs" (to describe students in special education classes). Gabe was on the basketball team and the vice principal, Woodman, blamed him for the cafeteria riots.

Ten years later things have changed. Gabe is married (to Julie) and is now a teacher who yearns to help students who are much like he was when he was young. He returns to Brooklyn and to Buchanan High where he is assigned to teach special guidance remedial academics to a new breed of incorrigible "sweathogs": Vincent "Vinnie" Barbarino (John Travolta), Juan Epstein (Robert Hegyes), Frederick "Boom Boom" Washington (Lawrence-Hilton Jacobs), Arnold Horshack (Ron Palillo), Rosalie "Hotsie" Totsi (Debralee Scott), Vernajean Williams (Vernee Watson) and Bambi Foster (Susan Lanier).

Gabe and his wife, the former Julie Hanson (Marcia Strassman), first live in a small apartment (3C) at 711 East Ocean Parkway (later, after the birth of their twins, Robin and Rachel, they move to a more specious apartment, 409, at 1962 Linden Boulevard). Gabe has a pressed flower in his high school yearbook that he bought for his date "But she never showed up." He says, about Julie, "If it wasn't for you, I would have married somebody else." When Gabe was nine years old, the neighborhood bully, Tommy Shaughnessy, picked on him.

Julie was born in Nebraska and is famous for her tuna casserole (which Gabe hates and says "it will deter dinner guests from returning"). Julie works as a volunteer at the Free Clinic and makes $5 for every 1,000 envelopes she stuffs with polyester fabric samples. When Gabe needed extra money to pay for his dental bills, he took a job as Captain Chicken, the greeter for Mr. Chicken Northern Fried Chicken. When Julie doesn't have money for Gabe's birthday present, she gives him a card that says "I owe you one giant favor."

Gabe, a social studies teacher, is looking for a meaningful relationship between himself and his students. His classes are held in room 11 and he is also the Sweathogs homeroom teacher. Gabe believes that the antics of Vinnie, Freddie, Epstein and Horshack are like those of the Marx Brothers

(Groucho, Gummo, Harpo and Chico): "Only I have four of my own— Wacko, Stupo, Jerko and Dumbo."

Vinnie is the leader of the Sweathogs. "Room 11 is my place and these [the Sweathogs] are my people." Vinnie believes he is the "Sweathog Heart-throb" and can date any girl he wants ("I have a stupefying talent with female girls of the opposite sex"). When it comes to homework "Barbarino don't do no reports for no one." (Vinnie once opened a book and studied for 15 minutes "but nothing happened." He hasn't read a book since.) Vinnie plays on Gabe's sympathies by saying "It will hurt my sainted mother if she hears bad things about me" (he also claims bad news causes his mother to throw her rosary beads at him). "Up your nose with a rubber hose," the expression associated with Vinnie, is a Sweathog farewell salute, according to Gabe (when one leaves the group, that saying is bestowed upon them).

Vinnie does a dance called the "Barbarino" ("Bar-bar-bar-Barbarino …"); when he ran for student body president with the slogan "Vote for Vinnie and Nobody Gets Hurt," he received 47 votes and lost. He had a "law and order" platform: Vinnie made the laws and Epstein, his secretary of fear and campaign manager, kept the order. When asked a question, Vinnie responds with "What?" when the question is repeated, Vinnie says "Where?" Vinnie later works as an orderly in the local hospital and would like "to be discovered in a drug store and become an actor" (the next Marlon Brando).

Juan Epstein, a Puerto Rican Jew, is the toughest kid in school and has been voted "most likely to take a life." Epstein would like to become a "typhoon" and open a string of Puerto Rican–Jewish restaurants (he has some experience already—"Don't eat the tuna casserole in the cafeteria"). When it comes to tests or being late, Epstein presents one of his famous "notes from my mother" excuses (usually a medical problem and each is signed "Epstein's Mother"). After 11 years of such notes, Juan actually handed Gabe a legit note (signed "Mrs. Epstein") when he was out with a stomach virus.

Juan has nine brothers and sisters and an array of pets: Wally, Eddie Haskell, Lumpy and Jerry Mathers as the Beaver (lizards); Jimmy, Darlene, Cubby and Annette (white mice; his "Mouseketeers"); Florence, Harpo and John-Boy (hamsters); Truman Capote (turtle); and an unnamed chicken "who escaped from a butcher shop and crossed Bay Parkway." Juan, who has a habit of smoking (on and off since he was 12), is the only Sweathog the school's principal, John Lazarus (voice of James Komack), has taken a liking to (he considers Juan his son). When it comes to book reports, Juan uses the *TV Guide* reports on movie adaptations of books.

"Hi There" is the greeting one hears from Freddie "Boom Boom" Washington. He would like to be an architect and build the world's largest building, "Boom Boom Towers." He wears jersey 1 on the school's varsity basketball team and says his nickname doesn't come from the fact that he plays the bass "But because I like Boom Boom." He and Vernajean were an item in many episodes. He calls Gabe "Mr. Kot-ter." As a kid, Freddie had an invisible duck named Ralph (who would sit on his shoulder) and hosted *Hi There*, a radio talk show on Station WBAD.

Arnold says that his last name, Horshack, "is an old and respected name. It means the cattle are dying." He also says that he is the last of the Horshacks "because after they made me they broke the mold." His father drives a cab and he originally only spoke when Vinnie gave him permission to do so. Arnold, whose catchphrase is "ooh, ooh, ooh," often raises his hand to ask a question then forgets why he did so when he is called on. Arnold was the only Sweathog to make it out of the "menagerie" (as Woodman calls them) when his grades improved and made him worthy of becoming a regular student (he eventually went back to Sweathog status, however). Arnold worked part time at his Uncle Harry's costume shop, "Orshack's of Fifth Avenue" (Harry, played by James Komack, doesn't use the *H*). Arnold's greeting is "Hello, how are you?" As a kid, he had a rocking horse named Pepper.

Rosalie, a very pretty and sexy young girl, hates to be called "Hotsie Totsi" "because it gives me the image of being easy and I'm not. I'm a lady." When asked which part of California she is from Bambi says "the beach." Bambi calls Gabe "Gabsee." When Gabe didn't care for that and asked that she call him something else, preferably Mr. Kotter, she called him "Captain Cosmic." "On second thought," Gabe said, "call me Gabsee." Bambi is original from Texas and attended 11 different schools in 11 states (her parents are divorced and she lives with her father, who is constantly moving). Bambi puts on a big act to be liked.

Michael Woodman (John Sylvester White), the sarcastic vice principal, was a nurse's aide during World War II and previously taught history at Buchanan High. He is ill-tempered and liked teaching history "because a good war cheers me up." Woodman claims "I have no sense of humor" and calls Gabe's unorthodox teaching methods "Nutty cuckoo." (Gabe finds normal teaching methods don't work with Sweathogs. "I talk, they listen" is how Woodman says he teaches his class.) Woodman hates "Captain Kangaroo" as much as he does the Sweathogs and wishes for only one thing: to get transferred to Scarsdale (where he believes there are no Sweathogs).

Seeing his students sitting in homeroom before the bell sounds would make Gabe happy (but "You wish" says Epstein). Gabe has established a late fund in room 11 (when a student is late he has to put a quarter in the kitty—

a rubber fish [a halibut]; Freddie is the late-fund treasurer). On test day, Gabe comes to school with a green bucket and detergent—to wash the answers off Epstein and Vinnie's arms. Arnold is Gabe's "official test distributor." Gabe has a knack for forgetting his lunch (which brings Julie to school for scenes other than those at the opening and closing where Gabe tells her a joke about one of his relatives).

The Sweathogs see movies at the Loew's Oriental Theater; Gabe and Julie were chaperons for the Sweathogs' first field trip (to the Museum of Natural History). Gabe is the faculty advisor for the school newspaper, the *Buchanan Bugle*. When the students needed to raise $700 to keep the remedial studies program going, the Sweathogs put on the *Sweathogs Telethon* on channel 52.4 (a mythical cable access station). Gabe hosted; Julie sang "Let Me Entertain You"; Vinnie sang "The Barbarino"; Freddie played the piano; Juan played the bongo drums; Arnold was a "dummy" to ventriloquist Gabe; Vernajean was the tote-board girl. The school's phone number is 384-9945.

John B. Sebastian sings the theme, "Welcome Back."

166.   Wendy and Me ABC, 1964–1965

Wendy and Jeff Conway (Connie Stevens, Ron Harper) are young marrieds who live at the Sunset de Ville Apartment Complex (Apartment 217) at 4820 Highland in Los Angeles. The building's owner is George Burns (Himself), a former vaudeville, movie, radio and television star, who lives in Apartment 104. George is the only one who is aware of a viewing audience and speaks directly to them. He loves to sing and practices singing five or six hours a day (George is the only one who thinks he has a good singing voice and "I have it in the tenants' leases that they cannot evict the landlord"). Jeff, an airline pilot, met Wendy, a stewardess, when they both worked for TGA (Trans Globe Airlines). They have been married one year when the series begins. Wendy is blonde, beautiful and totally scatterbrained. George says "People gave up wondering why Wendy does things a long time ago. I'm glad I own the building. People can go to Wendy's apartment, get confused and come to my apartment to hear me sing." Danny Adams (James Callahan), Jeff's copilot, is a ladies' man who gets withdrawal pains if he is without a woman. He lives in Apartment 219 and has two dating guides: his little black book and a red one he calls the "Red Star Edition." George Duning composed the theme.

167.   **Who's the Boss?** ABC, 1984–1992

Angela Robinson (Judith Light) is an attractive divorcee and the mother of a young son named Jonathan (Danny Pintauro). She lives at 3344 Oak Hills Drive in Fairfield, Connecticut, and is the president of the Wallace and McQuade Advertising Agency in New York City. Living with Angela are her mother, Mona Robinson (Katherine Helmond), her housekeeper, Tony Micelli (Tony Danza), and his young daughter, Samantha (Alyssa Milano). Angela's address is also given as 3334 Oak Hill Drive and her phone number is KL-5-6218.

Angela was born on October 16 and attended the Montague Academy for Girls. At this time Angela was, as she called herself, "a geek." She had a small bustline and felt bigger breasts would make her "one of the cool kids." She tried padding her bra with tissues but was still rejected. She tried to suppress her sorrows with food and became overweight, but cleaned up her act when she learned to accept herself. Angela later attended Harvard Business School. Beginning with the third season, Angela is seen as the owner of her own company, the Angela Bower Agency, at 323 East 57th Street in Manhattan. Angela, who is in the 39 percent tax bracket, manages a softball team called John's Giants. Her first job was rowboat manager at the Fairfield Boat Club. The TV show *Eye on Hartford* did a segment on Angela as successful businesswoman.

Tony, a widower, was born on April 23, 1952, in Brooklyn, New York; his middle name is Morton. He is a Catholic, attended P.S. 86 and was an altar boy at the Blessed Sacrament Church. At Pitkin High School, he was a member of a band called the Dreamtones. After a hitch in the Navy, Tony played second base for two seasons with the St. Louis Cardinals (jersey 14). After an injury ended his career, he returned to Brooklyn to work as a fish truck driver. Several years later, after the death of his wife, Tony applied for the position of housekeeper in an attempt to give Samantha a better environment in which to grow up.

Tony likes to barbecue outdoors in the winter time ("It's invigorating") and does his grocery shopping at Food Town. He first had a 1967 Chevy van (plate 780 AGN), then a black Jeep Cherokee (plate PH 3925) and finally a sedan (plate 518 G8Q). He plays golf at the Ridgemont Golf Club and is a member of a bowling team (Dr. Whittier's Drill Team). Tony posed as the Machismo Man for Machismo Scented 7-Day Deodorant Cream (for Angela's client, Lankersham Cosmetics).

Tony managed a softball team (Tony's Tigers) and became a sportscaster for the Ridgemont College sports channel (where he also took night classes in business). As the series progressed, Tony changed his major to education and became a substitute teacher at the Nelson Academy for Boys (he taught history, English and science; classes were held in room 103). Tony also taught history and was the athletic coach at Wells Junior College in Iowa. He proposed to Angela in the episode of 11/16/91.

Samantha, affectionately called Sam, is a young girl fascinated with sports (she wears, for example, a 5½ hockey skate). She receives an allowance of $15 a week and has a teddy bear named Freddy Fuzz Face. Her favorite foods are French toast ("Mr. Frenchie") and pasta ("Mr. Linguini"). Sam's tomboyish ways came to an end when she turned 12 and asked for a bra—"the one with the little pink bow" (what she got, however, from Tony was the no frills model D134 "My First Training Bra"). Angela and Mona stepped in, took Sam to Bloomingdale's and the tomboy returned home a beautiful young lady.

Samantha attended P.S. 86 grammar school (in Brooklyn), then Fairfield Junior High and finally Ridgemont College (she later moved into the college dorm and shared room 214 with Melinda, played by Andrea Elson). Samantha was a member of the Bulldogs baseball team and first worked as Angela's Girl Friday; she later held a job at the Yellow Submarine, a fast food hamburger store. Her first car was a yellow 1968 Oldsmobile (plate SAM'S CAR) with red reflectors on the sides, five rear brake lights, and an old tire on the rear bumper (Sam called it "My yellow nightmare"). In last-season episodes, Sam marries Hank Tompolus (Cunal Aulisio), a hopeful puppeteer.

Mona, Angela's ultrasexy mother, works as Angela's assistant at her ad agency. She is very proud of her large breasts (her mother called her "All boobs and no brains") and is constantly reminding Angela that she lacks cleavage. Mona also feels Angela is "controlled, conservative and uptight." Angela can't change her ways and is jealous because her mother is a free spirit. Mona appeared on the cover of *Mature* magazine and has a dog named Grover. When Angela was a kid, Mona discouraged her from playing the cello (she was so bad that Mona had to hide the cello in the attic).

Jonathan first attended Oak Valley Grammar School and then Fairfield High. He has a pet snake named Wilbur and a complete Lawrence Welk record collection. His favorite TV show is *Nightmare Theater* and he is learning to play the accordion. Rick Riso sings the theme, "Brand New Life."

168. WKRP in Cincinnati CBS, 1978–1982

WKRP, located at 1590 on the AM dial, is a 5,000 watt radio station in Cincinnati, Ohio. It was founded on December 7, 1941, and ranks 16 in an 18-station market. Its mascot is a fish (a carp) and it broadcasts from Suite 1412 of the nine-story Flem Building. The station's phone number is 555-WKRP.

Arthur Carlson (Gordon Jump) manages the station for his mother, "Mama" Lillian Carlson (Sylvia Sidney, Carol Bruce), who inherited it from her late husband, Hank. Arthur, a family man, has been married to Carmen (Allyn Ann McLerie) for 27 years and has managed the station since 1955. He rarely listens to the station (he dislikes the rock format), enjoys playing with toys or practicing his fishing or golf in his office, and reads *Ohio Fisherman* magazine. Employee Herb Tarlek calls him "Big Guy" (when Arthur ran for city council, he used the slogan "A Big Guy for a Big Job"). In his youth, Arthur was nicknamed Moose. Herb calls Arthur's son Arthur Carlson, Jr. (Sparky Marcus), "Little Big Guy."

Jennifer Elizabeth Marlowe (Loni Anderson), the receptionist, is the highest-paid employee at WKRP ($24,000 a year). She dresses in tight skirts, shows cleavage and says "I'm a very sexy and desirable woman" ("Other women," Jennifer says, "see me as beautiful and a threat to their husbands"). Jennifer belongs to the International Sisterhood of Blonde Receptionists and will never take dictation or make coffee. She was born in Rock Throw, West Virginia, and lives in an apartment (330) that is filled with appliances (gifts from the older, wealthier men she dates. She won't, however, lend men money—"It makes them weak"). Her doorbell plays the song "Fly Me to the Moon." Jennifer later moves into a $125,000 Victorian home in the town of Landersville.

Jennifer gets upset if something doesn't go her way ("Things always go my way," she says). She also hosted a call-in advice show (*Ask Arlene*) but quit when her flip answers caused a woman to become a victim of battery. Jennifer protects Mr. Carlson from pushy salesmen (whom he fears) and her work philosophy is "Do your job but don't do too much of it."

Herb Tarlek (Frank Bonner) is the obnoxious sales manager. He has been married to Lucille (Edie McClurg) for 12 years and is the father of Bunny and Herb III (Stacey Heather Tolken, N.P. Soch). Lucille believes that sex is a reward (for example, "Mow the lawn, Herb, or no num num tonight"). Bunny has a frog named Greenpeace (that Herb accidentally sprayed pink while refinishing the kitchen cabinets). When it comes to petitions, "Herbert R. Tarlek doesn't sign anything." Herb has a crush on Jennifer and fears getting fired for his constant failure to come through with advertisers (when a meeting is called he wonders "Am I in trouble?"). His catchphrase is "O.K. Fine."

Lester "Les" Nessman (Richard Sanders) is the news director (he uses his motor scooter as the WKRP mobile news unit). He is a graduate of Xavier University and the proud recipient of the Silver Sow Award (for his hog reports) and the Buckeye Newshawk Award. He was born in Dayton, Ohio, and took violin lessons as a kid. He thought he would make a good handyman until he tried making a footstool and blew out the back of the garage.

Les, the self-proclaimed "news beacon of the Ohio Valley," has a nasty dog (Phil) and one record in his collection ("Chances Are" by Johnny Mathis). He reads *Pig American* magazine and is a member of the Ho Down Square Dancing Club. He enjoys exploring dark basements and attics (hoping to find a ghost or some unearthly being). Les signs on with the 8 A.M. news and ends his day with the 6 P.M. newscast. He borrows Herb's comb "because I have to look good for my audience." Les also does the sports, *Show Beat* (his celebrity interview program), and the *Eyewitness Weather Report* ("I look out the window for that eyewitness aspect"). Les works in an open office atmosphere but has imaginary walls and a door (marked with tape on the floor) that the staffers respect.

A deep-voiced announcer opens Les' show with "London! Madrid! Bangkok! Moscow! Cincinnati! From the four corners of the world, from the news capitals at home and abroad, the day's headlines brought into focus. The issues and events that shape our times. WKRP, information bureau of the Ohio Valley, presents Les Nessman and the news." Les ends shows with either "This is Les Nessman saying this is Les Nessman" or "This is Les Nessman saying good day and may the good news be yours."

Venus Flytrap (Tim Reid) is the night disc jockey. His real name is Gordon Simms and he has been in hiding ever since he went AWOL (absent without leave) from the Army after serving ten months and 29 days. He plays a mix of hard rock and romantic music and usually burns scented candles when he is at the turntable (the station plays records, not tapes). Venus is also a ladies' man and, although it is against the rules, romances his many women friends with candlelight and wine in the broadcast booth.

Dr. Johnny Fever (Howard Hesseman) is really Johnny Caravella, the spaced-out disc jockey who earns $17,500 a year (most of which he loses on gambling). He was fired from a Los Angeles station for using the word "booger" on the air and has a picture of himself with Mick Jagger. Johnny has been called Johnny Cool, Johnny Midnight and Johnny Sunshine; he calls the station the "Mighty KRP." Although liquor is not permitted at the station, Johnny keeps a bottle in the broadcast booth (Jennifer once tasted it and remarked "I think Johnny gets it in a hardware store"). Johnny has a habit of listening to conversations from behind closed doors (his way of knowing whether or not to join in). He has an apartment at the Gone with the Wind Estates and is always late paying bills.

Bailey Quarters (Jan Smithers) is the only other female employee at the station. She majored in journalism in college and works as the traffic manager (schedules commercials). She crusades for causes she believes in and eventually became an on-the-air personality doing two of the ten daily "WKRP News Roundups." Golden Bean Coffee sponsors Bailey's shows and she upsets Les by not giving the hog reports (Les feels the farmers need to know this information). Bailey was originally depicted as a "Plain Jane" (glasses, pulled-back hair); as the series progressed, she became more glamorous and as much of a looker as Jennifer.

Andy Travis (Gary Sandy) is the station's program director (it was his idea to change the station's format from beautiful music to rock and roll). Andy has a dog named Pecos Bill and is the only one who realizes that WKRP will never fare better than 14 (which it achieved in one ratings period). He is the only one who can stand up to the stern Mama Carlson and often puts his job on the line to oppose her misguided ideas about the station. Andy believes "I'm an easygoing young guy with a natural ability to lead. Except no one listens."

The office intercom is yelling in the hallways. The show's gimmick is a bandage Les wears in each episode (but in a different place) to remind Sanders of an injury he sustained on the first day of taping. WPIG is the station's main competition.

Update

The New WKRP in Cincinnati, Syn., 1991–1993. Arthur Carlson (Gordon Jump) still manages the station; his wife, Carmen (Allyn Ann McLerie), has a business called Carmen's Crystal Corner in the Pinedale Mall. Arthur has high hopes that the station will crack the top ten and still spends most of his time dreaming about fishing and playing with toys.

Les Nessman (Richard Sanders) still delivers the news. He still wears the bandage and still has the invisible walls. He leaves for work each day at 6:32 A.M. and has a bird named Hilda.

Herb Tarlek (Frank Bonner), the station salesman, still calls Arthur "Big Guy" and still hits on every beautiful girl he sees (despite the fact that he is married to Lucille, played by Edie McClurg).

Mona Loveland (Tawny Kitaen) is the late night D.J. She has a sexy voice and opens her show, *Mona 'Til Midnight* (it begins at 9 P.M.), with "This is Mona Loveland, I'll be your guide to dreamland. It's just you and me and music 'til midnight." Mona is a Leo, loves to show cleavage and sobs

"I have a hard time finding bikini tops that fit." She lives in a former firehouse and has overcome a gambling addiction. Her show is also called *Music 'Til Midnight*.

Ronnie Lee (Wendy Davis) is the first receptionist. She is a Virgo and not as glamorous or buxom as Jennifer Marlowe, the girl she replaced. Ronnie was dropped (she was said to be attending night school to get her master's degree) and was replaced by Nancy Brinkwink (Marla Jeanette Rubinoff), a busty blonde graduate of Dennison College. She has a B.A. in communications and worked previously as a buyer for Strudor and James in Cincinnati (she left because all the men were either gay or married). At WKRP, she finds an uncontrollable passion for Herb.

Dana Burns and Jack Allen (Kathleen Garrett, Michael Des Barres) are divorced D.J.'s who host the music and talk program the *Burns and Allen Show*. Radical D.J. Razor Dee (French Stewart) replaced Burns and Allen and works as "Razor Man" (he was previously a monks' barber for two years in the Order of Our Lady of the Forgetful).

Claire Hartline (Hope Alexander-Willis) is the new traffic manager; Donovan Aderhold (Mykel T. Williamson) is the new program director. Assisting Herb in sales is Arthur Carlson, Jr. (Lightfield Lewis), Mr. Carlson's obnoxious son.

Jennifer Marlowe (Loni Anderson), a wealthy widow, is now engaged to Reynaldo Roberio Ricky Ricardo Goulegant III (Robert Goulet), the European prince of a country called Rosario Roberto. Venus Flytrap (Tim Reid) lives in Washington, D.C., where he is a chief executive officer with the BET cable network.

Dr. Johnny Fever (Howard Hesseman) rejoined the series in the second season as the overnight D.J. (midnight to 6 A.M.). Johnny was previously living in New York's Greenwich Village where he was attempting to write a book on rock and roll music.

Tom Wells wrote the theme for both versions.

Performer Index

References are to entry numbers